Praise for *Roads Not Taken*

"Via the literary time machine, Terry Keenleyside crafts in *Roads Not Taken*, we are delivered to the harrowing centres of major 20th century war zones. These historic scenes and the media machine documenting them are vivid, palpable, and riveting. A parallel journey parachutes the reader deep down into the tender, sensitive, psyche of the characters while they grow, study, love and work in this time period not so long ago, but far enough to fascinate as to what has changed and has not changed. Keenleyside paints this world so realistically: dreamlike, film-like, fast and brilliant."

—DAVID TIERNEY, PUBLISHER,
BOREALIS PRESS, OTTAWA, ONTARIO

"This is a dramatic story that includes a turbulent account of one man's love affairs and two journalists' lives covering major international crises around the world. On assignment, they are frequently at risk of being wounded or killed, and, as a result, the two are at odds with each other over whether or not the risks are worth taking.

—JOHN FLOOD, PUBLISHER,
PENUMBRA PRESS, ONTARIO, CANADA

ROADS NOT TAKEN

A NOVEL

T. A. KEENLEYSIDE

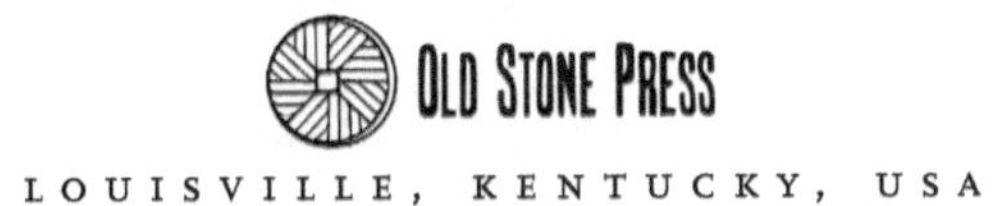

LOUISVILLE, KENTUCKY, USA

© 2024 by T. A. Keenleyside

All rights reserved.

This book may not be reproduced in whole or in part without written permission from the publisher, Old Stone Press, or from the author, T. A. Keenleyside except by a reviewer who may quote brief passages in a review; nor any part of this book be reproduced, stored in a retrieval system, or transmitted in any form or by any means, electronic, mechanical photocopying, recording or other, without written permission from the publisher or author.

No photograph, image or illustrations may be reproduced without written permission of Old Stone Press, the publisher or the author, T. A. Keenleyside

For information about special discounts for bulk purchases or autographed copies of this book, please contact John Clark, Old Stone Press at john@oldstonepress.com or the author, T. A. Keenleyside at keenleysideterry@gmail.com

Library of Congress Control Number: 2024907332

ISBN: 978-1-938462-71-9 (paperback)

ISBN: 978-1-938462-72-6 (eBook)

Published by
Old Stone Press, an imprint of J. H. Clark & Associates, Inc

Louisville, Kentucky 40207
www.oldstonepress.com

Published in U.S.A.

ROADS
NOT
TAKEN

Other Books by T. A. Keenleyside

Novels

All the Way (2019)
In a Spin (2015)
The Common Touch (1977)

Literary Travel Books

At the Table: Nourishing Conversation and Food (2012)
Roaming the Big Land: Flavours of Canada (2010)
Missing The Bus, Making The Connection (2008)

To Dot with love

Acknowledgements

MEMBERS OF MY own family have always been the first to read and comment on anything I have written. I am especially thankful to my spouse, Dorothy, who travelled with me to most of the locations where this story unfolds. More than that, she has always encouraged me to keep writing, even though, as a lonely pursuit, it has often deprived us of time we would otherwise have spent together.

A number of people were helpful at different stages of this novel's development. First, I wish to thank my longtime publicist and sometimes literary agent, Rachel Sentes of GalFriday, for her astute understanding of what I was trying to accomplish in writing this novel and for her input of ideas to improve what I wanted to convey.

Dr. Dennis Dalton, a distinguished political philosopher and activist, offered insightful commentary on the political crises explored in this novel. As a Professor Emeritus at Barnard College, University of Columbia, and a longtime friend from our graduate school days at the University of London, his perspective on issues of racial discrimination in the United States was particularly valuable.

Sara Cummins, a cherished friend since our time in Jakarta, Indonesia, has generously read and provided valuable feedback on all of my books. I am deeply grateful for her unwavering support and encouragement throughout the years, which has inspired me to continue writing.

Felicity Garrard, whose husband is a former colleague in the Canadian diplomatic service, offered insightful suggestions on all aspects of the novel, with particular expertise on the sections set in her native England.

Liz Etherington, a specialist in documentary film-making, read an early draft of the novel, visualizing it as a film to determine if it present-ed vivid images of events to the reader. Her conclusion was positive and, I hope, correct.

I would like to thank the late Dr. Joel Niznick, who was willing to review and, at some points, correct the many Yiddish expressions em-ployed in this novel.

Finally, I am grateful to John Clark for agreeing to publish this work and to his dedicated team, who scrutinized the text to catch any errors in spelling and grammar, designed the cover and interior, and, generally, did all they could to produce a quality book.

The various international and domestic events covered in this novel are all true, and I have attempted to recreate how they unfolded as accu-rately as possible. While I have inserted some fictitious characters into these situations, in most instances, the individuals mentioned are real, and I have characterized their roles in what transpired as accurately as possible.

While the fictionalization of global, Canadian, and American events is rooted in historical records, the sections of the novel pertaining to the *Toronto Star* during the early 1960s are drawn from my personal experi-ences as a staff writer. These portions are based on firsthand accounts and are presented as accurately as possible.

Finally, I take responsibility for any remaining errors in the text and affirm that, except as indicated above, the characters in this novel are fig-ments of my imagination, and any resemblance to people living or dead is purely coincidental.

Chapter 1
Selma, Alabama

• • • •

March 7, 1965

"THEY'RE GOING TO cross the bridge. Come on! Hurry!" Peggy Mortimer shouted to her colleague. "We need to get as close to the front as we can."

"It's not easy with all this goddamn gear," Alistair Parker retorted. He was weighed down by his Rolleiflex twin-lens camera and a black bag full of lenses and film. What concerned him more, however, was that he was not a trained professional. One of the *Herald's* photographers had simply given him a brief lesson on how to use the camera after the city editor told him to fly to Alabama along with the principal reporter assigned to the story.

"How many demonstrators do you think there are?" Peggy asked. She was not only Alistair's senior colleague, but a close friend as well.

"Maybe five hundred. Hard to tell when they're strung out like this to stay on the sidewalk."

"Mostly poor folks, I'd say. A lot of farmers. Former sharecroppers, maybe," Peggy observed. "Holy shit! Those are state troopers up ahead, blocking the whole road. They've got pistols in their holsters, and they're carrying billysticks."

"Mean-looking bastards. I think we're in for trouble."

"Wallace said he'd do whatever is necessary to prevent the march. Obviously, he meant it. Those are county police irregulars with the state troopers."

"Who?" Alistair asked.

"Young white men deputized to help deal with the demonstrators."

"Geez! What a way to operate."

"Fucking awful."

Suddenly, the march slowed and then stopped. The commanding police officer shouted at the protesters through a megaphone, but what he was saying was barely audible to the reporters.

"Seems one of the demonstration leaders wants to speak to the officer," Peggy noted. "Who is it? Can you see?"

Alistair stepped onto the road to get closer. "That's the Reverend Hosea Williams, I think, of the Southern Christian Leadership Conference. You know, King's people."

"Oh, shit, no! The troopers are putting on their gas masks. They're attacking the demonstrators, pushing them back."

Marchers were being knocked to the ground by burly state troopers wearing helmets strapped under their chins—angry bulldogs dressed in costume to instill fear. They were beating the fallen demonstrators with their billysticks. "Geez, it's absolute bedlam. They're firing tear gas now! I can smell it." Alistair pinched his nose to block the stench.

Police on horseback charged after the terrified demonstrators, flailing at them with long whips. Marchers with blood streaming down their faces, arms, and legs were lying on the bridge, and others were fleeing in terror. From the sidewalk, the reporters could hear white onlookers cheering the police as they pounded the heads and bodies of the demonstrators. People were wailing in pain, and others in horror at the violence of the assault.

A crowd was gathering around one victim in particular. "It's a woman. And she's been beaten unconscious," Peggy said. "Come on! Get in closer. We need a picture of her."

"I'm trying for Christ's sake!" Sweat dripped down Alistair's forehead, and he could feel his heart pounding from physical exertion and fear of a billystick striking his head. "I'm doing the best I can."

"I know. Sorry. But move closer if you can and get her name. We need her name."

Alistair shoved his way forward until he was crouching next to the woman. But at that moment, a policeman shouted, "Stand back!"

"I'm press." He continued to take pictures. "I'm covering the march."

"I don't care who the hell you are. I said stand back."

Alistair estimated he had all the photos he needed and began retreating, but the policeman grabbed him. "That's a northern accent I'm hearing, isn't it sonny boy? Where y'all from?"

"Toronto. Toronto, Canada."

"Well, well. Canada, huh? What in hell are you doing down here, except stirring up trouble? You don't have no problem like ours, do you?"

"We have a multi-ethnic population, and everyone's rights are respected," Alistair responded boldly, though his body trembled so hard that it had been a struggle to hold the camera steady. His perspiring face turned crimson with the realization he was being drawn into the fracas.

"Well, then, why don't you just get your ass out of here and shift it back to your goulash?"

The policeman pushed him in the back. "Bama is for real white guys. Not lefty pansies like you."

"Hey, leave him alone." Peggy saddled up to the officer.

"Oh! A sassy bitch, huh? Get out of my sight. Both of you!"

"We're done. We're going already."

They walked off the bridge, where wounded demonstrators lay at the side of the road receiving aid and comfort from other marchers. "Did you get the woman's name?"

"Of course, I got it."

"Good work. Let's get your film off to Toronto and phone in our story. I hope you got a pic or two that are better than what the paper will have from the wire services."

"Well, at least my images will be of higher quality."

• • •

Two days later, the 54-mile march along the highway to the state capital in Montgomery started again. This time, Martin Luther King, Jr. led the protest against the violation of the constitutional rights of African Americans, including the slow pace of voter registration.

"How many demonstrators this time, do you think?"

Alistair scanned the marchers filing onto the bridge. "I don't know. Two to three thousand, maybe."

Suddenly, the marchers on the bridge stopped and knelt in prayer.

"Hey, wait a minute," Peggy cried. "Look at the state troopers up ahead. They're standing aside…. They're going to let the marchers through. Yippee! We're on our way to Montgomery!"

But moments later, she realized that that was not the case. The protesters were turning around and moving off the bridge. "Holy cow, they're dispersing. They've decided to go home. There isn't going to be a march at all. Fuck this! It's over, and we have practically nothing to report. After this fiasco, I doubt the editors will be ready to send us here again."

"Well, let's go and scope out what the hell happened. At least we have pictures of the marchers turning around."

"And of the troopers standing aside. You got that, too, didn't you?"

"Come on, cut me some slack."

Alistair felt a hand squeeze his shoulder, forcing him to turn around. "Hey, you're the smart-ass photographer from Canada I talked to on Sunday, aren't you? Time to go home, sonny boy. Now you've seen what these people are really like. No guts for a fight. They stay in their place. You should do the same."

"Don't be so sure." Alistair's diminutive partner stood on her tiptoes raising her face close to the policeman's, her dark green eyes glaring defiantly into his. "The marchers will be back—here or somewhere else. And we will be, too."

"Ah, the uppity bitch again, I see."

Quickly, Alistair raised his camera and took shots of their confrontation until the policeman spotted what he was doing and covered his face with one hand. "Hey, stop that, you little shit." He grabbed Alistair by the arm. "Give me that camera!"

As the policeman tried to pull it from him, an image from Alistair's childhood appeared before him—his brother urging him to ask their neighbour, little Ruthie Frogmore, to pull down her underpants so that they could inspect her nude body. But by then, Alistair had already learned to calculate the risks in any such action and had rejected his brother's appeal. *This is different. I'm a reporter now. I have to show more courage.*

"Come on, give me the camera, or I'll arrest you," the officer repeated.

Still, Alistair resisted until Peggy intervened. "Look, don't be such a jerk. Do you want to be at the centre of an international incident?"

The policeman hesitated and slowly let go of the camera. "Well, take out the film and give it to me."

"Over our dead bodies. You have no right to confiscate it."

Again, common sense prevailed, and the policeman retreated to verbal abuse. "You're nothing but foreign scum, both of you. All you want to do is stir up trouble."

Peggy started to respond, but Alistair gently pulled her away. "Don't provoke him. Let's bail before we get arrested."

She relented, but not without turning for a parting shot. "You're the ones causing the trouble by denying a whole community its civil rights."

"Shut up, you northern slut, and get the fuck off this bridge."

Chapter 2

According to his self-diagnosis, Alistair had an affliction that emerged in early childhood and continued to plague him. It was a tendency—he used to call it the ability—to anticipate the likely outcome of any particular action. He was inclined to see it as negative, precipitating caution on his part even though he overcame that impulse at Selma. For example, as a young man, he developed the habit of imagining himself on the shore at The Beaches in Toronto just as someone was dragged unconscious from the water.

In his mind, he could see a small crowd gathering, but no one had started working on the victim. Alistair had learned to administer mouth-to-mouth resuscitation as a camp counsellor, but did he see himself rushing to assist? No, because, in his estimation, he would have convinced himself that, if he did, he would gag and probably throw up—maybe even catch some horrible disease. He was pretty sure that he would have hung back waiting to see if someone more courageous—someone with a less negative conception of the consequences—took charge. That's not to say that he would have done nothing in this situation if no one else came to the person's assistance. He hoped that he would, but he didn't really know because he'd never faced this particular circumstance. He had only mused about it—with thoughts that did not presage courage, even if the victim was a stunningly beautiful chick!

The earliest recollection Alistair retained of this cautious aspect of his personality was when his older brother, Jonathan, egged him into committing an act he lacked the courage to perform himself. He was five at the time, and his brother eight. Late one Friday afternoon, they were throwing a ball at the edge of their elementary school playground when Alistair's errant toss left the property and rolled across the road to a yard facing the school.

As Alistair ran to retrieve the ball, Jonathan called, "Hey, see the old greenhouse beside that house? I dare you to throw a rock at it."

"Why? You do it if you want to."

"I might miss if I threw from here. Besides, there aren't any stones near me, but I can see a whole pile by the greenhouse."

"I'm not doing that. We might get in trouble." Alistair was, however, as tempted as his brother to hear the awesome tinkling of breaking glass.

"Naw, we won't. It's just a dumb old greenhouse. It doesn't look as if they even use it anymore."

"What if Mom finds out?"

"She won't. There's nobody around, and she doesn't even know the people who live there."

"How do you know?"

"I just do. I'm positive. Come on. What are you, chicken or something?"

The classic taunt. Alistair quickly ran over to the greenhouse, picked up a rock from the pile, and hurled it onto the greenhouse roof.

The sudden, delightful clinking of breaking glass resounded throughout the slumbering yard, and Jonathan roared with approval. "Throw another one. Quick, throw it!"

Alistair obliged, returned hastily to his brother, and they ran out of the schoolyard like escapees from a maximum-security prison, which was pretty much how they saw the place.

Boys, of course, usually get these things wrong. Their mother did not know the lady who owned the greenhouse, but the woman recognized the boys because, through a living-room window, she had often seen them playing in the schoolyard, especially on weekends. Unbeknownst to them, she was home at the time of the assault and watching it, though, in the late afternoon light, the boys could not see her through the darkened panes. How she located their home and telephone number, they did not know. But less than a half hour after they returned from the schoolyard, they could hear their mother stomping up the stairs to Jonathan's bedroom, where they were innocently sprawled on the floor reading *Dick Tracy* comic books.

"I'm shocked and mortified by your behaviour." Alistair remembered clearly what she said because he had never heard the word "mortified" before and had to ask Jonathan what it meant.

"That she wishes she were dead," Jonathan explained, not being one ever to admit ignorance.

"I've never been so ashamed of you both. You are turning into little hooligans." Their mother's eyes welled up. "Wait until your father gets home. He will deal with this," she said, leaving the bedroom and slamming the door.

"Those were only crocodile tears," Jonathan assured Alistair, but that sounded even worse to him, as if their mother wanted to eat them alive.

Waiting for their father to get home, waiting for the prosecutor, judge, and executioner, all wrapped into one forbidding personage to stride into the room, axe in hand. That was always the worst part of misbehaving: the agonizing delay before their father announced the sentence and administered justice, plus the anticipation of pain as a slipper struck a bare bottom repeatedly.

The wait was always much worse than the punishment, however, for, in truth, their father was a kindly man who understood the behaviour of little boys better than their mother. Who knows? As a boy, he had probably liked the tinkle of breaking glass, too. "This is going to hurt me more than it will hurt you," he always intoned as he ordered them to bend over before raising his slipper. He was right. It hardly hurt at all, so soft was his slipper, so light were his blows. Still, his sons always cried out, "Ouch! Dad! Ow! Ow! That really hurts!" They knew he hated punishing them,

and they wanted him to feel free to stop, yet at the same time, they wanted to be able to tell their mother that justice had truly been meted out.

That experience with the greenhouse affected Alistair's behaviour
thereafter. It made him alert to the possible negative consequences of
acting impulsively, and from that moment, he started making a "will I,
won't I?" calculation, more often than not coming down on the side of
inaction. He also never forgot the first time he opted not to act, much
as he wanted to, because of his analysis of the likely consequences of
following his heart rather than his head.

That moment arose not long after the greenhouse incident. Once
again, he was with his brother, but this time they were in their garage
on a wintery, Saturday afternoon. They were building a sailboat out of
scrap wood they had collected throughout the neighbourhood, and they
planned to sail it in Toronto Harbour and make money by ferrying their
friends across to Centre Island and Hanlan's Point. Of course, they had
no construction plans for the boat, no carpentry skills, nor sailing experience, and no hope of the project ever reaching fruition. It was just
a pie-in-the-sky idea of Jonathan's with which Alistair went along to
pass some boring weekend time. They had been busy hammering boards
together for several hours when Ruthie Frogmore, a girl a little younger
than Alistair who lived two houses away, suddenly appeared at the garage door, interested in seeing what the boys were up to. Jonathan set
her to work, using his hammer and nails while he sat on an orange crate
supervising.

To Alistair, Ruthie was a cute little thing who sometimes came over
to play when her girlfriend down the street was away. She had red hair
with pigtails, and her face was a mass of freckles that seemed to take on
extra size and colour hammering in the garage. She wore a short yellow
dress, white socks, and black patent leather shoes. Alistair saw her only
vaguely as a neighbourhood friend, someone who just happened to live
on their quiet street, west of Spadina Road and south of Eglinton. Girls

were pretty much an enigma to him and Jonathan and, indeed, to most of the boys nearby—not exactly an alien species, but definitely different. Still, there was something that made them intriguing. They seemed soft, innocent, and incredibly clean: no dirt on their hands and feet, their faces scrubbed and rosy. Boys couldn't help wanting to touch them and discover if their smooth skin felt different, too.

Jonathan watched Alistair talking to Ruthie for several minutes and then motioned him over. "Ask her to pull down her underpants, so we can see what she looks like," he whispered. Neither of them had ever seen a girl naked. They knew that she didn't have a penis, but beyond that, they had no idea what was inside her lily-white underpants, and they were fascinated to find out.

"You ask her," Alistair retorted.

"No, you. She's your friend, not mine."

"No, she's not. She just lives near us."

"Well, she's your age."

"I don't care. You're the big shot. You ask her."

"What's the matter? Are you chicken?"

The same taunt. But this time, unlike in the greenhouse caper, Alistair didn't bite. Instead, he reflected on what would happen if he did his brother's bidding. First, it struck him that Ruthie might be so shocked that she would run away and tell her mother, and her mother would contact theirs. It would be the same old story and end in another spanking—probably one that was more than ritual, since their father would doubtless see this as a serious offence.

But then Alistair calculated that there was another possible outcome as well. Ruthie might not mind the proposition all that much. She might even welcome it, but only because she might be equally eager to see what a boy looked like uncovered. So, it occurred to Alistair that he could end up confronted with a trade-off; he might have to agree to pull down his pants as well and give her a good look at his penis. That was something he simply wasn't prepared to do. As a result, that potentially exciting moment passed, and for both boys, it was a long time before either of them had another opportunity to gaze upon the intimate parts of a female body.

There were other moments in childhood when visualizing the outcome of a potential action prompted caution and, hence, inaction on Alistair's part. Sometimes, several boys in their gang would carry their bows and arrows into the school playground for target practice, no doubt under the watchful eye of the lady with the greenhouse. It was a large area with baseball diamonds, a football field, and a cinder track, but none of it was grand. What grass survived was hard and rutted from cleats digging into it and the track needed a fresh spread of cinders. The grounds did, however, provide plenty of space for several Robin Hoods and Will Scarlets to shoot their arrows simultaneously without striking one another.

"Okay, now everyone lie on the ground head up," Melvin Steinberg, Alistair's school chum, ordered after they had all grown tired of watching their feathered weapons fly aimlessly around without striking a target. "I'm going to shoot an arrow as high as I can. No one move until the arrow hits the ground."

Some but not all in the merry band were willing to participate in this risky dare. But Alistair never did despite Jonathan's bullying and taunts of chicken. "What about you? You're a chicken yourself," Alistair shot back one day.

"Yeah, we've never seen you do it," the others joined in.

Jonathan was humiliated and offered a compromise. "I'll shoot an arrow into the sky and lie down with everyone else until it lands."

Only Alistair noticed that he did not aim directly skyward, but on a slight angle so that the arrow lodged in the earth a safe distance away. Alistair did not, however, bring this trickery to the attention of the other boys, for he was certain they would tease Jonathan for being a coward and that, to end their taunts, he would agree to lie down again while all the boys shot their arrows straight overhead. Alistair could visualize the outcome. He could see his brother lying dead on the ground, an arrow piercing his chest. That in and of itself was not too bad to contemplate, but what, he worried, would his parents say or do when they learned that Jonathan's death was a consequence of Alistair revealing him as a coward?

There was also the pond that Alistair, on a dare, declined to cross one March when the ice was growing thin. There were the houses and apartment buildings under construction he wouldn't break into, although tempted by the joyful shouts of the other boys as they ran up and down the freshly cemented stairs. There were the snowballs not hurled through the open windows of passing cars, prized vegetables not rifled from proud neighbour's victory gardens, and gum and candy never lifted from corner stores. Alistair had mastered the art of anticipating outcomes and believed that this trait served him well.

This is not to say that, after the greenhouse incident, his childhood was pure innocence, but simply that decisions became carefully calculated. He joined other kids in playing nicky nicky nine doors, but he resisted ringing the same doorbell more than once, and he never approached the home of the lady with the greenhouse. They ran lemonade and flower stands on their front lawn with the proceeds not always reaching the charitable organizations for which they were intended. With their parents' permission, they also sold flowers taken from the family garden, but they didn't reveal to them that these supplies were often supplemented by climbing roses cut from the fences of their neighbours. There was also the evening when Alistair, born in the darkest days of World War II and thus strongly influenced by anti-German propaganda, stood at his bedroom window, bellowing to the street below, "Hitler has only got one ball, Göring has two, but very small. Himmler is rather sim'lar, but poor old Goebbels has no balls at all."

Jonathan heard him and ran from his room to join in just as their mother appeared. "Boys, that is appallingly vulgar. What will the neighbours think? If you ever do something like this again, your father will deal with you."

A week later, they were at it again. "Hitler is a jerk, Mussolini bit his weenie, now it doesn't work."

Alistair had calculated correctly that their mother would be unable to persuade her husband to punish them—that he would see their song as patriotic and funny. So, when there was no sound of angry footsteps mounting the stairs, Alistair simply asked his brother, "What happens when your weenie doesn't work?"

"You go on the floor, and you have to clean it up yourself every time."

Alistair was impressed by the authoritative way he answered.

Although he was not aware of it at the time, there were also instances where Alistair's growing caution and penchant for assessing the probable consequences of any action led him to avoid initiatives that, in hindsight, he realized, probably would have been desirable. One was his decision, after graduating from the Royal Conservatory of Music's Grade 1 program, to give up any further lessons. The final exam included singing "God Save The King," which he performed off-key and discordantly. Nevertheless, he had somehow passed the test, perhaps because the baffled examiner mistook his strange rendition as the work of a budding and creative young artist.

But that outcome simply led to another trapdoor: the annual spring recital of his music teacher, where the varying talents of all her pupils were on display for parents, relatives, and friends. At the end of the first stanza of his unique interpretation of "Oranges and Lemons," Alistair came to a complete stop having totally forgotten what keys to strike next.

"Take a deep breath, relax, and start again," his piano teacher whispered offstage. He did so, but once again faltered at the same place.

"Stand up!" his teacher hissed at him. "Now bow to the audience and … get off the stage!" He was so mortified that he never took another lesson, and never attempted to play the instrument again. Much later in life, he came to regret this decision. Had he been willing to carry on with lessons, there was, he realized, at least some chance that he could have been the one at the piano leading the singsongs at the nursing home he regularly visited with spirited renditions of "Blue Moon," "Que Sera, Sera," "Bill Bailey," and "My Way"—yes, "My Way" played *his* way!

After one season of dance lessons at the Heliconian Club in midtown Toronto, Alistair never returned to that pursuit either. He reached the point where he could just about manage the foxtrot without looking at his feet, but almost all the other dances—the tango, the bossa nova, the cha-cha-cha, even the waltz—were beyond him. Whenever he contemplated dancing, he could see himself with sweating palms, lurching around the floor out of rhythm with the music, incapable of leading, confusing his partner with unannounced turns, scuffing her dance shoes, and not even offering interesting conversation due to his focus on his feet.

Because of this ineptitude, he also wasn't comfortable enough to invite a girl to his high school formal at Forest Hill Collegiate in grade twelve. By then, he had gone out with several girls, but nothing had ever come of these intermittent dates. Making his inevitable calculations, none of them had tallied a high enough score to risk embarrassing himself in what would likely be a failed pursuit. He did, however, very much want to go to the dance and had a couple of prospects in mind. One of them, in fact, was the infamous Ruthie Frogmore, who, though a grade behind him, had suddenly flamed into a red-hot number. It wasn't that he was still keen to see under her skirt; it was simply that she was a stunner, and he knew her well enough that he thought he might be able to chance an awkward night of dancing with her. But once again, as he visualized how the evening would likely go, he lost his nerve and never asked her or anyone else. So, after helping with the decorations and setting up the tables for the intermission supper, he went home and spent the evening alone and unhappy, reading, as he remembers it, Hugh MacLennan's *Two Solitudes*.

In a fortuitous twist of fate, however, Alistair's unreadiness to invite someone to his grade twelve formal—his reluctance to travel new, uncertain roads—had a positive outcome, a happy one, for it was the very next winter that he met Virginia Sloan whom he subsequently invited to the formal in what was for both of them their graduating year. Had he gone to the dance in grade twelve with Ruthie Frogmore, it was possible he would not have been on the prowl for a girlfriend the following year. And, had that been the case, their lives might never have intersected in the way they did.

Chapter 3

Toronto

. . . .

March in The Present

ALISTAIR IS SITTING in the one, not-so-easy chair in a bedroom of a long-term care facility, watching a woman fall asleep. Her eyes, once the hue of the prized marble in her childhood collection, are shut tight, concealing the vague layer of film that covers them now, a curtain drawn over her life. There is, however, a steady, nervous flutter to her eyelids as if she is not at peace—in the midst of a nightmare, perhaps. Her mouth is half open as if anticipating a spoonful of unappetizing food will be coaxed into it—a dollop of lumpy mashed potatoes, creamed squash, or apple sauce. Mucus drips from her nose, and her nostrils emit an intermittent gurgle like a baby's rattle, gently shaken. It's less irritating than a full-blown snore, but unpleasantly repetitive, not a sound she would ever have contemplated making. Well, at least it blocks the incessant clacking of the heating system and helps Alistair ignore the stench of disinfectant coming from the hallway where one of the cleaning staff has just dealt with the output of a libertarian bowel.

The person Alistair Parker gazes at is barely recognizable compared to the woman he used to know and still loves, the sickly skin of her face stretched and wrinkled like a discarded sheaf of yellow paper, her arms like the brittle lower limbs of a dead spruce, her hands an opaque swamp covered in a mealy, black and purple scum with lumps of bone looming above the mixture like menacing shoals.

Less than an hour ago, while she was sitting vacantly in a chair in a corner of the recreation room, Alistair was dancing with three of the residents. He did his best to lead them gently around the floor, to make them laugh, and to encourage them to talk—to tell him as much as they could remember about their lives—their careers, their families, their good times and bad. He had felt rather like he had when he went to dance classes as a teenager at the Heliconian Club. The eager girls would sit in a row on one side of the hall, the reluctant boys on the other, fearful of dancing with someone of the mysterious other sex, terrified of treading on a toe, at a loss for what to talk about. Eventually, under the insistent urging of the dance instructor, the obedient boys would timidly shuffle across the room to the girls' benches and invite them onto the floor. Alistair always sought out the one who looked the most compassionate. "You, you, you, I'm in love with you, you, you." That's all he can still remember of the dance music. They played it over and over at every session.

Alistair thought all the ladies at the dance tonight were after him. It is, however, an assumption that hasn't gone to his head, for he knows they have nothing but scattered and disconnected recollections of their past, even of what happened to them a few hours earlier. They live in the present, and, at the dance, he was the one man to whom they felt vaguely attracted. Of course, that's not saying much. There were only two others in the room, one of them running a crooked, arthritic finger along a blank wall as if he were looking for cracks to be filled with plaster, the other pacing anxiously, perhaps anticipating life-threatening results from a recently concluded physical examination. Twice, he rushed out, crying that he had an urgent appointment to make. Angela, who was running the dance, chased after him and brought him back, reassuring him that he wouldn't be late if he waited until the party ended.

Like the staff, almost everyone living in the home is female. Their husbands are mostly dead or visit infrequently, as do their sons and grandsons. Their daughters have assumed most of the responsibility for their well-being. Until Covid-19 struck with a vengeance, they would drop in once or twice a week for short, awkward conversations with their failing mothers and then spend most of the time with the staff, dispassionately checking on changes in health and behaviour, asking about medications, paying bills, and sometimes taking their mothers out for walks or lunch. Occasionally, they would even attend social events at the home, like the dance that just ended.

No, this is very much a woman's world. And it's a world in which Angela plays a leading role, a sort of conductor of a discordant orchestra that has existed for many years, but whose members rarely stay for long, their musical talents steadily diminishing, and a long list of applicants waiting to assume their orchestral positions. Angela is a physiotherapist by training but has broader responsibilities than that. Apart from meals, she organizes virtually all of the home's daily program of events: exercise classes, the quizzes, news discussion groups, films, concerts, parties, and dances. At this evening's function, Alistair admired how she made a point of dancing with all the women in turn. And not demurely, but with abandon, sexily even, waving her arms over her head and swinging her hips to "It's Now or Never" as if she were—who knows—Priscilla Presley maybe.

Alistair would have taken a turn around the floor with her, except they were both there to entertain, not enjoy themselves. But now he is wondering where she is. She often drops by at this hour for a conversation before he leaves. Alistair likes that. She's bright and vivacious with eclectic interests, and there is no affectation to her. He sees that as one of the strengths of everyone who works in the home. They are frank and open. There is no artifice about people who work with Alzheimer's patients. Alistair guesses that Angela is about forty-five. Given her professional background, she knows that fitness is important and as a result, she still has a good figure. Of course, leading the exercise classes and the dances, taking the able patients on walks, and staying abreast of the latest nutritional information pertinent to Alzheimer's all help her to stay fit. She's a reminder to him of the importance of eating his broccoli and going regularly to a gym. There is one just a few blocks from the nursing home, and before the virus struck, he often went there to ride a bike for an hour or more. Four hundred calories burned, his heavy heart lifted a notch. But now his legs are too stiff and sore to return to his former routine.

There is a serenity about Angela that he likes as well. He can see it in her face—in the absence of frown lines, in the upward curl of her mouth, and in the hazel eyes that fix on people steadily and confidently. He feels that whatever he says to her, she can handle and won't be perplexed or at a loss for words. By now, they know most of each other's life stories, so there is an easy familiarity to their conversation, a calm, unsurprising flow of thoughts and emotions.

If she stops in tonight, Alistair is tempted to ask her if she'd like to go out for a drink. Her shift is over now; it ended with the dance, or at least with the clean-up afterwards. And there is no point in his staying any later; yet, it is only eight-thirty. *Hell, we could even go for a bite to eat.... But do I have the nerve to ask her?*

If he invited her for a drink, he wouldn't mean anything by it. It's just that the evenings are long and lonely after he leaves. But he is afraid that she might take it the wrong way. She might think it was pretty strange, coming after they'd spent so many hours together, but always within the confines of the nursing home. He supports the Me-Too movement and doesn't want to seem aggressive and chauvinist. All he yearns for is companionship and lively conversation. So, on reflection, he decides he'll head home, pour himself a beer, and scramble some egg whites to eat while he reads. He certainly doesn't want to risk offending Angela.

But is this just the old me reasserting itself? He glances at the frail body lying sound asleep in the bed and then at his watch, trying to convince himself that Angela isn't stopping in anyway. *Am I thinking my way into inaction, cutting myself off from someone I like who is interesting and helpful to talk to, and who, for some reason, seems to enjoy my company as well?* He stands up, stretches his legs until they feel limber, and tiptoes out of the bedroom. *Am I,* he wonders as he has in the past, *the proverbial victim of roads not taken?*

Chapter 4

WHEN VIRGINIA SLOAN was young, her parents thought of her as a shy, lonely girl. They were determined to try everything they could to change her—to alter what they perceived as an unhappy childhood, or what was likely to become one without corrective action. They would invite other girls from their Etobicoke neighbourhood for playdates, but when they came, the outcome was not what her parents had envisaged. Sometimes, Ginny—her mother preferred Virginia, especially when cross—would play with them, but she saw her daughter as making only a half-hearted, unenthusiastic effort out of politeness.

And often, she noted, Ginny would just sit and watch the other girls sprawled out on the floor, filling out the black and white images in colouring books with Ginny's large giant box of crayons and fighting over the most sharply pointed ones. Sometimes, the girls would make rows of paper cut-outs of gingerbread men or Santa Clauses. Ginny would initially participate, but quickly grow bored and pick up a book to read until the other girls were finished. Not only were children from her class at school invited to Virginia's annual birthday party, but her mother often hosted parties for other kids as well. Yet, on these occasions, Ginny's mother considered her daughter as quiet and restrained, letting others dictate the order in which presents were opened and even on her own birthday, involving them in the unwrapping of her presents, and blowing out the candles on her cake.

Virginia was, however, much more than just an aloof and boring goody two shoes who never misbehaved. At one birthday, after the girl sitting next to her licked chocolate icing off the cake, Ginny smeared her with it and, before her table companion could retaliate, shouted, "Come on, everybody gets icing on their face!" A battle ensued until everyone was splattered dark brown.

"Time for the conga," she cried at another party. A neighbour she barely knew hitched onto her waist, and soon a long line of girls was parading through the house and out to the street, accompanied by tinny blasts on a cheap party horn.

No snivelling snitch was Ginny either. Once, when she spied a girl lifting candy from someone's bag of goodies, an act of which she totally disapproved, she neither squealed on the culprit nor reported the incident to her watchful mother.

Even though Virginia's behaviour was sometimes boisterous and sociable, her parents, especially her mother, did not perceive her that way since her socializing efforts did not result in Ginny cementing new and close friendships. So, she tried another tack: persuading her daughter to invite friends for dinner and sleepovers. But Virginia always said there was no one she wanted to ask—no one with whom she was ready to share her bed and bedroom other than her cat, Christopher Robin.

Eventually, her parents shifted from such tactics to enrolling her in various extra-curricular activities, hoping that would prompt new friendships and lead her out of what they saw as unhealthy self-absorption. First off were ballet lessons, a perceived rite of passage for all young girls who, if they didn't take easily to pirouettes and pas de deux, would at least fancy themselves in the frilly, pink costumes.

"Oh, my, don't they all look adorable!" Virginia heard one mother exclaim as the pupils paraded onto the studio floor for the first time, grasped the practice bar, and turned to admire themselves in the mirror. But that comment was too much for her. When she was little, she had never liked the blue ribbons her mother tied to the end of her blonde hair, and now, she was embarrassed to be seen the way she apparently looked in a tutu—feminine and cute. That was not the way she saw herself, and she hated the idea of projecting a false image. So as not to upset her mother, she endured one term of lessons, but then persuaded her to be allowed to drop ballet on the understanding she would agree to try something else.

Next up was figure skating. To start, her mother enrolled her in singles' lessons while she learned simply to skate proficiently, to do loops and spins, and jumps involving a single turn.

"Now I'd like you to take dance or pairs lessons," her mother said when she turned thirteen. She had concluded that Ginny's social aloofness might be because she was not attracted to playing with other girls, that she was ready for and perhaps even wanted the companionship of boys. "How do you feel about that?"

Ginny just shrugged her shoulders.

"I think dance would be better at the start. It takes a lot of trust in pairs to be spun over your partner's head and thrown so that you land backwards and gracefully on the ice. How do you feel about that?"

"Well … I like dancing, just not ballet."

Ginny's mother located a boy the same age as her daughter who seemed to have the necessary attributes to be a dance partner and, perhaps, eventually, a friend. Norman Peabody was somewhat shy, but that seemed acceptable, perhaps even desirable; he wouldn't come on too strong, and it might even induce sympathy on Virginia's part, leading her to talk to him more and bring him out of his shell.

None of that was to happen. From the outset, they looked stiff together, uncomfortable holding hands, and barely a word passed between them. Despite the constant urging of the instructor, they never learned to look natural, relaxed, and happy dancing together. As with ballet, Ginny bore it through a whole set of lessons, but then told her mother that that was it.

"Why? What is the matter? Norman seems like a nice young man, and technically, you both look good."

"He's like yuck, Mom. Completely yucky."

"Yucky? What do you mean?"

"I don't know. Just yucky. Like … like, he's *so* effeminate."

Aha! At last, her mother figured she had grasped the problem. *She's ready for a more meaningful relationship, perhaps a boyfriend even.* Her mother scoured the skating club for a suitable choice, a pairs skater this time, and not finding an appropriate partner, she enlisted the services of knowledgeable coaches to come up with a list of prospects. Ginny found the whole process distasteful and embarrassing rather as if she were a lower caste East Indian girl whose mother wanted an arranged marriage with a Brahman that would elevate the family's status in the community.

The person eventually chosen was Charlie Bernamthorpe, a strapping young sixteen-year-old lad who was already over six feet tall. He had curly, sandy-coloured hair, muscular arms and legs, and a confident grin that would help any anxious partner relax before a throw. What's more, he had a gift for gab. Everything started out well with their partnership. They skated beautifully together, cutting sharp, clean edges in the ice. They were synchronized in their side-by-side jumps and, before long, smooth in overhead spins and throws. Equally noteworthy was the fact that Ginny seemed to like Charlie. She smiled easily while they skated and she chatted with him amiably at the end of their performances. "I like him," she admitted to her mother. "He is handsome and funny, and I feel confident skating with him."

A romantic connection seemed to be developing. But then Charlie asked Ginny out on a date. It was to the movies, which Ginny normally loved, but it was to see *The Ten Commandments*, and despite rave reviews, she disliked the film. To her, it was boringly melodramatic and too fervently religious. Worse still, shortly after the start, he put his arm around her shoulder. Ginny tightened and gently removed it, but halfway through the film, he leaned over and tried to kiss her. Ginny was totally taken aback. "Stop it! I can't follow the movie." He yielded, but as the credits were rolling at the end, he tried again, and she pushed him away. "I'm not ready for that."

"Why not? Don't you like me?"

"Yes, I like you, but not that way." She thought of adding "not so fast," but something kept her from saying more. So, the upshot was that Charlie never asked her out again, and after one season of skating together, he told Ginny that he was moving on to another partner at his old club. Ginny carried on with skating lessons, but she told her mother that she had decided now to focus on singles.

So, all through her growing years, Virginia's parents continued to regard her as a sort of lonely outcast, shy, quiet and bereft of friends. But that is not at all the way Ginny saw herself. She was never conscious of being all alone or anti-social, nor did she see herself as unhappy. Quite to the contrary, she felt content with her life and surrounded by family and friends who loved her. She was, she realized, different in her interests from most other girls her age; it wasn't other kids she saw as her real friends, but rather, from aged four to fourteen, her collection of animals stuffed and alive—with her cat, Christopher Robin, her closest friend and confidant.

With her social life relatively limited, when she wasn't tending to her menagerie, Virginia focussed most of her attention on school, especially in grade thirteen as she prepared for the provincewide, independently graded Senior Matriculation examinations. "Make three major grammatical errors in English Literature or Composition and you automatically fail; then you don't get into university," she had frequently heard her teachers say, so careful attention to her course work was important to her.

Virginia was one of those students who, at the beginning of a course, a teacher was unlikely to notice because she neither asked questions nor volunteered answers. It was only when the first test of the term was being graded that Ginny's answers stood out, especially in English, for they were invariably right on the mark and articulately expressed. "What would you say is the principal weakness in Hamlet's character?" the teacher asked in the first class after the test.

No hands raised.

"Mark, how about you?"

A shrug and shake of the head.

"Sally?"

"I…I sort of know, but I can't express it?"

"Well, Virginia, we haven't heard anything from you in class yet. What is your answer?"

All eyes turned on Virginia as if she were a new girl at the school when, in fact, she had been there all along. "Um…um."

"Yes? Go on."

"He…he has a tendency to procrastinate."

"Exactly. Very good, Virginia. Succinctly put."

Whispers around the room. "Procrastinate? That's heavy. What does it mean?"

Thereafter, that was the pattern. Whenever the rest of the class was stumped, the teacher would turn to her, "Well, Virginia?" and she would provide the correct answer. As a result, some of the pupils started describing her as a brown noser, clearly an unfair charge, given her efforts not to stand out in class. But that was not true of everyone. Indeed, in several cases, the result of her being noticed was the formation of new friendships, although Virginia was suspicious that in most instances the students were simply looking for someone to help them with their homework, or to whisper answers to them in exams.

There was, however, one classmate who initiated a conversation with her for a different reason—simply because he liked her responses to teachers and admired her apparent intelligence. Richard Cartwright had just turned eighteen and at the same time had pretty much defeated a bad case of acne. He was neither handsome nor particularly homely, just rather ordinary looking: five-foot, eight, pale, light brown hair and eyes of a similar, undistinguished colour. He wore glasses to read and had a habit of tapping his feet in concentration, but that didn't bother Ginny as it gave him a scholarly look that she rather liked. They struck up a friendship and eventually Richard asked her if she'd like to go to the ice carnival at Maple Leaf Gardens.

"The Ice Carnival? I…I don't know."

"You're a figure skater, aren't you?"

"Former."

"But you still dig the sport, don't you?"

Ginny simply nodded.

"Well then?"

In the end, she consented to go and actually had a good time, thanks in part to Richard's never laying a hand on her. But then, like Charlie Bernamthorpe, he asked her to the movies—to see *A Night to Remember.*

What is it about darkened movie theatres that makes young men horny? Virginia wondered, for, part way through the movie, Richard wrapped an arm around her shoulder. This time she didn't lift it away, but that simply raised his hopes. Slowly, the hand slid down to her chest and a fumbling Richard attempted to fondle her breasts. She pulled away and sat up straight, fussing with the tie on her ponytail.

"Sorry," Richard said. "I didn't mean to touch you there if you didn't want me to."

That wasn't the end of their friendship. They went on occasionally talking with each other at school. But Richard never asked her out again. *Why is it that guys drop you if you don't want the relationship to be physical?* She wanted to ask her mother that question but kept it to herself.

Shortly after the incident with Richard, there was, however, another much happier result of Virginia's being drawn into answering questions in class and standing out as an articulate student. One day in October of her graduating year, her history teacher asked if she would join the group of Etobicoke Collegiate students she was bringing together as a delegation to the Toronto High School Model United Nations General Assembly, scheduled to be held that December. Not particularly knowledgeable about contemporary world affairs, she was reluctant to participate, but pressed by her teacher she eventually agreed. It was a decision that changed the course of her life.

Chapter 5

THE MODEL UN was to be held in the legislative chamber of Queen's Park, adding such an aura of dignity and high expectation to the event that, once selected to the delegation, Ginny set about in her usual assiduous way to inform herself on General Assembly procedures and the issues that would constitute the agenda. Her school had fortunately drawn Canada which facilitated her research on topics about which she knew very little and augmented the value of participating as a lesson in Canadian international affairs.

Virginia was contemplating taking psychology or sociology at university and was particularly interested in the subject of child behaviour. It's not surprising, therefore, that the first UN topic that she researched pertained to the United Nations Children's Fund. Quite quickly, she was able to persuade her colleagues on the delegation that they should introduce a resolution seeking more financial assistance from member states for the organization. Apartheid and racial conflict in South Africa was another issue she read about and induced the students to introduce a resolution on the practices of the South African government. Since 1959 was World Refugee Year, the delegation also worked up a resolution calling for more financial assistance to aid refugees and greater efforts at voluntary resettlement.

Another member of the group had informed himself about Canada's prominent role in the creation of the first-ever UN peacekeeping mission in 1956, an initiative that had earned a Nobel Peace Prize for Lester B. Pearson, the Secretary of State for External Affairs. Lieutenant-General E. L. M. Burns, a Canadian, had been the first commander of the force and was now relinquishing that position, so it seemed natural that Canada should sponsor a resolution expressing appreciation for his leadership.

Armed with draft resolutions and supporting speeches on these topics, Virginia and her fellow students walked into the legislative assembly at Queen's Park on a snowy day in December 1959, taking their seats in the imposing, wood-panelled chamber behind the desk with the cardboard sign labelled Canada. If the allegedly shy and retiring Virginia was at all nervous and socially ill at ease in that setting, she managed to hide her feelings well when she got up to introduce her resolution on the United Nations Children's Fund. "Madam President, this fund is of ever-expanding importance in delivering aid to developing countries to enable them to provide health, nutrition and welfare services to their children in need. Assistance provided through the Fund is a practical form of international cooperation by means of which member states can fulfill the goals set out in the Declaration of the Rights of the Child."

She spoke slowly and clearly in a smooth, even voice that reflected true conviction. "In particular, the Fund is central in international efforts to help developing countries raise their standards of living and augment their capacity for economic and social progress. The opportunities are clearly there for the effective use of larger amounts of assistance than are currently forthcoming."

A young man across the floor from Virginia whose head had been buried as he busily drafted a resolution suddenly looked up and took notice of the person speaking. Occasionally as she talked, he watched her brush wayward strands of her blonde hair to one side. To him, her skin seemed as white as the snow that was falling in Queen's Park, an illusion perhaps, conjured by her rosy cheeks that glowed like the bulbs on the government Christmas tree. Her full lips were also red, though he couldn't tell at that distance if that was their natural shade or if she had applied some lipstick. He also couldn't discern the exact colour of her eyes, though they were clearly dazzling in the strong chamber lighting;

and he thought he could detect frown lines on her forehead as if she were not at all pleased about the parsimony of the UN's wealthier nations. She wore a soft, downy blue sweater and what he assumed was a pendant on a chain, but, beyond that, her body was annoyingly hidden behind her desk.

"Canada wishes to congratulate the Fund and its staff on the outstanding work that has thus far been accomplished, and it urges all nations to support this resolution and, in keeping with its spirit, to give as generously as they possibly can to the Fund. Thank you, Madam President."

It seemed to Ginny that she had no sooner sat down than the youth from across the chamber had bounded over to her desk, hand outstretched. "Alistair Parker. India. Well… Forest Hill Collegiate actually. Excellent speech. I really enjoyed it. Very passionate and moving."

"Thank you." Ginny felt hotter on her cheeks than she had throughout her delivery. "Would you…I mean would India be willing to co-sponsor?"

"Hmm. Maybe." There was a mischievous twinkle in Alistair's eyes that she liked, but not the rest of his response. "Quid pro quo is the name of the game around here. If India co-sponsors your resolution, will you support ours to incorporate on the agenda the question of seating the People's Republic of China in the United Nations and excluding the Government of the Republic of China?"

"Taiwan, you mean? We can't do that!" Ginny had done her homework on this subject.

"Why? Because you don't want to anger the Americans?"

Ginny declined to answer.

"You know, Canada's position doesn't make sense. The People's Republic of China is the *de facto* government of China and has been since 1949. It's not in keeping with your traditions to ignore objective international realities. Don't forget what Churchill said, 'The reason for having diplomatic relations is not to confer a compliment, but to secure a convenience.'"

Ginny had no idea what Churchill's views were on recognition nor knew much about the argument Alistair was making. She simply felt let down after his praise of her speech and assumed that that was the end of their conversation and opportunity to collaborate.

Alistair had chosen to dress for his role. He was wearing a Nehru jacket buttoned to the neck and the white Gandhi cap of the Indian National Congress. He had even placed a red rose in his lapel. For several seconds, he stood head cocked to one side as if deep in thought, but then suddenly he broke into a broad smile. "Okay, what the heck, I'll co-sponsor your resolution anyway."

"Really?"

"Sure. Who could reasonably oppose more funds for children in developing countries?"

He's not really handsome, Ginny thought. *But he's sort of cute. I like that dimple in his chin, and his dark brown eyes really shine when he looks at me. Even with that hat, I can see that his hair is certainly a mess… I wonder if he ever brushes it. Certainly not this morning.* "So, we have this draft resolution on apartheid in South Africa. Would you be willing to co-sponsor that one, too?"

"No sweat. The East Indians in South Africa have been discriminated against, too, for many years. Gandhi was in South Africa protesting their treatment even before he launched satyagraha in India."

"I didn't know that." *Satyagraha? He sounds pretty intellectual.* "I have a speech ready, but maybe you have one as well."

"No, no. You introduce the resolution. You'll do a better job than I would."

Does he mean it, or is he just trying to flatter me?

"So, if not our China resolution, how about quid pro quo on this one?" Alistair drew a sheaf of paper from the folder he was carrying. "Are you willing to co-sponsor our resolution on the Palestinian refugees? Theirs is a terrible situation. Virtually no progress has been made on repatriation, resettlement, and compensation since the crisis started in 1948."

Virginia reddened. "I…I don't know much about the subject. It's not one I researched."

"Well, this is something I feel passionate about, a delegate of India or otherwise." *Back off, you idiot! You sound like an arrogant know-it-all.*

Virginia's instincts told her that if she were going to represent Canada accurately, she had to be wary of resolutions pertaining to the Middle East, especially if they entailed implicit criticism of Israel. On the other hand, her personal preference was to support the resolution—not to please India really, but rather this earnest young man who was spending so much time conferring with her. "I don't think I can co-sponsor, but I'll try to get the rest of our delegation to agree at least to vote for yours."

"That would be cool. Thank you."

Their meeting seemed about to end, but neither of them really wanted it to, and it was Alistair who surprised himself by taking the initiative to postpone its conclusion. *I like her. She's cute and enthusiastic. She's obviously bright as well. Compassionate and earnest, too.* "So, anything else up your sleeve?"

Ginny hesitated. "Well…we have this resolution we've just drafted on the suspension of nuclear and thermonuclear tests."

"No. Let's not get into that one."

"I thought you might say that. Also, one of my colleagues has drafted a resolution of congratulations to General Burns as he steps down as commander of UNEF."

"An obvious one for you. That's fine by us, assuming, of course, that the resolution also welcomes the appointment of Major-General P. S. Gyani as his successor." Once again, Virginia felt embarrassed. There was no reference to him in the resolution her colleague had drafted. "You know he's Indian."

"Of course," she fibbed. "I don't know why he wasn't mentioned in the resolution."

"Well, with that addition, obviously we'll co-sponsor." Alistair's lips curled into a subtle grin, leading Ginny to wonder if it was because he enjoyed catching people out or because a happy, easy-going disposition mixed with his seriousness. "No harm in congratulating Burns, I guess, but he's a hard-nosed, taciturn guy, you know, cold and sarcastic. Not the sort of commander you'd think would ever have a mistress."

"How do you know he does?"

Alistair just shrugged. "I guess I just have a nose for news."

"Or gossip?"

"No, it's true. But everyone who needs to know that sort of thing is aware of it, so he isn't a security risk." Alistair stood at her desk for a few moments, struggling to find something else to say, something that hinted at wanting to talk to her again—to get to know her better. "Well…I guess I better go…Maybe something will come up where we need to confer."

"Yes, maybe." Ginny almost added that she hoped so but checked herself and then was immediately annoyed for not appearing more interested in talking to him again.

"Well, see you…maybe." Alistair lingered for a few seconds and then left.

"Oh!" Ginny called after him, "Are you going to the dance at the conclusion of the Assembly?" She held her breath, wondering if he would swallow her bait or go on swimming away.

Alistair turned back. "Gee, I don't know. I'm not much of a dancer. Are you going?"

Ginny felt that little tug on the line, and despite her bad experiences in the past, she reeled in what she was hoping might be a good catch. "I will if you go."

"Oh, great! I'll see you there."

Geez, *why didn't I offer to drive her to the dance, get her phone number and her address?* Alistair was annoyed with himself as he made his way back to the India desk. But as he thought about it, he decided he had done the right thing—to have gone further might have appeared too forward; after all, he didn't know much about her and especially if she were involved in another relationship.

That was Alistair. Always cautious about the road ahead. Always calculating before acting. But this time, given Ginny's past experiences with the opposite sex, he had been wise to move slowly.

Chapter 6

Ginny and the rest of the Etobicoke Collegiate delegation arrived at the UN dance before Alistair, but not really knowing anyone there, they simply stood at the edge of the floor, talking—and in Virginia's case searching the room for sight of the apparently nice, young delegate from India.

Not surprisingly, Alistair was late arriving because, in his inimitable way, he was picturing how the evening might develop and having second thoughts about going at all. *What if she's a good dancer? She'll be put off by my unorthodox moves. Maybe we can just jive…But she'll catch on quickly if every time the music slows, I suggest taking a break. What will we talk about? I hardly know her. I could be in for a big disappointment.* He adjusted his tie in the mirror, turned down his shirt collar and ran a brush quickly through his hair. *Still, there is something about her. She seems sweet but also serious. Her eyes look so bright and inquisitive. It's as if they hide layers of depth and complexity. And that long, blonde ponytail, her smooth, rosy cheeks. Wow! Of course, that's all superficial. What is she really like? Well, only one way to find out.*

Alistair drove his father's car to the dance and joined the rest of his delegation across the floor from Ginny's, just as they had been in the Ontario legislature. With so many students gathered at the edge not dancing, he found it hard to spot her, but Ginny saw him the moment he entered the room, though she went on talking to her school chums and only occasionally glanced in Alistair's direction. He missed her the first time his eyes circled the room, but not the second when their glances met, and she gave him a tentative wave. Alistair reciprocated. *Well, this is it*, and he strode across the floor, pushing past the delegates from Poland and the United States, looking far more at ease than he actually felt.

"Hi," Ginny greeted him. "Are you always late?"

"It's a UN tradition. But, yes, I guess so. It takes me a long time to get my hair just right."

Ginny laughed. "It would be harder still if you wore a duck tail."

"I don't have the hips and voice for that…nor the dance moves. You look nice. Pretty dress."

"Thank you. My mother made it."

"So, your Mom's a seamstress?"

"Just for me. Dress-making is a fussy business, and she likes to fuss."

"Over you, you mean?"

Ginny just smiled.

Only child, I'll bet. "So, how does she fuss?"

"It's a long story. Would you like to dance?"

"I'd rather hear the story, but okay." They walked onto the dance floor with Ginny surprising herself by hoping that Alistair would take her hand as they searched for an open space to begin. In fact, he wanted to, but decided that that would be too forward. Instead, he warned her, "I'm not very good at this."

Jive music was playing—"That'll Be The Day"—so Alistair managed to get by without too much difficulty, only vaguely shuffling his feet while leaving it mainly to Virginia to do the spins and overheads and only twice confusing her about which way to turn. Ginny, he noted, was better than other girls had been at interpreting his intentions. But soon the music slowed: "When I Fall in Love." *Here we go. Disaster time.*

Simultaneously, they both assumed the fox trot position. "Hold me a little closer." Ginny blushed. "I mean then it will be easier for me to follow your lead."

Now Alistair could detect a light, appealing fragrance drifting from her—not a perfume, perhaps a lavender oil that she had added to her bath. Whatever, it was subtle, and he felt it suited her disposition. "Wow! You're good! You must have taken lessons."

"Yes."

"Me too, but they didn't stick."

"Well, I was a figure skater and that helped."

"So, now I know a bit about you. You have a mother who fusses over you, you're a figure skater—"

"Former."

"Okay, former. And…oh yeah, you're concerned about the welfare of children in developing countries."

"And about the plight of the Palestinians!"

Alistair laughed. "Well, I've demonstrated my ineptitude as a dancer long enough. Now can we sit down somewhere and talk about all this stuff?"

They got two plastic glasses of an insipid punch and brought them to a vacant table near the dance floor. Each took a sip, grimaced, and put their glass down. "So, I assume you're an only child."

"Why?"

"Because your mother fusses over you?"

"Don't all mothers fuss?"

"Not mine…Well, not unless we get into some sort of trouble."

"We? So, you have siblings. How many?"

"Just one."

"A brother."

"How do you know?"

"Because you said you get into trouble. Is one brother more than enough?"

"Actually, most of the time we get on well. Better than when we were little. The only problem now is when we both want the car at the same time, like tonight."

"You won."

"Yes, for once." Alistair didn't add that he'd urged Jonathan to let him have it because there was someone he was hoping to meet up with at the UN dance. "Okay, Romeo. It's about time you played a little back seat bingo."

"So, he's the older brother."

"You got that right, too…So how does your mother fuss?"

Ginny was struck by how Alistair brought the conversation back to her. It seemed he really did want a meaningful answer, so she briefly described for him her parents' concern that she was a loner and her mother's efforts to involve her in ballet and skating to make her more sociable.

"Why did you stop figure skating if you were good at it?" Alistair eyed his drink but couldn't bring himself to try the sugary concoction again.

"I was okay… I guess I just lost interest." Virginia avoided mentioning the unpleasant dates with Charlie Bernamthorpe and Richard Cartwright. "Besides, I knew it was going to be a busy year at school with the Matric exams, and then this UN thing came along."

"And you didn't want to miss stepping up to the plate for the Children's Fund."

"Of course not," Ginny laughed again and attempted to bring the conversation back to Alistair. "You say your mother fussed only when you and your brother were naughty. What about your father?"

"Oh, not him. But then he was always kind of in the background. Mom did most of the child-rearing. Dad was just there to mete out punishment, which he hated. Oddly, I don't think I've ever really known him that well. He's always so busy with his work. I wish he'd played with us more, you know, shinny on a backyard rink, pick-up baseball. What about your dad?"

"Similar, I guess."

"But I bet he spoils you."

Ginny just smiled. "If I have kids, I want to play with them a lot, not just watch them perform the way my mother did with me."

"Them? Not just one?"

"No. Too much fussing."

I like her openness to repartee. "You know I don't blame my dad for doing so little with us when we were young. It's got to be really tough being a parent. He comes home from work every day dead tired. All he wants to do is put up his feet, have a beer and talk to Mom about how the day has gone."

"There are certainly big sacrifices you have to make being a parent, but I think they're worth it…Would you like to dance again?"

"'Like' may not be the operative word—"

"But as a preamble then to more conversation?" Ginny sustained the UN analogy.

"If you are resolved that we do so."

As they were walking onto the floor, one of Ginny's school chums approached her and explained that the rest of the group had decided to leave. "We're going to Fran's Restaurant for a bite before going home. Are you coming?"

Ginny was unable to hide her disappointment and Alistair, detecting it, jumped at the opportunity. "No problem. I'll drive you there. I'm pretty hungry myself."

Back on the dance floor, Alistair did his best to talk and simultaneously move his feet in time with the music. To his relief, he found he could just manage it, thanks again to Ginny's expertise. "So, are any of the kids in your delegation good friends at school?"

"Not really. My cat, Christopher Robin, has always been my closest friend. He's still alive at fourteen. During the day, he curls up on the bedspread at the foot of my bed. At night, when I was little, he used to tuck himself in at the head as close to me as he could get. Now, though, when I climb in, he moves to a wicker basket on the floor. He doesn't like being kicked."

"So, no one sleeps in bed with you anymore?"

"Nooo!" Ginny pretended to scowl.

"Why was he so special?"

"He was a good listener. I talked to him every morning and evening. We had long animated conversations and every night I gave him a report on what I had done that day. I confided in him about everything—my hopes and dreams, my likes and dislikes."

"You know that sounds like you've flipped your lid, don't you?"

"Yup. That's me, I guess."

Hopes and dreams. I'd like to learn more about those. But Alistair realized that it was time they left for Fran's, the flagship location, he automatically assumed, at Yonge and St. Clair.

"I don't see the others anywhere," Ginny sounded concerned as her eyes roamed around the restaurant for a second time.

"Maybe they got lost or stopped somewhere on the way. Let's go ahead and order something. I'm sure they'll show up shortly."

They both chose cheeseburgers and, sniffing the fried onions on the grill, Alistair asked for some. Ginny hesitated, her blue eyes focussed quizzically on Alistair, trying to guess his intentions, but then she did the same. "So, who besides C. R. was in your live menagerie?"

"My hamster, Edgar. He spent most of his waking hours, spinning the wheel in his cage. But every morning and evening I'd let him out to hop around the room."

"To engage in a different calisthenics routine?"

"Exactly. I had a budgie, too, Hiawatha. He would fly onto my bedside table, snatch a dime in his beak, and flip it in the air to make it spin."

"Sounds like he had an instinct for gambling."

"I guess. And I had an aquarium on top of my chest of drawers, full of goldfish. They were the first to go. Eventually, I couldn't stand any longer watching them press their heads against the glass."

"And did you talk to them as well?" Alistair asked as they munched on their hamburgers.

"Yes. Every time I fed them."

"Like what? 'Don't forget to wait an hour before you go swimming again'?"

"That sounds like my mother talking… I don't know what has happened to the others. It doesn't look like they're coming."

"Maybe they got lost. I don't know how, though; this place is pretty easy to find… Oh, you know what?" Alistair slapped his forehead. "I bet they went to a different location. The Fran's at Yonge and College maybe. I never thought of that because this is the main outlet. I'm really sorry… But no sweat. I'll drive you home."

"It's a rather long way."

"All the more time to…ah…", Alistair hesitated, searching for words that would not sound too forward, "to…to continue our conversation."

Ginny couldn't help wondering if Alistair had intentionally shaken off the rest of her schoolmates. It was, however, a thought that she found didn't bother her, and, in response to another question, she went on to describe to him her other companions—her similarly chatty, stuffed friends, Winnie the Pooh, Tigger and Piglet.

"I suppose we should get going," Alistair said at last. "It's a pretty long drive to Etobicoke."

"It's not that far if you take the Lakeshore."

"Yes, but I'd rather drive out Bloor."

"Why?" They stood up and put on their coats.

"Ah, now that would get us into discussing a peculiarity in my personality."

"Then we better save that for the drive." As they walked to the car, their arms momentarily brushed together, and Ginny thought Alistair was going to take her hand. She had already contemplated the possibility and had decided to grasp it willingly so long as he was the one to take the initiative. But Alistair held back, uncertain if either of them was ready for that so soon.

As they drove away, Ginny said, "Now tell me about this mysterious feature of your personality."

Alistair had left the radio on, tuned to the CBC, but as he answered her question, he switched it off. "I have this habit of thinking things through for a long time while I examine the pros and cons in a situation and then often I decide against doing something that would make perfect sense to do."

Like kissing me? "What does that have to do with choosing this route home?"

"Well, I haven't had my licence that long, and there is a lot of traffic on the Lakeshore, so when I start thinking of going that way, I can see myself getting into an accident. Someone ahead of us will stop suddenly and there will be a multiple car pile-up. We'll get rear-ended and one or both of us will end up with neck pain at best, or maybe in hospital with a more serious injury."

"Or dead?"

"Even that!"

"Gosh, you really *are* a worrier! You're like Piglet."

"Oh, thanks a lot."

"I don't mean you're small, just that, like him, you fret." *And you seem sensitive and other-oriented, too.*

"Yes, I do worry, that's for sure. Like, what if we're just in a small accident and blow a tire or something. I'd have to phone my dad and tell him about it."

"And he'd be angry even if it wasn't your fault?"

"Not really. He's not like that. But my brother—Jonathan is his name—might use it to make sure he gets the car the next time I want it."

"Well then, I'm glad we're driving safely out Bloor Street… I mean going this way, there's not much traffic to bother you at this time of night."

When they reached the driveway of her house, Alistair got out to walk her to the front door. Ginny followed him, moving slowly. *If he wants to kiss me, I'm going to let him.*

At the doorstep, Christopher Robin suddenly appeared from around a corner of the house. He brushed the side of his body against one of Ginny's legs and then he did the same to Alistair. "Hello, old boy. You seem to be a friendly guy."

Ginny smiled. "He is…most of the time."

It wasn't really the cat appearing that kept Alistair from kissing her. He had thought about it throughout the drive but had decided that the safe option was simply to say that he had had a great time and that maybe they could get together again before too long.

"I'd like that," Ginny answered. "Now you know my address, and if you have some paper and a pen, I'll give you my phone number."

Alistair had to race back to the car to get them from the glove compartment. When he returned, there was an awkward silence as they both contemplated taking the initiative—just a simple peck on the cheek or maybe the lips. But nothing happened. Alistair simply said, "goodnight. I'll call you."

Damn. How do you let a guy know it's okay if he wants to kiss you? And then a horrible thought struck Virginia, *what if he doesn't?*

Chapter 7

I T WAS THREE weeks before Alistair called Virginia and she had pretty much given up hope that he would, concluding that she had misread what seemed to be tentative signs of interest in her. But it wasn't that; Alistair had calculated that the very next weekend was too soon—it might appear to her that he was pursuing her aggressively—and the following one he had car issues with Jonathan. "Get with it, man, you didn't even get to first base with her at that dance." When he did call, it was Ginny's mother who answered the phone in their living-room. She motioned to her daughter that the call was for her, and she rushed to pick up the receiver on the extension line in her parents' bedroom, shutting the door behind her. Alistair had called to invite her to the movies.

Hmm. Some Like It Hot. Interesting choice. A romantic comedy, no less, but quirky apparently. They both enjoyed the film, but unlike her experiences on her previous dates, it appeared that Alistair was not going to put his arm around her shoulder. Summoning her courage, she leaned towards him and whispered in his ear, "Marilyn Monroe is stunning, isn't she?"

"Yes, but is she capable of playing a role other than a dumb blonde?"

"*I* happen to think so."

"Tony Curtis is certainly handsome and not a bad actor. Is he your type?"

"Not really." Ginny moved her mouth from his ear but stayed close to him. And with that final signal that it was okay for him to touch her, Alistair tentatively wrapped an arm around her shoulder. There was no resistance, and he felt her head drop gently into the crook of his arm. A surge of excitement coursed through both their bodies.

After the movie, they decided to go to a Honey Dew for a drink and a hot dog. Once again, walking to the car, their hands brushed together, but this time simultaneously they held on. Their grips tightened as they crossed a road and stayed that way. Alistair felt his face and legs tingle and, weeks later, Ginny told him that she had had the same sensation at that moment for the first time.

Driving out Bloor Street on the way home, she recalled their conversation from three weeks earlier and asked Alistair to give her another example of his proclivity for protracted reflection.

"Well, I really like walking, but I'm nervous about heights. So, if someone invites me hiking, I make them go over the route with me beforehand to be sure we won't be climbing up a narrow path with a steep edge dropping hundreds of feet. Even when I'm told it will be perfectly safe, sometimes I still say no because, as I think about it, I visualize myself getting dizzy or tripping and then falling to my death. If I do go, I have a rule: any path I walk must be wide enough for me to faint without plunging to my death."

Ginny smiled. "That seems perfectly sensible thinking to me, hardly peculiar behaviour."

"Here's one related to food. I happen to like raw oysters—"

"Yuck!"

"But I never order them in a restaurant because I don't really know how fresh they are and where they're from. I anticipate that they might make me sick, and I'm a terrible vomiter—"

"Yuck, again."

"Ergo, I don't eat oysters unless I've collected them myself at a beach where I know there hasn't been a red tide."

"I wouldn't eat them anywhere. You don't have a problem with me on that score." She changed the subject and asked him how he felt about Forest Hill Collegiate.

"It's okay I guess, a bit too rigid for me. I'm looking forward to university and a more open environment where there will be lots of options."

"What do you plan to study?"

"Probably political science and economics."

"I thought so. Where? Have you decided?"

"Maybe Queen's or Toronto. I'm applying to both. It's the economics courses I'm worried about. I'm not much good at math."

"Neither am I."

"You're better than I am, I bet. I can never finish the problems in geometry and algebra."

Ginny didn't answer directly. "Are you involved in any extracurricular activities?"

"I'm president of the Public Affairs Club and I'm on the debating team."

"I assumed so."

"Why? Have I been argumentative?"

"No, just informed. Any sports?"

"I was on the swim team in grades ten and eleven—the breaststroke—but I was terrible. When I started, the butterfly had just been introduced and you were free to use it instead. Almost everyone else switched and they'd beat me by a pool length. I was humiliated."

"Poor thing. Why didn't you switch, too?"

"I could never master the stroke."

"So you quit?"

"Yes, but it was also because I hated the smell of chlorine. It made me gag."

Ginny laughed. "Like giving mouth-to-mouth resuscitation."

"Exactly. I've never really been able to get into team sports and the rah-rah spirit of high school anyway. Football seems to be the only sport that matters for guys, and I wasn't going to break a leg or blow a knee for the sake of the team and the school. All the hype seems so artificial.

You know, someone with a bullhorn telling you to shout, 'Hold that line.' It's bad enough having teachers order you to stop throwing paper darts."

"Oh, you're one of those pranksters, are you? But I know what you mean. My mother wanted me to be a cheerleader; the whole idea just revolted me."

You would have looked beautiful, though, in a short skirt and knee-high boots.

When they got out of the car in Virginia's driveway, Alistair took her hand as they walked to the front door. She hoped that his inherent caution wouldn't keep him from taking the initiative and kissing her this time. But just as they reached the doorstep and the critical moment was upon them for a second time, a frightening screech reached them from a tree beside the house and a second later Alistair felt a heavy weight drop onto his right shoulder and claws dig into his coat.

"Christopher Robin, get down!" Ginny scolded the cat as she pulled him off Alistair. "Sorry about that."

"Well, it's certainly not like the welcome I got the first time."

"No. Now…now he is jealous of you…I think."

"Maybe he knows I'm more of a dog person."

"I like them also, too, but my mother won't let me have one."

"Too much fuss, eh?"

"I guess." Ginny slipped the door open and pushed C. R. inside, closing it behind him.

They stood awkwardly for a moment, but then Alistair bent forward and kissed Ginny lightly on the lips. "That was a fun evening. Maybe we can do something next weekend."

Damn, he certainly is slow moving.

"Jonathan doesn't need the car. Can I phone you?"

Well, at least he's been thinking ahead. She smiled at him, looking straight into his dark, shining eyes. "Of course, you can. I'd really like you to."

"Great. I'll be in touch early in the week," he said, and he walked to the car with Ginny watching him until he drove away. *He just doesn't get it! He's certainly different.*

When Alistair called her, Ginny suggested going dancing at Casa Loma.

"Dancing? That's not my strength. Swimming would suit me better."

"I don't want to watch you throw up. Besides, I thought you did very well at the UN dance, and you'll get better the more…I mean if we go dancing again." And Alistair did get better the longer they danced that evening, eventually jiving with some flair and foxtrotting and waltzing without staring at his feet. "Now, I'm going to ask you a question to see if I can go on dancing while talking. Um, let's see. Who were the authors you read growing up rather than playing with other kids?"

"I guess A. A. Milne, E .B. White and Dr. Seuss were my favourites. "Oh, and I also loved Robert Lawson's story about Ferdinand, the bull who wouldn't fight. Later, I read Charlotte Brontë, Harper Lee, and Gerald Durrell. I especially liked *My Family and Other Animals.*"

"Because you thought if only your parents read it too, they would understand your preference for animals over people, right?"

Ginny laughed. "Oh, so you know it. What books did you like best as a boy?"

"Oh, adventure series, I guess, like the novels of Arthur Ransome."

"Me too! I never cared for the series other girls were reading like the *The Bobbsey Twins,* but I loved Ransome's novels, especially *Swallows and Amazons.* Titty Walker was my favourite because she had such a great imagination. It transported her from the Lake District to exotic, far-off places." She refrained from adding, however, that she sometimes imagined that Titty's older brother, John, was her boyfriend and mad about her. She liked him because he seemed sensible and serious though not opposed to having fun and even being naughty in a controlled way. "So, who was your favourite character?"

"As a younger brother, I suppose Roger Walker, ship's boy. Then he added slyly, "I think he and Titty are rather alike. Roger has a good imagination as well."

"They are alike!" Ginny's eyes burned at Alistair as she said it, hoping he would read the feeling of excitement that was steadily growing inside her.

"Do you mind if we take a break? I can't imagine dancing and talking any longer without crushing your toes."

"You won't. You've done very well." They walked out on a balcony with an uninterrupted view of downtown Toronto, but Ginny, clothed only in a semi-formal yellow dress her mother had made, shivered in the early spring cold, prompting Alistair to put an arm around her. "Ah, that feels much better," she said, but they couldn't stand outside much longer, so they returned to the dance floor and left a little later.

"So, who are some of your favourite authors now?" Ginny asked, as they started out Bloor Street again.

"I really like Graham Greene and Kingsley Amis, especially *Lucky Jim*. But now my reading is more political, James Baldwin's *Go Tell it on the Mountain*, and Martin Luther King's *Stride Towards Freedom*, books like that." Ginny tried hard to hide her discomfort. *Maybe we're not that alike. I must seem pretty superficial to him. He must have wondered what I was doing at the model UN.* "Oh, I almost forgot about Jane Austen. She was so incredibly socially astute for her time. Her satire is brilliant."

"Oh, I love her, too!" Ginny's spirits lifted again. "I don't know how I forgot to mention her. She's probably my favourite author. So you *are* a romantic!"

"If that's what liking Jane Austen means, then I guess I am…Oh, and here's another book I loved, *Fair Stood the Wind for France*. What an incredible wartime love story!"

Ginny had read it and now she relaxed completely. *He may be complex and serious, but he's also warm and sentimental. I think he's really sweet.*

So, what are you going to study at university?" Alistair asked.

"Psych or Sociology. Maybe both. I'd like eventually to work with disadvantaged kids."

"That figures. At a UN agency maybe. What university?"

"I'm not sure yet." Ginny tried to read the expression on his face, but all she could go by was the vague upward turn of his lips which she had seen before; she decided to take that as a good sign.

When they got to her driveway, they walked to the front door holding hands. Alistair bent and kissed her on the lips, lingering a little longer than he had before. Looking straight into his dark, shining eyes—closer to her now than they had ever been—she said softly, "I think we can do better than that." Neither of them hesitated then. Alistair drew Ginny close to him and their lips joined for a long time. A tingling sensation enveloped Alistair once again, accompanied by an embarrassing erection. Ginny felt it happening, but it didn't bother her. Instead, it made her heart pound harder and between her legs she felt a dampness she'd never experienced before. It was then that she realized that she had fallen in love with him, and that she didn't want simply to kiss him. She was thinking how nice it would feel to have Alistair inside her.

Chapter 8
Alabama

* * * *

March 21, 1965

"WE HAVE A problem."

"Why?" Alistair asked his colleague Peggy. "The marchers won't turn back this time. President Johnson federalized the National Guard yesterday to make sure they have protection."

"No. Not that. The highway is going to narrow when we get to Lowndes County. From there it is two lanes until the Montgomery County border. According to a court order, there can be no more than three hundred participants while the march is on the two-lane section."

Somewhat to their surprise, Alistair and Peggy had once again been dispatched to Selma to cover the event. The *Herald*'s editors had been delighted with their reports on the first two aborted marches, and especially with Alistair's close-up shot of the unconscious body of Amelia Boynton lying on the Edmund Pettus Bridge as the first protest was violently halted. It had been sharper and more graphic than the wire photo published the day before Alistair's had arrived, so they had printed his as well in the first edition they could.

"For how long will we be on the two-lane section?" Alistair asked.

"Tomorrow and the next day. We won't reach four lanes again until the twenty-fourth."

"So, what are we going to do?"

"I think most of the marchers will go back to Selma tonight by bus or car and sleep there before rejoining the march somewhere tomorrow."

"Including us, right?"

"No! I don't want to do that. We need to schlep the whole way to Montgomery. That's what will give us big, front-page coverage."

"I don't mind walking that far, but where will we stay at night?"

"Apparently, there are campsites set up in fields along the route."

"Oh, no! I'm not doing that. When I was a camp counsellor, I loathed canoe-tripping because I could never get a decent night's sleep lying in a tent on the rocks of the Precambrian Shield."

"But this will be on grass."

"No! Not in this cold weather and with rain forecast for Tuesday. We can't anyway. We don't have any camping gear."

"Don't worry, we'll figure something out."

"You figure it out. I'm taking a bus back to Selma."

"Oh, come on. Get a grip. Don't be such a dick. I'm a big city girl. If I can do it, you can, too."

"Have you ever slept in a tent?"

"No."

"Well, I have, big city girl, and I tell you it's no fun."

"Alistair, we've got to do it. That's how we get a story different from most of the others. That's how we get ahead in this business. You told me you want to be a foreign correspondent some day. Well, this is how you get there. You do articles that the brass notice—human interest stories, movingly and eloquently told."

Alistair relented. So, for four nights, they slept in borrowed sleeping bags in a large tent reserved for the media. It was one of four erected by the organizers each evening. The first three campsites were in fields owned by local residents who sympathized with the marchers' cause and the fourth was in the grounds of a Catholic church. The first night they had a spaghetti dinner, served on paper plates as they sat around a blazing incinerator, stuffed with scraps of wood, the only source of heat in the encampment. "Hey, compliments to the chef. This stuff is pretty good." Alistair used a plastic fork to scoop up the last of his meal and then tossed his plate in the fire. "There were certainly a lot more people marching today than last time, eh?"

"Around eight thousand I'd guess," Peggy answered. "Mostly African Americans, but there are a number of whites, Latinos and Asians here as well."

"And religious leaders from several faiths, I discovered…Well, no point turning in early. We're not going to get to sleep." So, they sat with some of the demonstrators gathered around the crackling incinerator, taking notes on their backgrounds and their experiences of racial discrimination.

"In Lowndes County, over eighty per cent of the population is African American," one protestor told them. "But there is not a single African American registered to vote. Yet, there are more registered white voters than the adult white population of the county."

"How so?" Alistair and Peggy looked incredulous.

"Because whites are often left on the voter rolls long after they've died or moved away."

"Incredible!"

When the conversation lagged, the campers turned to singing hymns and protest songs, "We Shall Overcome", "A Change Is Gonna Come" and "The Times They Are A-Changin.'"

It was cold in all the tents and hardly anyone slept long or soundly. For breakfast, they had what was billed as porridge. "This tastes like gooey paste," Alistair complained to Peggy. "Like the stuff we used to make in kindergarten from flour and water. Bring on the spaghetti again!"

On the third night of the march, it rained. "Jesus, it's freezing in here," Alistair griped when they finally climbed into their sleeping bags near one edge of the media tent. He lay on his back, staring at the canvas roof, wondering how long it would be before raindrops started seeping through the fabric.

"Stop kvetching. This is an experience you're never going to forget."

Alistair rolled onto his side. "With that I can agree. I'll have nightmares about it the rest of my life."

Their legs were so close together that they could feel each other shifting positions inside their sacks in hopeless efforts to get comfortable, and that only added to the difficulty of falling asleep, especially for Alistair. But there was warmth to be gained lying that way, so he didn't move away closer to the wall of the tent. Of course, he was also aware that to do so was to risk causing leaks on the side as well as from the roof. Eventually, he could hear his tent companion breathing more heavily. "Shit! You don't snore, do you?"

"Of course not. I'm a bitch, don't forget. How about you?"

"Well, duh. All men snore."

Peggy groaned sleepily. "Thank God I've vowed I'll never marry."

The next day they marched across the line into Montgomery County where the highway widened again to four lanes. "This is fucking amazing," Peggy said with surprise late in the afternoon. "Our numbers have been growing all day."

"Yeah, people keep arriving by bus and car. More and more media as well."

The final campsite was at the City of St. Jude on the outskirts of Montgomery where they were entertained outdoors at what was billed as "The Stars For Freedom" Rally" with the performers singing from atop a flatbed trailer. "Holy shit! That's Harry Belafonte! And there's Sammy Davis Junior, too."

"Yeah, and Tony Bennett and Joan Baez. They're all here, my boy. And so are we!"

From their isolated locations, it was hard getting stories and photos out to the paper, but, nevertheless, they managed to several times. They wrote their final piece just after Martin Luther King, Jr. addressed the joyful demonstrators from the steps of the state capital, closing with a sobering, personal reflection:

> The very night that King spoke, Viola Liuzzo, a white Detroit woman and mother of five who had come to Alabama to support the right of African Americans to vote, was assassinated by members of the Ku Klux Klan while she was assisting marchers in returning to Selma.
>
> It was a tragic and also ironic incident in light of Dr. King's prediction in his speech that it would not be long before a society that could live with its conscience was achieved. "How long before justice really is assured for all?" we asked ourselves before leaving Montgomery. That moment still seems far away.

"We did it, Alistair, we did it!" Peggy hugged him hard around his chest and, despite her small size, lifted him off his feet, twirling him in a tight circle. They had just phoned in their final story and dispatched the last of their photos to the airport by taxi. "We walked the whole fucking way, and we got some great stories and shots. Time to chill out over a few beers and a good dinner before we fly home and accept our editors' plaudits. My treat."

Chapter 9

AFTER THAT NIGHT at Casa Loma when, afterwards, Ginny and Alistair expressed their incipient love for each other, they started in effect "going steady." Neither of them, however, called it that. They disliked the term, regarding it as a convention of the time that did not mesh with their own personalities and their predispositions not to disclose too much of themselves to others. From that night onward, they did, nevertheless, see each other as often as they could and, when distance and absence of a car of their own, made that impossible, they regularly talked to each other on the phone, finishing each call with a pretend kiss.

Ginny's parents were delighted that she had emerged from the shell that they had long perceived as shutting her off from others. Indeed, they even installed a phone extension in her bedroom so that she could talk to Alistair in private for as long as she liked. At the outset, of course, they knew little about this young man who had suddenly entered their daughter's life other than the modest amount of information Virginia volunteered about him. "He's sweet and good-natured and he has a nice sense of humour—a little offbeat maybe, but that's part of what I like about him. And he's bright and concerned about world issues."

That sounded fine to the Sloans, but it didn't include all the information Ginny's mother in particular wanted to hear. "What church does he go to?"

"Gosh, you know I've never asked him that!"

"Really, I would have thought that that was something you would want to know." The Sloans were members of the United Church and Ginny's mother attended the service every Sunday, she and her father less often. When Mrs. Sloan was busy finding friends for Ginny, one of her proposals had been that her daughter join the Young People's Christian Club at their church. But Ginny had resisted the idea: "That sounds as yucky as ice dancing with Norman Peabody."

"Oh, Ginny, really! What a terrible thing to say."

When the date of the graduation formal at Forest Hill Collegiate arrived, Ginny and Alistair both knew that on this occasion, when he picked her up, he would have to go in while corsages and boutonnières were pinned in place, and photographs were taken. Inevitably, there would be several minutes of small talk and Ginny had had the presence of mind to warn Alistair that one thing her mother would want to know about him was his religion.

"Hmm. That could be a tough one, but I'll do my best. What else?"

"Just be yourself. But don't say anything too obscure or radical."

"Just be conventional, you mean?"

Ginny playfully stuck out her tongue at him. "No, be your UN self. Be…diplomatic."

As soon as he entered the Sloans' home, Alistair was struck by how different it looked from his own. Even in the vestibule, there was a vase of fresh-cut flowers on a small walnut table, gleaming after a fastidious polish. The hallway between the living-room and dining-room was covered by a Persian carpet—an old one from Bukhara so bright and clean that it looked as if it had just been removed from a washing pond in Teheran, dried on the rocks, and its grey fringe neatly brushed into place. Around the edge of the hallway, the hardwood floor was visible, and it was clear to Alistair from the aroma that it had been recently and vigorously waxed with every scrap of dirt and dust carefully extracted. *Geez, what will Ginny think when she sees our house?* There were always unemptied gym bags in the hallway, books and papers lying on the floors, and shoes and socks on the staircase, all of it strewn about like the residue of a receding flash flood. *Still, I think C. R. would like our house better. No place here for a surreptitious pee!*

Religion did dominate Alistair's conversation with Virginia's parents as they sat on a couch in the formal living-room under an original oil painting of a brigantine under full sail in a heavy sea. In Ginny's estimation, Alistair pulled off the encounter brilliantly. Her mother seemed not at all concerned to learn that he had been "raised" an Anglican and apparently took for granted that he was still one. Asked if he went to church, he responded honestly though vaguely that he did sometimes, but "not regularly." That prompted her simply to look disapprovingly at her daughter.

Alistair managed quickly to deflect the conversation away from the contentious subject of frequency. "I must say that, while I'm not a member of the United Church, I am impressed by its preoccupation with social issues. It seems far ahead of other denominations in its concern about poverty in developing countries and its support for organizations working for social justice. It's even taken a progressive approach on issues like the recognition of the Chinese People's Republic."

Ginny's mother seemed pleased by his observations even though they pertained to church matters that were not central to her own preoccupations. She dropped the interrogation at that point and shortly after Ginny and Alistair left for the dance. "You did splendidly," Ginny kissed him on the cheek as she snuggled close to him in the car. "What is your religion anyway? I guess that's a conversation we ought to have, but not right now. You need to focus all your attention on the road, oh nervous one!"

When Alistair and Virginia walked into the school gym holding hands, several of Alistair's friends spotted them right away. "Hey, where did he flush that quail? Never seen her before."

"He met her at a dance at the end of the UN model assembly." It was Alistair's friend, Melvin Steinberg, from primary school days and arrow-shooting fame who answered.

"Seems he lucked out. But another idealist, I suppose. Pretty, though."

"Yeah, no wonder Alistair looks jazzed."

Indeed, Ginny did look beautiful that night, even more than usual in Alistair's view. Her mother had made her a new dress for the occasion, knee length, cobalt blue satin, and full at the hem so that it billowed when she danced. The dress was the perfect shade for her sapphire eyes and the dangling, gold plate earrings that she had purchased for the occasion seemed purposefully chosen so that she would match the blue and gold colours of the school. Enhancing the effect were the streamers strung on all the walls of the gym and the balloons bunched together in big nets hanging from the ceiling, all in Forest Hill's colours. Ginny had discarded her ponytail and let her blonde hair flow in light curls to her shoulders. Altogether, there appeared to be a new confidence about her; even Alistair had noticed it over the preceding weeks. Her frown lines had almost disappeared, and she didn't purse her lips when put off by an awkward question or an impertinent remark. Alistair had altered the arc of Ginny's life and it clearly seemed for the better.

Right away, they stepped onto the dance floor and began to jive, closely observed by Alistair's friends. "Hey! He's not that bad. He even looks like he's having a blast." When the music changed to a fox trot, they carried on comfortably dancing with Alistair leading Ginny with relative ease. "Dig our lover boy. He's a new man!"

At the supper intermission, they sat at a table for four along with Melvin and his date, munching on chicken and egg salad sandwiches served on small paper plates. Along the walls of the hall where the tables had been laid, there were large, hand-painted posters of falcons, the school's mascot, peering down at them as if intent on following the course of the conversation. Below each falcon were the words "Non Nobis Solum"—"Not for Ourselves Alone," the school's motto. Often through his years at Forest Hill, Alistair had reflected on that injunction, more so in his last year there than ever before. *It's good moral advice, I guess. But can we really make a difference to others—to humankind?*

When Melvin and his girlfriend left to resume dancing, Ginny finally asked her mother's question. "So, what is your religion anyway?"

"I'm not sure I know any longer. I guess that makes me an agnostic."

"But not an atheist? You believe in something?"

"I guess, but not in any organized religion. I used to, though. When I was little, Mom made us go to Sunday school and to the Anglican service afterwards. I don't think I ever enjoyed it, but for a while going made me feel good and I slept better at night."

"No nightmares about dying?"

"No. I think I saw God as a kind of Super Dad who protected me from evil and bad things happening."

"Not a Super Mom?"

"No, the God I believed in then didn't fuss. He had everything under control."

Ginny laughed. "So, did he fly through the air in a blue cape with a picture of a boy on his chest?"

"I guess. Anyway, when I was eleven or twelve, going to church and praying didn't work for me any longer. I got to thinking about people in other countries—in Africa, the Middle East and Asia, for instance. If they didn't have any exposure to Christianity that was hardly their fault. They deserved salvation and eternal life as much as anyone else. And what about Melvin and all my other Jewish friends? If I had been born a Jew, wouldn't I view religion the same way they do?"

"Probably, but I'm not sure this means you're beyond salvation. You—"

"Hey, what about all the other animals on the planet? Are they excluded from the hereafter, even poor old C. R.? That's a totally human-oriented view of life that I can't buy."

"It's a good thing you didn't say any of that to my mother."

"But I didn't lie to her either. I still go to church…like for weddings and funerals."

"Good thing also that you weren't explicit about how often."

"Anyway, I don't make a big deal about my beliefs—about being an agnostic. Quite frankly, I don't know what I am. Nehru said once that he was interested in the problems of this world, not in some future life. I guess that's sort of the way I feel."

"Golly, Mr. Ambassador, you certainly read widely preparing for the General Assembly! But I agree with you about organized religion. I do believe in God…at least I think I do, some omnipotent power that made life happen…a Super Mom who doesn't fuss."

"Is there such a being? So, think about this. Do you have any recollection of anything at all through the infinite space of time that passed before you were born?"

"Not really. But I do have moments when I feel that what is happening now has happened to me before."

"You're likely vaguely recalling events from much earlier in your life that are still in your subconscious. Isn't it probable that when we die, it will be like it was before we were born, just nothing?"

"That's just too awful to contemplate. Anyway, I think there is a God. We just have to have faith that there is. That's what religious people always say."

"In an age of reason? That's not possible for me. I need evidence."

Now, Ginny did frown and purse her lips. "The problem with you is that you think too much—too many gloomy ideas." She stood up and held out her hand for Alistair to take. "Come on, my brooder, let's dance again. I need to cheer you up—both of us actually."

"Hold on a sec." Alistair rose. "Here's a happier thought…maybe. What if there is a God and we all get to live forever. Like, I certainly don't believe in hell. Perpetual fire and damnation are too much punishment for any sins. So, supposing we all get to live forever in a perfect place called Heaven. Can you imagine what that would be like—how boring it would be after, say, ten thousand years? How about a million, or a trillion, trillion? Isn't that more terrifying than dying? At least without a God and Heaven, when you're dead, you're totally gone. Admittedly, it's not great to contemplate, but you won't even know what's happened to you. It will just be nothing. No pain, no worries, no fussing."

Ginny grabbed his hand and pulled him down the hall to the gym. "I'm sorry I ever asked you about your religion. Next time I'll try politics!"

"With your mother, too?"

A week after the formal, they went to Alistair's home for dinner with his family. Mrs. Parker greeted Ginny politely at the door. *Gosh, she looks older than she really is. Worn out, I guess from raising two rambunctious boys.*

Alistair's brother sidled up to her and gave her a hug as he took her coat. "It's nice to meet you at last. Welcome to our humble abode." Ginny liked him right away. *He seems warm and casual. He even looks like Alistair only taller with the same little grin, but no dimple.*

Mr. Parker came down the stairs, appearing relaxed and younger than his wife. He greeted Ginny warmly but then apologized, "I'm sorry I have some work to do but I look forward to talking with you at dinner."

"So, you're the person who has been making it hard for me to get the car lately," Jonathan said as they stepped into the Spartanly furnished living-room. "We've heard a lot about you."

"What? That I am kind of kooky?"

"No. Nice and as beautiful as a dozen roses—which is true by the way—as sweet as a cherry pie, as—"

"Come on!" Alistair interjected. "To describe Ginny, you need more creative similes than those."

"But I don't want to steal your lines. Anyway, whatever, you'll have to look after him." Jonathan poked his brother jocularly in the ribs. "He needs a lot of tender care."

Alistair shook his head. "I hope that Jennifer knows what she is in for going out with you."

"Dates without a car unfortunately." He winked at Ginny.

"We could double date," she retorted.

"Only if we get the back seat."

"And leave the driving to Alistair?"

"Hmm, good point. I withdraw that condition."

Chapter 10

GINNY SPENT THE summer of their graduation year at her parents' cottage on Long Lake in Muskoka while Alistair worked as a counsellor at Camp Comak in Haliburton. By mid-summer, she was wishing that she had taken a job in near-by Bala, perhaps at Gerry Dunn's where "All Muskoka" danced. She found she was rather bored with only her parents at the cottage and spent much of the time painting the old boathouse and reading—*The Flame Trees of Thika, Cider with Rosie,* and *This Side of Jordan,* Margaret Laurence's first novel. The rest of the time she sun-bathed, swam, and wrote long letters to Alistair, full of how much she missed him and did not want to spend another summer apart. Every other day, she paddled across the lake and walked into the Bala post office hoping there would be a letter from him. Alistair did write frequently though not as often. He was busy looking after several cabins of ten- and eleven-year-olds and accompanying them on short canoe trips where they slept in tents perched on bare rocks. He found the job challenging and it made him feel guilty for the antics he and Jonathan had inflicted upon their parents. Once in mid-August, he managed to get three days off and made a brief trip to Long Lake to see Ginny. A fellow counsellor with his own car drove him to Dorset and he hitch-hiked from there, leaving only two nights and a day that he could actually spend with her.

The cottage was starkly different from the Sloans' home in Etobicoke. It was an old one, lighted only by coal oil lamps. All of the cooking was done on a wood stove while water came from a well to a hand pump mounted on the kitchen sink, and propane tanks had to be hauled across the lake by boat to run the refrigerator. An outhouse constituted the only bathroom, and the lake the only means of washing other than using the kitchen sink. None of these limitations particularly bothered Ginny, but what she didn't like was that the flimsy, plywood bedroom walls did not reach all the way to the ceiling so that, when you were in the living-room in particular, you always felt that others in the bedrooms could overhear your conversation. That especially concerned her with Alistair's visit. The first evening they had dinner with Ginny's parents and then she and Alistair had to wait patiently through a group game of Scrabble before her parents went to bed.

When that moment came, Ginny lighted the fire that she had already laid in the living-room's rough-stone fireplace. It wasn't so much that the evening was chilly, and they needed warmth as it was the hope that the crackle of the wood would prevent their voices from carrying to the cocked ears of her parents in their bedroom. As the fire noisily blazed, she turned around and flung herself into Alistair's arms for a long embrace. "Oh, gosh, how I've missed you! I don't want to be away from you for so long ever again."

"No, I certainly don't either and speaking of that, I've been thinking about university in the fall. I'm leaning towards going to the U. of T. rather than Queen's. I want to be near the action."

"In that case, I'm going there, too." Ginny guided Alistair onto the pull-out sofa in front of the fire for another deep and lengthy kiss, their mouths opening and their tongues searching until Alistair felt Ginny wrap her mouth around his curled tongue and glide firmly along it. They were by now fully sprawled on the sofa that was to be Alistair's bed and he was lying on top of her. It wasn't easy at that point to stop, for they both wanted desperately to make love. But they had been brought up to believe that intercourse was something you saved for marriage, for only then would it be a special symbol of intimacy and preserve its status as an enduring bond between two people deeply in love. There was, of course, another reason for their parent's' position: the risk of an unintended and perhaps unwanted pregnancy. In fact, so eager was Alistair to have sex with Ginny that he was prepared to abandon their parents' restraining influence, were Ginny to signal that she felt the same way. But so far as he was able to tell, despite the deepening physical nature of their relationship, she had not yet reached that point. So, Alistair held back, and when he returned to camp, they were still virgins.

That autumn, they both enrolled at the University of Toronto, Virginia at Victoria College because her mother took seriously its affiliation with the United Church, and Alistair at University College since he wasn't under pressure to reflect his parents' faith by going to Trinity. U. C. appealed to him because it was non-denominational and less populated by students from private schools. "No budding stock pickers in crew neck sweaters and penny loafers. Lots of faux leather briefcases and bag lunches."

"You're so snide! Switch to Vic. We're in between."

"I would if it meant I would be lying between your legs."

"Behave yourself or I'll sic my mother on you!"

The U. C. and Victoria campuses were not far apart, and Alistair and Virginia were able to see each other fairly regularly. Going to the U. of T. also enabled them to live at home for the first two years of college, saving their parents the expense of room and board in residence. They were rewarded for this after their first year when their parents agreed to help them meet the costs of a two-month trip to Europe.

Travelling together in 1961 as an unmarried couple did, however, pose a problem. Staying in youth hostels was uninviting since that invariably meant sleeping in separate dormitories. On the other hand, hotels required the submission of passports at registration, and they generally frowned on providing a room for young, unwed lovers. Not wanting to risk being discovered using fake documentation nor to face the embarrassment of being refused a room after a hotel clerk scrutinized their passports, they chose to stretch their resources and book separate rooms.

That required selecting the cheapest hotels they could find, but at least almost always they were able to sleep together undetected. As a precaution, they always left suitcases and clothes in both rooms and they either moved to separate quarters in the morning or made sure that the blankets and sheets in the unoccupied room were properly dishevelled.

Their tour started with a week in London where, in addition to the classic tourist sights, they visited Hampstead because Ginny was keen to see Wentworth Place, the Regency villa home of the poet, John Keats. His "Ode to a Nightingale" had been required high school reading, though much enjoyed by both of them. "I didn't know that he was a surgeon as well as a poet," Ginny exclaimed.

"No. I didn't either. So much accomplished in such a short life."

Listening to the birds chirping in the small garden at the rear of the house, she burst into verse, "'… thou, light-winged Dryad of the trees … singest of summer in full-throated ease' I think that's right."

"I bet you can recite from memory the whole poem, 'thou still unravish'd bride of quietness.'"

"Hey! That line isn't in it."

"No. 'Ode on a Grecian Urn.'"

"That wasn't required reading."

"It was in the same volume of poems, and Keats composed them both while he was living here."

"You never cease to surprise me, oh brilliant one."

"Nor you, me," Alistair said as he kissed her.

"But I'm not the quiet woman in that poem, only compared to you."

"You are, however, unravished, much to my regret."

"Well…partly ravished, I guess."

Given Ginny's interest in psychology, they also walked past the fashionable, red-brick house that Sigmund Freud had occupied during the last year of his life after fleeing from Vienna following the Nazi annexation of Austria. They could not see the interior because Freud's daughter, Anna, was still living there, but Ginny had heard that it contained the ornate couch on which Freud's patients had reclined during his famous analyses. "I wish I could get you on it. Then maybe we could get to the bottom of your over-analysis of everything."

"If the couch is more comfortable than our bloody hotel bed, I'd simply fall asleep."

In reciprocation for visiting the two homes, Ginny agreed to go to Highgate Cemetery so that Alistair could reflect on the state of humankind at the tomb of Karl Marx. "I don't know why you wanted to come to this dreary place," Ginny chided him gently. "You're not a Communist as far as I know."

"No but take away the advocacy of violent revolution and a lot of his thinking made good sense. 'From each according to his ability, to each according to his needs.' It's not a bad way to order a society to make it just by serving the interests of ordinary people rather than the rich and powerful. Socialism achieved without violence and coercion seems pretty good to me. That's why I'd vote Labour if we were living here and why, when we get to vote for the first time, I'll support the new party that's replacing the CCF."

"While you go on enjoying yourself, travelling all over Europe."

"Yes. I'll vote left and live right."

"Hypocrite!"

"I know. But at least I'm honest about it. I owe my good fortune to chance. I don't say that the poor deserve their fate because they are lazy. And if my guys happen to win a federal election one day, I'll happily pay the price of my convictions –higher taxes– because everyone else will be doing the same."

"But that's not likely to happen, so you're safe voting your conscience."

"Right."

Ginny shook her head. "You're sick, you know. Your calculating mind has led you to pretend to be virtuous when you're as selfish as anyone else."

"I know I'm sick. I need you to look after me." Alistair examined the eyes in the large, bronze bust of Karl Marx in front of them. Bearded and long-haired, he was set atop a marble plinth with the inscription, "Workers Of All Lands Unite." Twelve feet high, the monument had been designed so that viewers would be close to eye level with the controversial philosopher. "Did you know that Marx was a hypocrite just like me? He wanted the destruction of the capitalist system, but that didn't stop him from playing the British stock market."

"Really? I guess that means you'll do something like that, too. But I don't mind…so long as you don't play around on me."

"Only if I meet a licentious Italian beauty with sleek black hair and olive-coloured eyes."

"Beware. You'll still have to behave. She will have her mother or an aunt on her arm."

From London, they took the train to the ancient Hampshire city of Winchester to visit its medieval cathedral, the burial place of Jane Austen. And from Winchester, they went by bus to Chawton to tour the simple cottage where Austen had written or redrafted most of her novels. "Golly! Look at the size of her writing table. It's barely big enough to hold two sheets of a manuscript."

"And to think that she had to hide her draft under it whenever someone entered the room. How far we've come since then."

"But not nearly far enough." Ginny gazed thoughtfully at the little table for some time. *Poor Jane. Her life was so short, and she never married. At least I don't think that will be my fate.*

From Winchester, they travelled by train and ferry to Dieppe and then to Paris where they walked all over the core of the city and visited the left bank cafés frequented by the authors they had read, Hemingway and Fitzgerald in particular. Much to Ginny's surprise, Alistair also proposed going to Cimetière du Père-Lachaise to pay their respects at the grave of Oscar Wilde, hounded out of England because of his homosexuality. "It's supposed to be a beautiful place—like strolling through a large park."

"Oh, as if the Tuileries and the Luxembourg Gardens aren't good enough? I think one cemetery is enough on our first trip abroad, thank you very much."

"Come on! Freud must have liked them. They're a bit like the archaeological sites he scoured for relics. You can find information in graveyards about people's forgotten pasts."

"You never give up, do you? I wonder if it is because subconsciously you are still troubled by arguments you lost to Jonathan."

This time, however, Alistair did yield and, rather than Père Lachaise, they went for a walk along the soft, crushed-gravel paths of the Luxembourg Gardens, admiring the formal flower beds, the numerous fountains and statues, and the central pond in front of the palace. "Come on, slowpoke." Alistair urged Ginny on as she stopped yet again to observe the young children enjoying the park. This time she wanted to see the outcome of a dispute between two boys in blue and gold football shorts and shirts who were fighting over a model sailboat at the edge of the pond. "Let's get going or we'll never cover the whole place. You're not their teacher, nor their mother."

"No, but I bet I could help them find a compromise that would satisfy them both."

"I'm sure you could." *And that you'd like to, maybe as a teacher, but certainly as a mother.* Ginny started walking again very slowly, looking backwards toward the boys. Alistair's pace also slackened as he stared at the dusty gravel beneath his feet. *That's what she wants—to be a mother. There's no doubt in my mind about that.*

After a few days in Germany where they saw rubble still being cleared from buildings flattened by Allied bombing, they travelled south to Italy where, despite similar wartime wounds, the infectious high spirits of the people shone through, lifting their own again. They visited Milan,

Florence, Venice and finally Rome, loving them all for their exquisite beauty, their rich cultural heritage, their food and wine. Yet surprisingly, it was visiting the Trevi Fountain in Rome—a commonplace tourist site compared to many of the unheralded spots they had discovered—that had the most immediate personal impact on them. Why that should have been so was not immediately evident to them even though they did find the fountain majestic. Searching for an explanation afterwards, they decided that the Trevi's unexpected effect on their behaviour stemmed from the fact that their European sojourn alone together was almost over. It was also, they believed, a result of the cumulative impact of spending more than two weeks immersed in Italy's historic art and architecture and the contemporary charm of its people—from observing men and women openly flirting, freely expressing their feelings for each other. Collectively, these influences had led them to renewed doubts about the sexual strictures under which they had been raised. On top of that there was the fact that they had taken to drinking more wine since their arrival in Italy—cheap, young chianti that was slightly bubbly and tended to go quickly to their heads.

Finally, there was the explanation for the change in their behaviour that was specific to that day spent in the heart of Rome. Ginny and Alistair had seen the popular romantic comedy, "*Three Coins in the Fountain*," released just a few years before their own European tour and, standing that day on the fountain's steps holding hands, they had softly sung the movie's hit tune. *I wonder if Alistair made the same wish I did*," Ginny thought to herself as they finished. *But why can't both our coins be blessed?*

That night after they climbed once again into their narrow hotel bed, it was soon apparent that all of the above factors had diminished their inhibitions. As they lay sprawled on the bed, their mouths opening to welcome each other's playful tongues, Alistair gently ran his fingers along Ginny's thighs. Her grip around his neck tightened and she removed her tongue from his mouth long enough to whisper, "More...I want more."

Slowly, Alistair's fingers slid to where they had never been before but where she wanted him to go.

He could feel Ginny dampen. "More," she sighed with pleasure. "Deeper." There were soft murmurs of contentment as Alistair obliged. Warm fluid oozed onto his fingers and Ginny's legs twisted, uncontrollably, awaiting impatiently an anticipated moment of ecstasy.

"Deeper," she pleaded again, and then she let out a little cry, "Ouch!... Ouch...Oh!"

Alistair didn't know what had happened nor if it was a cry of pain, surprise, or both, but he began withdrawing.

"No! No! It's okay now. I want you...I want you where you were!"

When her orgasm was over, Ginny took his penis in her hands and thrust it in her mouth. A few minutes later, as they lay quietly side by side in bed, with Ginny's head wresting contentedly on Alistair's shoulder, she suddenly giggled. "Well, I'm not sure my mother would consider me any longer a virgin. But I do. Your thing still hasn't been inside mine."

Chapter 11

Returning from Europe in the autumn of 1961 was difficult for Ginny and Alistair. After the freedom of a summer spent together, they were back living in their parents' homes without the same opportunities for intimacy. Making out in movie theatres and in the car that Alistair borrowed from his father—even when they parked it at the end of a quiet street—was far from the pleasure of sleeping together in the same bed. At university, while they sometimes found carrels where they could hug and kiss undetected, these physical moments were limited and short.

They did, however, have one memorable winter evening together that year—at the university farm in Caledon, 150 acres of rolling land owned by Hart House, an hour's bus ride northwest of Toronto. They went there with a number of classmates and late in the evening, when the party turned boisterous, Alistair and Ginny climbed onto a wooden dinner table in the rustic farmhouse and jived. "This is my Ginny," Alistair called out as he swung his arms over her head and, with her back to him, he twisted her from side to side. "She rocks to the left, and she rocks to the right."

As the music stopped and everyone around the table clapped, Ginny turned to face Alistair for a kiss. "Ritchie Valens, no? You're *so* cool."

"Half-way there maybe, thanks to you."

Because Alistair was leaning towards a career in journalism rather than trying to enter the Canadian diplomatic service, he started working as a reporter for the *Varsity* student newspaper, and this also consumed a large chunk of his time outside study and classes.

The problem was compounded the following summer when he was

offered a position in the *Toronto Star*'s training program for potential future staff writers. "The Apprenticeship of Alistair Parker," Ginny congratulated him, but there was a hint of jealousy, even of possessiveness in her remark.

"Yes, but a man without land is nothing." Alistair said, referring to the principal character in Mordecai Richler's novel, *The Apprenticeship of Duddy Kravitz.* "You have a cottage at least."

"It's not mine, silly." In fact, for the moment it was a contributing factor to her frustration and disappointment. Ginny had been unable to find a suitable summer job in the city and had opted for the only position that seemed open to her to make enough money to repay what she owed her parents for their support of the European trip: she had chosen to work as a waitress at Gerry Dunn's where the prospects were good for supplementing her modest salary with generous tips. As a result, they managed only three weekends together that summer when Alistair visited her parents' Long Lake cottage.

Ginny was unhappy all that summer, viewing their relationship as having taken a significant step backwards and finding herself in a situation she had vowed not to have happen again: long stretches of time living apart from Alistair. During his cottage visits, he took obvious delight in seeing both Duke Ellington and Louis Armstrong perform at Dunn's and in obtaining their autographs after the shows, but it also became clear to her that he was enjoying being in Toronto working at the *Star*. After the *Varsity,* he was enthralled by the size and efficiency of the paper's operations. "The editorial room is always noisy and sometimes frantic with activity," he told Ginny the first weekend that summer that he managed a visit to the Sloans' cottage. "Several dozen typewriters clack at the same time, telephones constantly ring, police and fire department dispatches blare over radios, and every so often you hear reporters shout 'boy, please' when they want a coffee or have copy to go to the rim where the editors sit. Oh, yeah, finally there is the loud pop of the vacuum tube as a story sails away to the composing room."

"Gosh, how can you concentrate working like that?"

"It wasn't easy at first, but I'm getting the hang of it. "Oh, another thing, I was given a bit of a tour the first day. The most impressive thing was the presses. Huge rolls of paper were spinning on a giant machine that clanged like…like, I don't know—as if it was a chained prehistoric beast struggling to break free and escape to the street. It grunted and snorted in the heat, or maybe it was because it didn't like the smell of ink that hung everywhere. Finally, it disgorged from its belly fully printed and neatly folded copies of the *Star*'s next edition, ready to be loaded onto trucks and whisked throughout the province."

"Good description, cub reporter. I don't think I can match that, talking about waiting on tables."

"You know, nothing has given me a greater sense of the responsibilities of being a reporter—to be accurate, articulate, complete and unbiased—than watching that press spin with such speed and seeing the finished product come out in such awesome abundance."

Alistair was also enthusiastic about the *Star* employees he was introduced to that summer. "We met the editor-in-chief, Beland Honderich, very briefly. He's the guardian of the paper's liberal social principles and a pretty intimidating guy. I wouldn't want to tangle with him. And I had lunch one day with Mark Gayn, the senior foreign correspondent. He's just the opposite, modest and mild mannered."

"That's the job you would like to have one day, isn't it?"

"Maybe. It sounds exciting living abroad most of the time. Oh! I forgot to mention that one of our first assignments was to do a practice interview with Pierre Berton, the *Star*'s best-known columnist and investigative journalist. 'Well come on, you people,' he goaded us as he sat at his desk wearing his customary bow tie, eyes twinkling. 'You're *supposed* to be reporters. Ask me something.' Everyone seemed dumbstruck, so finally I asked him, '"How do we get your job?"'

"Cheeky, you!"

"Yeah, there was stunned silence and I thought I was done for, but then I added, 'Go and work for the *Telegram*, I guess,' and everyone laughed."

"You were lucky."

"Did you know that Ernest Hemingway worked there as a reporter in the 1920s?"

"Yes, you told me that before."

"But did I tell you about his resignation? Apparently, he had several clashes with Harry Hindmarsh, the city editor, who didn't like him. Hindmarsh had special clout because he was the son-in-law of the publisher. He was known for giving reporters the 'Hindmarsh treatment' and when Hemingway had had enough of his criticisms, he resigned. The story I heard—it may be apocryphal—is that he wrote his resignation on a ream of toilet paper that stretched from the executive washroom to the desk of the city editor."

"That sounds like something Hemingway would do."

Most of all that summer, Alistair was excited by the political reporting he got to do and that had the effect of cementing his leaning to the left. "I interviewed Tommy Douglas on the telephone," he told Ginny on his second visit to the Sloans' cottage that summer. "It was to get his reaction to the end of the doctors' strike in Saskatchewan. What a man! You could just tell listening to him how special he is. He was so polite with me—and so modest about his role in the achievement of public medical insurance."

What particularly appealed to Alistair that first summer at the *Star* was, however, covering the federal election in June shortly after his twenty-first birthday. "I got to attend a couple of David Lewis's campaign events." They were paddling the Sloans' Peterborough canoe close to the shore on the far side of Long Lake, looking for a secluded place to land where they would be away from prying eyes. "He was the NDP candidate in York South, my own constituency. Even though the *Star* is staunchly Liberal, I voted for him. He's ethnically Jewish, but what they call in Israel a 'Bund Socialist.'"

"What's that?"

"An atheist who is at the same time a secular humanist. He was opposed to the creation of Israel and that probably cost him votes in the Jewish community, but he won anyway. Personally, I wouldn't have opposed the creation of Israel, nor do I question today its right to exist, but, like him, I do sympathize with the plight of the Palestinians."

"Yes, Mr. Ambassador. You sound more like a diplomat than a neutral reporter. And is there anything else you feel compelled to report about the *Star* before we turn to a more important matter on the agenda: where we can safely lift this canoe from the lake?"

Alistair playfully splashed Ginny with water from the end of his paddle.

"My naughty little boy," she pretended to scold him. "You deserve a licking."

"Great!"

Ginny splashed him back as the canoe slowed and Alistair eased it towards a flat ledge on the shore. "Not what you're thinking. The kind your father gave you."

"A gentle licking, you mean."

In their third year at university, Alistair and Ginny both moved into college dorms. This gave them more freedom than living at home, but they had room mates who could not be relied upon to withdraw obligingly to give them privacy. There were restrictions as well on the hours that "guests" could be in their rooms, although these were sometimes broken. That happened, for instance, during the hysteria of the Cuban Missile crisis in October when no one paid attention to the registry of dormitory visitors and a number of students left the residences, seeking security outside the city. Their numbers included Ginny's roommate who fled to her family's farm, enabling Alistair to move in for three nights.

The pleasure of being together was, however, diminished by Ginny's anxiety that they were about to be annihilated in a nuclear war when they were just on the cusp of a lifetime together. Alistair, on the other hand, was sanguine about the situation. "Khrushchev won't challenge the blockade. The Soviets are realists. He'll stick to Lenin's dictum, 'If you strike mush, push forward. If you strike steel pull back.'"

"I should have known you'd calculate it that way. Communist!"

"Fusser!" Alistair wrestled with her playfully and she pretended to struggle in his arms until her body went limp, her hands tightened around his neck and her lips fastened on to his.

In the summer of 1963, Alistair was back at the *Star*, but Ginny, determined that things would be different than the year before, took a job in the city at the Clark Institute, administering psychiatric tests to patients. She hoped that would mean that they would have time together in the evenings and on the weekends that Alistair wasn't working. That was not, however, the way it turned out, for, in the first half of the summer Alistair was assigned to the "graveyard shift" from midnight to eight in the morning, and, in the latter half to a time slot from four in the afternoon to midnight. Both positions placed him on the rewrite desk, revamping stories not written to the liking of the editors, typing up ones dictated by phone, and sometimes rewording items the *Star* had missed, but that had appeared in the latest edition of its principal competitor, the Toronto *Telegram*. In addition, when through the speakers perched on the rewrite desk—to which he kept one ear constantly cocked—there was notice of a major fire or crime, he was often the reporter obliged to drop what he was doing and rush to the scene.

The two shifts severely limited his opportunities to spend time with Ginny, especially since, at the end of work with his adrenalin high, it was impossible to go to bed right away and expect to sleep. So, on the graveyard shift, when he got home, he would have a beer and breakfast with his parents who tolerantly adjusted to his unorthodox behaviour, and then go to bed in the late morning. He would get up around eight in the evening, but by then there wasn't sufficient time to drive out to Etobicoke and back, and still get to work before midnight. The eight to midnight hours might have been less of a problem because Alistair could have relaxed for a bit after work and still got to bed early enough to be up in time to have lunch with Ginny somewhere downtown. That happened occasionally, but not often. The problem was that there were other young reporters on that shift as well and they tended to go out together afterwards for a few beers. Sometimes, Alistair didn't join them, but it was hard to resist their persistent appeals. Getting together like that was an integral part of the hard-living, hard-drinking newspaper culture. It was then that young reporters discussed the key stories they had covered that day, shared their opinions about senior staff and management, and discussed their future journalistic plans. It was hard not to be a participant in these exchanges and Alistair feared he would fall out of the loop if he were frequently absent from the gatherings.

Moreover, 1963 was a heady year at the *Star*. The Liberals had just been returned to power in April and, under pressure from the New Democratic Party, ambitious plans were afoot to establish a federal health care program and Canada pension. Most of the reporters ardently supported these measures since they were consistent with a key principle of the *Star*'s founder and publisher—promoting social justice. So, for several reasons, Alistair was doubly enthusiastic about his job that summer and being engaged with his colleagues in addressing the key issues of the day.

While Alistair did his best to explain this situation to Ginny and while she contended that she understood, in fact, she didn't entirely. She felt hurt and rejected. And when she and Alistair did get together, these sentiments were compounded by the fact that, in his reports on what was happening at the paper, the name of one young reporter in particular kept arising.

Chapter 12

THE PERSON IN question was a short, feisty woman with black hair and an undersized but pugnacious nose. When she was working, her mouth and jaw were set tight and her chin arched slightly upwards as if she were a boxer inviting an opponent to take a jab, confident she could bob and weave away before it landed. Her most striking feature, however, was her dark green eyes, uncommon in women of her background. They flashed like port lights, made brighter by the contrast with her tawny skin. "She graduated from Western in the spring," Alistair recounted to Ginny. "The *Star* has hired her full time, so her status is different from the rest of us. A couple of the trainees don't like her because management went outside our program to get her and that takes away a position for one of us when we graduate, and maybe more if it becomes a precedent."

"But you do…like her, I mean?" Ginny was already churning inside.

"Yeah. She's nice. Cheerful and spunky. She's made a real effort to fit in with everyone. She goes drinking with other reporters, plays poker with them and even places bets on the horses via the track reporter. She also cusses as badly as any of the guys, and with the trainees she doesn't make a big deal of being a fulltime employee."

"What did you say her name is?"

"Peggy Morganstein."

"Oh. From Forest Hill Collegiate?"

"No. She grew up in Montreal but went to Western because she wanted to study journalism."

"It seems you already know quite a bit about her."

"Ginny! She's just a colleague at work. There's nothing in it. We don't even see major issues the same way. She's a Zionist, for instance. She hates the Palestinians."

"Oh, well then there is an irreconcilable difference between you!" Ginny stuck out her tongue only half in jest.

That August, Peggy got a major break that helped to secure her position at the *Star*. She managed to convince the city editor to send her to the U. S. capital to cover the March on Washington for Jobs and Freedom, led by Martin Luther King, Jr. and other Black leaders. A senior reporter was being dispatched to provide the hard news stories, but Peggy persuaded the editor that the demonstration was important enough that his copy should be supplemented by colour pieces she would write to give readers a feeling of actually being there.

"Hi, is that you Alistair?" It was he who was on the rewrite desk the evening of August 27, 1963, when Morganstein filed her first report. "I was hoping it would be."

"Geez, I don't know. There are others who are faster typing."

"Maybe, but you'll be patient if I mess up a paragraph and have to start again. So, how is everything in Toronto?"

"Busy."

"Too busy to see your shiksa?"

"My who?"

"Never mind."

After his years at Forest Hill Collegiate, Alistair was fairly familiar with Yiddish expressions, but he hadn't heard this one. "So how is it down there?"

"It's fantastic. The atmosphere is terrific. People are already gathering, and expectations are running high that the demonstration will lead to major progress on civil rights."

"Bugger, I wish I were there."

"You'd love it, but don't worry; your chance will come…Anyway, here goes. Tell me to slow down if I get going too fast."

As Peggy reached the point where she reported that five thousand policemen, reservists, and National Guardsmen were going to patrol the actual area of the demonstration and close to 20,000 federal troops were being stationed on alert in Washington suburbs, Alistair interrupted. "It sounds like there will be trouble. You'd better be careful."

"Just an occupational hazard. Can't do anything about it."

When Peggy finished, Alistair told her the story was great and he didn't anticipate that there would be much if any editing. "Thank you. You're a mensch, but there will be changes. Those guys always have their pencils sharpened. Anyway, I'll file another one tomorrow afternoon as late as I can to catch the last edition, but it will probably be before the whole thing is over. So, I'll do a wrap-up at night. Are you on then?"

"Yup, I'll be waiting for it."

"Good."

At four o'clock the next day when he got to work, the first thing Alistair did was phone his old high school friend, Melvin, to ask the meaning of "shiksa."

"It's derogatory. A gentile girlfriend you're attracted to because she is young and beautiful. Why? Did someone say that about Ginny?"

"If I heard it right."

"A woman? Sounds like she's jealous."

"Not at all. Just sarcastic."

Peggy didn't call until after nine that night. "Okay, here it is, the best I can do with so little time." She opened by describing the atmosphere at the Washington demonstration as "an odd combination of a revival meeting and a picnic," and was in the middle of explaining how, despite their important role in organizing the event, no women were invited to speak, when Alistair interrupted her.

"Oi, vey! We've got to stop for a bit. Something important is coming in on the police radio. Hold on and I'll get back to you as quickly as I can." He listened to the police dispatches for several minutes and then summarized what he had heard for the assistant editor on the rim. It was a shooting on Yonge Street that the editor decided needed covering, but at that hour he had another reporter he could send, enabling Alistair to return to his call from Peggy.

"'Oi, vey.' You've got to come up with a better expression than that to convince me you're not one of those goys who boasts he isn't anti-Semitic—that some of his best friends are Jews."

"No, I don't do that," Alistair answered sharply. "It just happens to be a fact. And, by the way, when you called Ginny a shiksa, that wasn't very nice."

There was silence at the other end for several seconds and then Morganstein said, "Oh, fuck, you're right. I can be a putz sometimes. Sorry. I didn't mean it. I don't really know anything about her, except that you love her."

"Apology accepted. Back to your story."

Peggy summarized briefly the speeches that had been delivered and explained how it was only because of an interruption by Mahalia Jackson, shouting at Martin Luther King to tell the crowd about "the dream," that King departed from his prepared notes to utter the words that would define the march. Then she closed with the line, "At least on this momentous day, it seemed that King's dream might be attainable."

"Thirty … So, what do you think?"

"Great, just like the others. And, by the way, there was practically no editing of them on the rim."

"Free of the pencil! Free at last!" Peggy shouted joyously. "Well, I could plotz. I'm off for a beer and bed. See you on Monday when I get home."

"Actually, I'm done here on Saturday. Back to university."

"Oh…of course. I forgot… So, are you coming back next year?"

"I don't know yet. We graduate in the spring. Lots of decisions to make."

"So, why don't you keep your hand in at the *Star*, you know, submit a few features over the year."

"Maybe, but I need to focus on my studies. I don't know what lies ahead."

"It's a great profession, Alistair. I love it. I feel at the centre of the action, and I think it's possible to have a real impact on public thinking and even policy at the *Star* in particular with its commitment to social justice."

"And to selling papers."

"You're such a cynic."

While Ginny and Alistair were back in dorms for their last undergraduate year, the circumstances were somewhat better. Alistair's brother, Jonathan, had already graduated from Osgoode Hall and completed his articling; he was now with a Toronto firm doing corporate law. When he and his fiancée, Jennifer, got married that summer, he offered his apartment to Alistair and Ginny while they were away on their honeymoon. "Better than hiding away in the stacks to smooch or whatever you do."

At the end of their time using the apartment, Alistair said, "What an opportunity this is to leave a little surprise, but what to do?"

"I know! Let's apple-pie their bed."

"Great idea! You *do* have a mischievous streak, don't you?"

"It's your bad influence. Do you think they will be cross with us?" Ginny was refolding the sheets to less than half their proper length.

"Just for a moment, but then Jonathan will probably laugh. It is the kind of thing he would expect to have happen."

"We can leave a bottle of wine to appease them."

"You're so sweetly naughty."

"Oh, it will be dry, of course!"

That moment of levity was followed by a jolt that Alistair feared would end his journalistic career just as it was beginning. He was back on the rewrite desk on the shift that ended at midnight and home in bed the next morning when his mother shook him awake. "There is a telephone call for you from the city editor."

"Aw, oh." Alistair rubbed his sleepy eyes, stumbling to the phone.

"You better get down here right away," he was told. "We have a problem and Honderich is steaming."

"Why? What's happened?"

"It's that fire you wrote about last night where no one was in the apartment looking after the three little kids."

"True, so the police contacted Children's Aid, but there was no room for them in a shelter. That's why I made that the lead. It was a social issue story."

"It's not that. You wrote that the mother was charged with criminal neglect."

"Yes, I checked with the police just before my shift ended and they said they were charging her."

"Well, the guys at Magistrate's Court say she's not on the docket, so you better get down here pronto and explain yourself."

In the end, it all blew over. The *Star*'s ace police reporter was asked to investigate and corroborated Alistair's account of what had transpired. Overnight, the police had determined that the mother had mental health issues and decided to drop the charge. "How was Alistair to know that would happen when he filed his story at the end of his shift? I would have done the same thing he did."

It was, however, another reminder for Alistair of the potential pitfalls journalists routinely faced. *You have to work fast but entirely accurately. I hope I'm up to this.*

In late November of 1963, circumstances arose again that enabled Ginny and Alistair to spend two nights together undetected in Ginny's residence. With the assassination of President Kennedy, there was another period of panic that precipitated an exodus from the dorms: fear that Lee Harvey Oswald had not acted alone and that his were only the first shots in a new conflict between the Communist bloc and the West that might end in nuclear war. Ginny shared this anxiety but not Alistair who vainly tried to lighten the atmosphere of gloom everyone felt after the assassination. "At least political crises are good for sex." In fact, however, faithful to their parents' principles they continued to stop short of full intercourse.

After exams ended in the spring of 1964, Alistair went back to work at the *Star*. He was surprised to discover, however, that Peggy Morganstein was no longer there. She had left three months earlier for a higher-paying position at the Toronto *Herald* with flexibility in the stories she chose to cover. Shortly after he started work, there was, nevertheless, good news as well. The city editor advised him that he had graduated from the training program and was now considered full-time staff. Ten days later, he had his first byline story—on the opening earlier that spring of the first Tim Horton's coffee shop, located in Hamilton, Ontario. Peggy called him from the *Herald* and insisted on taking him out for lunch along with several reporter chums to celebrate. "'Alistair Parker, Star Staff Writer.' Doesn't that make you feel good seeing it in print?"

"I'm enough of an egotist that I have to admit that it does."

Ginny, on the other hand, wasn't at all sure what her future held. She had expected that as soon as classes ended, Alistair would propose and when that happened the course ahead would be set, but he hadn't, and now she anticipated that he was waiting until their graduation ceremony. In the meantime, she decided to go back to work for the summer at the Clark Institute. Their graduation, however, came and went with still no initiative on Alistair's part. Their parents all attended the event and afterwards engaged in polite small talk together as they posed for pictures outside Convocation Hall. Tulips of various shades were in full bloom in King's College Circle, providing needed contrast to the surrounding sombre and grimy academic buildings. Everyone in the group smiled dutifully, yet the shots had an air of stiff formality about them. In part that was due to the graduation dress code; the women were in fashionable, spring dresses suitable for a tea party at Buckingham Palace and the men in dark suits and conservative ties, clothes that would have done equally well at a wedding or a funeral. Ginny and Alistair, of course, had the added discomfort of wearing graduation gowns and headache-inducing mortar boards that pressed against their temples. But there was more than that affecting the atmosphere. There was a quiet soberness to the group induced by the universal expectation that Ginny and Alistair would have been engaged by then. With that not having happened, uncertainty, even anxiety pervaded, weighing everyone down.

Ginny wasn't prepared to wait any longer and two weeks after convocation, she suggested to Alistair that they go out for dinner at the Old Mill in the west end of Toronto. With its oak ceiling beams and half-timber walls and its views to the Humber River flowing swiftly in the spring run-off, the Mill was an attractive place to dine now that Alistair had a fulltime job and they could afford the occasional splurge. Ginny had prepared herself to match the aesthetics of the setting. She wore a little more makeup than usual, employing blue eye shadow and black mascara to bring emphasis to her eyes and some rouge to her cheeks so that they glowed in the table candlelight. Her dress was a blue velvet one her mother had made two years earlier, cut across the chest to reveal just a hint of cleavage. It was one that she knew Alistair particularly liked, though he complained it had not been made low enough. He, too, had done the best he could for the Mill, retrieving from deep in his closet grey flannels, a Harris Tweed sports jacket and a thin, checkered wool tie. His hair, however, was rather dishevelled, but then it usually was, so Ginny didn't see it as an affectation he had adopted as a newly minted full-fledged journalist scoffing at social convention.

"You look lovely as always," Alistair complimented her as they studied their menus.

"You don't look bad yourself." Ginny reached across the table and swept his hair into place. "My Star Staff Writer, so busy he doesn't even have time to brush his hair."

"I do really. I just forget. It would be better if I got a crew cut and could just leave it alone."

"Gosh, not now, silly! You need a more distinguished look that suits your new role...and your age."

Alistair wasn't sure if she was flattering him or being sarcastic. *Does she think I'm too enamoured of my job?*

In fact, Ginny was trying to shift the conversation from Alistair and the *Star* to the two of them and their future. Alistair, however, didn't grasp her intent and she waited patiently for him to bring up the subject, but he didn't. At last, over replenished glasses of wine at the end of the meal, she decided she had to broach the subject herself. "It was nice having Jonathan's apartment to use, wasn't it?"

"Sure was, and it's still there for us whenever they are away."

"But...Now that we've graduated, maybe we could...you know..." She waited for Alistair to finish the sentence, but he just looked at her quizzically. "Maybe...maybe we could get one of our own."

"Oh! Yes! That would be great."

"But in that case...we'd have to do something about our...our situation first."

"Our situation?"

Ginny sighed with exasperation. *Is he so focussed on his work that he's not thinking about us at all? Surely, he knows what I'm getting at.* "Well, we couldn't just live together. Our parents wouldn't approve."

"I don't think mine would mind."

"Well, mine certainly would, so ......So..."

"So?"

"First, we'd have to...you know...get married." Alistair said nothing and turned his head towards the window beside their table even though the sun had set, and it was too dark now to see the river. "Well?" Ginny's throat tightened and she felt her heart pounding, not with excitement, but fear of the reply. "What do you think of that idea?"

"I…I don't know." Slowly Alistair's eyes turned back to Ginny's with what she thought was a look of both sadness and dread. He had, of course, in his inimitable way, reflected a lot on their future, but he simply hadn't been able to come to a definitive conclusion.

"What do you mean you don't know?" Ginny struggled to stay calm, to avoid appearing angry or upset.

"I…I don't know if I'm ready to get married."

"But we've been together for over four years now. We know each other completely, all our quirks and faults. And we love each other. At least, I love you. Don't you still love me?"

Alistair reached across the table and pressed one hand on top of hers. "Of course, I do."

"Well then? Why not get married so that we can be together whenever we're not working? Don't you want that?"

"Yes, living together sounds great."

"You mean having an apartment of our own, not getting married?"

"Yes…I guess…for now at least."

"But why not get married if you really do love me like I love you?"

"I don't know. I guess I just don't feel ready yet."

Tears were gathering in Ginny's eyes. "Is it Peggy? Have you fallen for her and just won't admit it?"

"No! No. I've told you before we're just friends. That's as far as it goes, honest."

Ginny started shaking. "Is it because you don't want to have children and you know I do?"

Alistair hesitated, searching for the right words to answer. "That's part of it, I guess. I can't visualize myself as a father. You know how hard I found the job at Camp Comak. I'm not sure I'm ready to make the sacrifices that having a family would involve—to accept the limitations that could have on my career. Journalism is very demanding."

"But others manage both successfully." Ginny's throat felt sore as she choked back her tears. "Why couldn't we?"

"Maybe we could. I just don't know."

"And you're not ready to take the risk?"

"No…Not yet anyway."

"Oh, gosh! I should have realized this might happen." Ginny dabbed at her eyes with a handkerchief and blew her nose. "I thought that by now you'd changed your mind about kids. We should have talked this out long ago."

"I know. I'm sorry. It's…it's just that I keep thinking of my father. I wouldn't want to have a distant relationship with my children the way he did. But I'm afraid it would be like that if I stay in this profession, especially if I get to be a foreign correspondent. It wouldn't be fair to them, nor to you either."

"But I would love to live abroad. I'll go with you anywhere. I can always find work and if we have children, they will be fine with that so long as we are together."

Alistair ran his hand up Ginny's arm trying to comfort her. "I'm sorry…I feel really terrible about this."

Ginny shuddered from the realization she had not altered Alistair's mind. "Kids are only part of what's holding you back. What's the rest?"

"I…I just don't feel ready. We're still so young, and I'm only just starting out on a potential career. I want to get established first, feel secure about the future before taking that step."

"But the future is never certain. If you really love me, we can face together whatever happens." Ginny was weeping uncontrollably now, and Alistair was also close to crying. He moved around the table and wrapped his arms around her. "I don't think you really love me, not the way I love you."

"No…no! That's not true. I love you deeply."

"It doesn't sound at all like that to me."

"I know. I'm sorry. I *do* love you, and I'm probably being really stupid… but I need more time."

Alistair pressed his lips to her cheek, but she shrugged him off and stood up. "I think we should go. Please take me home."

When they got to Ginny's house, they sat in the car in the driveway silently for some time in the awkward way they had felt on their first date, each trying to come to grips with what was happening. Tears were once again running freely down Ginny's cheeks and, at the sight of them, Alistair, too, began to cry. He put an arm around her and drew her trembling body close to him. She lifted her face towards his and, clinging desperately to him, pressed her lips to his. "I love you," she blurted through her tears. "I love you and I don't want to lose you." Then she pulled herself from his arms and opened the car door. "Please don't get out. I'll let myself in." She rushed to the front door, opened it, and disappeared inside without looking back.

Chapter 13

AFTER THAT DINNER, weeks rolled by without Alistair calling Ginny. He felt miserable about what had happened and on several occasions was on the verge of contacting her. Yet, every time, he came to the same conclusion that had caused the rift: he didn't feel ready to get married much less assume the responsibility of having a family, and since his position hadn't changed, he realized it would be unfair, even cruel, to phone and raise her hopes only to dash them again in another unhappy, emotional scene. He was , nevertheless, wracked with guilt over his treatment of her and failure to discuss earlier his reservations about marriage. "I've been a total shit," he said to Peggy one day over a beer and pastrami sandwiches at a restaurant halfway between the *Star* and *Herald* offices. "I don't know what it is. There must be something wrong with me."

"Don't be so hard on yourself. You probably didn't really know fully how you felt about marriage until you were forced to make a decision. Maybe, like me, you're not cut out for it. I value my independence too much. I don't want to be someone's baleboste. I—"

"Homemaker?"

"Right. Being in charge of a well-run home is not my dream. I have bigger plans and to fulfill themn I need to be free to come and go as I like. Maybe deep down you feel the same way."

"Maybe. Right now, I just feel like an enormous prick."

"Well, think about it. If you're really committed to this profession, it wouldn't be surprising if you don't want to be tied down. Your piece on the Lions Club International Convention here and Governor Wallace's racist speech condemning the Civil Rights Bill was terrific. And look at the public outrage that resulted from the negative media coverage Wallace got. In journalism, you can make a real difference, but it's hard if you have a family because it's demanding, all-consuming sometimes, and it can be dangerous if you become a target because of where you are or what you've written."

"I just don't know. I've fucked things up. That's about all I'm sure of."

Ginny was even more upset and confused than Alistair after that night at the Old Mill. She, too, was longing to talk to him on the phone—to get back at least to where they had been in their relationship before that night, to tell him that she was okay with not having children and ready to wait longer before making a decision about marriage. But whenever she reached for the phone, she thought to herself, *If he really loves me, he will call. The onus is on him. He knows that I love him and want to spend the rest of our lives together. If he feels that way, too, he will get in touch somehow.* Yet, Alistair never did and day by day, Ginny's hopes grew fainter. It was at this time , too, that her old cat, Christopher Robin, died. To Ginny, that signalled an end to her childhood world at the same time that what had seemed realistic hopes and dreams for the future were suddenly vanishing as well.

Apart from going to work and dropping in at the School of Social Work to submit an application for graduate studies in the fall, Ginny spent almost all her time at home, shut away from her parents in her bedroom. It did not, however, offer the solace and escape it had in childhood and throughout her years in high school. The aquarium that had been on top of her chest of drawers had been given away and so had the cages for her hamster and budgie. Most of her stuffed animals had been shut away in a box that was now at the back of her clothes closet, although her mother had left the most cherished one, her old teddy bear, Winnie the Pooh, on the pillow in the middle of her bed. The extension phone on which she had so often talked privately to Alistair was also gone, relocated to the kitchen since it was seldom used any longer.

After Ginny had moved into residence at university, her mother had also stripped the wallpaper—a pattern of farmyard animals—and had it replaced by one with small pink roses clinging to twisting, thorny vines that reminded Ginny of barbed wire. To her, the bedroom now had a cold, almost hostile look that only added to her longing for an apartment with Alistair that they could decorate to their own tastes.

Ginny's mother feared that her daughter was reverting to her old, introverted self. She was angry with Alistair for wounding her so badly, but equally concerned that she recover and, if their relationship was truly over, have a social life again. So, she kept urging Ginny to get in touch with her friends from high school, Victoria College or the Clark Institute. "You need to stop feeling sorry for yourself. It's been weeks now. You need to get out and back in circulation. Then you'll feel better and who knows what might happen."

Ginny resisted, but then, in late summer, she received an unexpected telephone call that did radically change her circumstances. It was from Jonathan. "I've been meaning to call you for some time. I know you guys have broken up...well...for now at least. I'm really sorry about that. I think you're right for each other, but you know Alistair can be a real dork sometimes and this is one of them. He thinks his way into stupid decisions. Listen, one of the young lawyers at the firm managed to snaffle some tickets for the Beatles Concert at Maple Leaf Gardens on September sixth. Jennifer and I are going, so why don't you come along with us? It's not really a couples' thing, and there will be several nice young guys in the group who are unattached. It would be good for you to get out and, who knows? When I tell Alistair that I've seen you out on the town that might just do the trick. He'll be so around the bend he may get down on one knee and beg you to marry him."

Ginny found herself smiling for the first time in weeks; the image reflected so much what she wanted. "I don't know, Jonathan. Maybe Alistair and I are less well suited than I always thought."

"But will you at least give this a try?"

Ginny paused, weighing Jonathan's proposition. "I'm sorry," she finally answered. "It was really sweet of you to call. But no thank you. I...I'm not ready yet to go out anywhere. I..." Her voice was trembling, and Jonathan realized she was about to cry.

"Okay, okay. I understand. I won't press you but think about it. The concert is still three weeks away. Call me anytime if you change your mind."

"Who was that?" Ginny's persistently inquisitive mother asked after the call, and while in the past Ginny had been reluctant to confide in her, this time she did. "You should go, darling. Jonathan is right. It might lead Alistair to get in touch and try to patch things up."

So, in the end, Ginny called Jonathan back and agreed to go to the concert. There, she met Colin Jameson, a tall, fair-haired lawyer, three years older than she was, one of several men to whom Jonathan introduced her. Two weeks later he telephoned and asked her out to a dinner dance at Casa Loma. "Um, how about somewhere else?"

"That's fine with me. We'll go to the Granite Club. I joined two years ago. It's good socially and also for business."

Ginny accepted the invitation, hoping the result might be the reappearance of Alistair on her family's doorstep. Rather to her surprise, however, she enjoyed the evening with Colin. When they first took to the dance floor, she was delighted by how light he was on his feet and confident in guiding them through complicated steps. *Hmmm... A lawyer with twinkle toes. What a surprise!* She also appreciated the solicitous way he treated her, inquiring as to whether she was comfortable sitting without a jacket when they took a break from dancing, offering to fetch hers from the cloakroom, or to get her a drink from the bar. On the other hand, she had to admit to herself that he lacked Alistair's wit and sense of fun, and, as a conversationalist he was rather limited. *He doesn't seem to have the breadth of knowledge and eclectic interests that Alistair has. Does he care about big public issues? I don't know. We haven't talked about any. I wonder if he reads, goes to the movies and things like that.*

When they left the Granite Club, Ginny let Colin take her hand as they walked to his car. *Golly, Iis this really me? Have I changed that much since Alistair and I first went out?* But when, at her front door, Colin leaned in to kiss her, she turned her face away. "Sorry. It's too soon for me."

Shortly after that date, Jonathan phoned her to find out how it had gone, and then reported to Alistair that Ginny had had a good time dancing with Colin. "Great. I'm glad she went out. That's what she needs to do. She loves to dance. It will do her a world of good."

"Call her, you idiot!"

In late September, Colin invited Ginny out again, this time for dinner and dancing to the Moxie Whitney Orchestra in the Imperial Room of the Royal York Hotel. Once again, she enjoyed herself and his attention to her every need. She decided that he wasn't arrogant, simply more self-assured than Alistair, and clearly very much focussed on corporate law and earning a large income. *But I miss Alistair's social concern... and also his eccentricities, his vulnerability. Funny, those are things it never occurred to me that I actually like about him.*

The next time Colin called, he seemed at a loss to suggest something that they might enjoy together. "How about a movie and a light meal afterwards?" Ginny proposed. "Did you ever see the musical, '*My Fair Lady*?'"

"No, but I heard it was good."

"Well, the movie version has just opened with Audrey Hepburn and Rex Harrison in the leads. How about that?"

"That's fine with me."

"I liked the ending better than in *Pygmalion*," Ginny commented over dinner afterwards at Murray's Restaurant. Colin, however, didn't respond. "You know... In Shaw's play Liza ends up marrying Freddy not Professor Higgins." Colin just shrugged his shoulders and offered no opinion. *I know what Alistair would say—that Shaw's ending effectively portrayed the impact of class on human behaviour while the movie was an enjoyable but romanticized version of real life.* Ginny filled the awkward silence. "Whatever, I liked the film because I'm a sucker for happy endings."

"Oh, oh yes! I am, too."

Perhaps it was the effect of the movie, but this time when, holding hands, they reached the doorstep of Ginny's house, she let Colin kiss her. It wasn't a passionate embrace, but it was more than a simple peck, and it was on lips that slightly parted.

After they had gone on yet another date, Jonathan called his brother once more. "Well, you've done it now, asshole. Ginny is seeing Colin pretty regularly. Why the fuck didn't you call her? Do you want to spend the rest of your life hanging around swilling beer with a bunch of overweight, jackass reporters?"

When Jonathan's call ended, Alistair sat by the phone for a long time, thinking. *I can't let this happen. I don't want to lose her.* He dialled Ginny's number, but just as it started to ring, he hung up. *I can't do it. I can't just apologize for treating her the way I have. I need to beg her to break up with Colin and come back to me if she's willing. No, it's more than that. I have to ask her to marry me.* As he sat twisting the telephone cord in one hand, he tried to visualize how his life would transpire as a married man, or how it might turn out if he remained a bachelor. *Would it be as bleak as Jonathan imagines?*

To his surprise he found himself suddenly humming his own version of the old sea shanty that Titty had recited at the end of *Swallows and Amazons*. "Leave her, Alistair, leave her while you can. It's time for you to leave her."

Tears were running down his face as he stood up and stared one last time at the phone, resting in its carriage. *I can't do it! I can't see myself settled down to a conventional life with a wife and two kids, maybe more, tugging at my shirttails for attention. And where? In a little bungalow somewhere in the suburbs? I want more from life than that. I want adventure and the chance to have an impact on global affairs. Peggy is right. Marriage is not for me.*

Chapter 14
Toronto

• • • •

The Present in June

ALISTAIR IS SITTING in an upholstered chair in the shared living-room of the long-term care home having a cup of tea and an Arrowroot biscuit. She is beside him rigidly upright in an ordinary hardback chair, munching slowly on a cookie Alistair is feeding her bite by bite. Her tea is in a cup on a small table, but her hands are too unsteady to raise it to her lips, so he does it and, after each sip, wipes away spills from her mouth. She tries several times to say something, but amidst her soggy, disintegrating crumbs, all that comes out is a stutter. "Don't worry. I know what you're thinking…Nice tea, isn't it?"

Angela is seated on the bench at the upright piano along with a neatly coiffed, white-haired resident in her late seventies. She is helping her relearn the right-hand keys for "Heart and Soul." Gradually, it comes back to her, and she hammers out the familiar central section of the melody without fault, so Angela joins her, playing a simplified version of the base. After several runs, they stop and high-five each other as the small, appreciative audience claps energetically. "Encore, encore!" Alistair encourages them and they play chopsticks several times, a tune they have previously worked on together.

"Apparently, she was a good pianist when she was young," one of the staff confides to Alistair as she passes around more cookies. "But she stopped for a long time until Angela got her playing again."

"If I lived here, I wonder if she could unearth in me some ability to read musical notes."

"So, what is your talent?" a woman sitting near him calls out. "Everyone has one."

"Not me, I'm afraid," Alistair answers.

"Oh, bless my soul, you're just being modest. Do you play any sports?"

"Not any longer."

"Oh, well, my husband does. He's a very good squash player. I'll ask him to show you how the next time he comes in."

"That would be fun, thank you."

Alistair is aware that the woman's husband has been dead for a long time but knows that it isn't helpful to dispel the residents' illusions. "Let them enjoy them," he's heard Angela say several times. "They're comforting."

He checks to see if this woman he loves—now little more than a tangled filament, her past forgotten—is ready for more tea, but she is still munching slowly on her cookie, so he lets his eyes roam around the room. To him, it seems relatively attractive, somewhat institutional to be sure, but not without warmth. The pale green walls have been freshly painted and a new carpet, a darker shade of green that hides most stains, has recently been laid. Inevitably, Group of Seven prints hang from the walls, but there are a few by other artists as well—James Morrice, Robert Bateman, and Walter J. Phillips, all safe, traditional choices. There is, however, nothing by Alex Coleville or Ray Mead, and certainly not by Edvard Munch, nothing dark or with hidden, uncertain meaning. Surprisingly, Alistair notes, there are also no female artists represented, not even Emily Carr, nor such easily appreciated painters as Kathleen Morris and Mary Pratt. There is a large LED television in one corner that was a recent gift from the family of a former resident. The television is often on, but it seems to Alistair that most of the time it is staff—never Angela, however—who watch it during breaks, endeavouring to stay up with their favourite daytime dramas. Rarely if ever is it tuned to sports, so little is the male demand for entertainment.

On this particular afternoon, there is an easel set up in the middle of the living room with a long sheet of light brown paper tacked to it. With a black magic marker, several headings have been printed:

> **Friday, June 14**
>
> **Partly Cloudy, High 26 degrees Celsius**
>
> **Record warm temperatures in Canadian Arctic**
>
> **Forest fires predicted for this summer**
>
> **New urban national park**
>
> **Canada-United States relations**
>
> **Monday, June 24. Group outing to the Aga Khan Museum**
>
> **Remember to wash your hands thoroughly and often**

Before the afternoon tea and coffee hour, Angela had held her thrice-weekly review of current affairs, coaxing news items out of the handful of residents who attempt to follow what is happening outside the home.

A woman with wispy strands of grey hair fidgeted into a shapeless ball, her face a Lucien Freud study of worry, unsuitable for the nursing home walls, rushes up to Angela. "I'm leaving. I must be ready when my mother gets here. I'm going home today."

Angela gently checks her. "Wait, my love. There's no rush. Your mother won't be here for a while. I'll help you pack before she arrives." She leads her over to the piano bench. "Come and sit here where I was. We'll all sing a song together."

Alistair notices that his own love is nodding off. He stands up, stretches to loosen his limbs and then he helps her to her feet. "Let's go. It's time you had a nap." He places one hand under her left arm and leads her slowly down the corridor to her room.

"Oh, good. You're still here." It's just a few minutes later that Angela slips quietly into the bedroom. "I was afraid you might have left. You're not coming back tonight, I guess?"

"No. The kids have invited me to dinner."

"That's nice. I hate to think of you all alone, wolfing down a take-out salad in five minutes."

"Some of them are pretty good actually, especially if I slice in some leftover cold salmon or bits of prosciutto. But you don't really think of me after I'm gone, do you?"

"Of course, I do."

"As a future resident, you mean, someone to help a little in balancing the gender ratio."

"No, as a compassionate man who has visited as often as he can when not prohibited by the pandemic."

"Maybe it would be better if I just moved in myself, and you gave me piano lessons."

"Stick to dancing," Angela jokes. "I need a coffee. I was too busy earlier to have one. What about you? Have you time for another cup of tea? I can heat up the kettle in the kitchen."

Alistair glances at the bed where his faded flower is now asleep and snoring. "Always time for tea."

When the tea and coffee are ready, they take their cups to the living-room and sit in easy chairs. The room is empty now in the unscheduled period before supper. Even the television is turned off. "Those 'kids' as you call them are good to you, aren't they?" Angela asks.

"Yes, indeed. I don't know why though. I don't deserve it."

"What do you mean? Of course, you do. You've been wonderful to them."

"I'm guilty of some pretty big cockups, personal and professional." Angela is aware of that. By now he has related to her most of his personal history.

"True, but who doesn't carry baggage by your age…or mine?"

"Yeah, but they don't usually need Sherpas to schlep it."

Alistair stares reflectively into his teacup and Angela assumes it is in disappointment that it has been made with tea bags. She knows he is fussy about his teas and always uses loose leaves at home. Still, he never complains about the selection at the facility; he just jokes about there being no leaves for reading fortunes, though she guesses he doesn't really want to know his own. "What does it mean to be good anyway?" he asks her.

"That you do what you can to help others, I suppose."

"Or does it require more than that—that you sacrifice your own well-being for their sake?"

"That would certainly be a higher level of goodness."

"Well, you're at that level. You're exemplary with everyone here. I never see you frustrated or angry. You're always patient and caring, looking after their needs, not your own. You've gone on working through these really tough times accepting the risks and fatigue involved without any complaints."

"I think it's because I had a grandmother I really loved. I talked to her about all sorts of things I never felt comfortable discussing with my parents."

"Or with me for that matter. Your boyfriends, for instance. That's a subject you always evade."

"Do I? Well, anyway it was easy to talk with my grandmother about anything. But then, when I was sixteen, she had a stroke that left her paralyzed on one side and affected her speech. I spent a lot of time with her during rehabilitation, walking her up and down corridors, talking to her and helping her read out loud. Gradually, she got better, never one hundred per cent, but a lot better. That's when I decided that this was the kind of job I wanted to have. Especially, I wanted to work with older people; they've all had such interesting lives, yet most of us don't have the patience to listen to them and learn from their experiences. I find what I'm doing very rewarding, bringing a little sunshine into lives that are often very dark."

"That's why I put you high up the ladder."

"But it is my job. I get paid for this. I think it takes more than that to be a really good person."

"So, how about this? I know several people who give fifty per cent of their income to charities—not friends of mine; they're all too hedonistic to do that; these are only acquaintances—but that would seem to make them good people, right? Me, I give one or two per cent. My aim is to stay ahead of our parsimonious federal government which is at about point three of one per cent of GDP in aid to needy countries. So, I don't come anywhere near this goodness mark."

"Fifty per cent is way more than I can imagine myself sacrificing either."

"That makes me feel better, not good but at least better."

"You mean to know that I fall short of the top grade?"

Alistair laughs. "Maybe but cheer up. Here's the snag. These particular acquaintances are religious. They all go regularly to church, or to the synagogue, mosque or temple. In their cases, it's religious teachings that inspire their generosity. That helps them to do good, even if it still isn't easy for them. But what about the rest of us, those who are only nominally religious and the atheists and agnostics like you and me? Our numbers are climbing, but are there good people among us, willing to make such major sacrifices?"

Angela pours herself another cup of coffee since it is clear Alistair is not in a hurry to go. "I think so. Look at all the people who sacrifice their lives to save others."

"In wartime certainly but then often they have been conscripted. Besides, they're conditioned to obey their commanders. Sometimes, they have guns pointed at them to ensure they follow orders."

"But in peacetime, too—saving others from violent assaults, from drowning, from being lost in the wilderness, rescuing people caught in fires, floods, hurricanes, earthquakes, you name it."

"Yes, they are undoubtedly courageous. All the people who make those kinds of sacrifices are, but mostly they don't have a choice. They are doing their jobs to the best of their ability. So, they are good in the same way that you and other health workers who haven't quit are, but we've put that sort of goodness at a lower level."

"Oh, thank you very much for reminding me." Angela pretends to throw the rest of her coffee at Alistair. "But some just make major sacrifices spontaneously and without a workplace obligation because they find themselves in situations where they feel instinctively that they must."

"Fair enough, but that is sacrifice without reflection. Personally, I'm not good at that. I'm more like the dog Jonathan and I had when we were young. He didn't last long because he had an unpredictable temperament and a penchant for biting. He was a cross between a Rotweiler and a Newfoundlander, so he was a big dog and that's why our parents got him—to protect us when we were out on our own. In those days, lots of people let their dogs run loose without a leash; we did, too. We were walking down a side street off Spadina Road when this Rotweiler approached us, coming the other way. Our dog took one look at him and quickly calculated that if they got into a fight, he would likely lose. So, he took off and crossed to the other side of the road, leaving Jonathan and me to deal with the Rotweiler."

"And what happened?"

"Nothing. The Rotweiler just walked past us, and our dog came back to our side."

Angela roars with laughter. "So, he analyzed the situation correctly, the sly devil. But no wonder he didn't last long in your family."

"Anyway, I hope I'd act more bravely than our dog did. I'm pretty sure I'd lay down my life to save someone in my immediate family. Some say that is because we are wired to do what we can to preserve our own gene pool. But beyond my closest relatives, I doubt I'd go much further. Many do, of course, as we've seen in Ukraine. We saw that during Trump's presidency as well when many experiencing racial discrimination and violence in their communities responded by demonstrating and taking other initiative regardless of the personal risks. But me? I don't think I'd act that bravely. I do a bit in support of worthy causes, but that's mainly out of guilt or gratitude for my own good fortune. It's sort of a casualty insurance policy against things suddenly going horribly wrong."

"I think you are being too hard on yourself."

"No, without religion, without a moral compass, I'm lost. I don't think there is any reward at the end for noble commitment. So, I'm guided by pragmatic self-interest. Maybe if I thought I'd get to know how things work out in the end—if due to the sacrifices and extraordinary efforts that good people make, we finally lick pandemics, cancer and other diseases, we achieve a truly just international order, and we save the planet from environmental destruction, then maybe I'd behave differently. But I don't believe that's what happens. I think we exit stage left in the middle of the play and that's our last scene. No ending, no applause, no encores."

"I never thought you could be so depressing to talk to."

"Sorry about that. You always lift my spirits when I come here. I should do the same." Alistair gets up to leave. "I'll have to lighten up before I go to dinner, won't I?" He pats Angela on the shoulder; she doesn't mind, not with someone his age, and she realizes that it is out of genuine affection.

"Give them my best. I don't know Rachel's spouse very well, but she is certainly a good person. And so are you by the way in my estimation at least."

"It's nice of you to say that. Shall I give myself a star? Not a gold one of course. That is reserved for you."

Angela just laughs. "Go and have a nice dinner. I'm sure that afterwards you'll help with the dishes."

Is Angela right? Am I being too hard on myself? He turns the ignition key in his car. *I don't think so. Most of my life has been pretty self-indulgent and I haven't had the impact I hoped to.*

The car moves slowly away from the curb and Alistair does his best to stifle his thoughts and to concentrate on driving safely. *But is there more that I can and should do—even at this late stage?*

Chapter 15

ALISTAIR WAS DEJECTED for weeks after Jonathan's news that Ginny was dating Colin Jameson regularly. Several times Peggy phoned to console him, but nothing worked until February of 1965 when she made a suggestion. "Why don't you come and work at the *Herald*. I know you like it at the *Star* but it's a big operation and it's not easy to get ahead. Here, I've got the city editor eating out of my hand. I'm sure I can get him to hire you. We could do some stories together. It would be fun, and this is the kind of change you need right now."

As always, Alistair spent time mulling over the idea, but in the end, he decided to give the *Herald* a try and submitted his resignation to the *Star*. *It doesn't have to be a permanent move. Reporters are always shifting allegiances. We're a paranoid bunch, perpetually afraid we're about to be fired.*

He had been at the *Herald* only a couple of weeks when Peggy told him, "I've been reading wire stories about growing racial tensions in the south, especially in Alabama. Looks like there may be a major protest shaping up in Selma. I've told the editors we should go down and sniff things out."

"We?"

"Yeah, you and me. I mean it's hard to tell right now what is going to happen. Maybe nothing, but whatever, it's time the *Herald* did some first-hand reporting on civil rights issues there. The brass agrees."

"So, we're going?"

Peggy pumped her fist. "We're on. Oh, you can use a camera, can't you?"

"Not professionally. I've only taken pictures for fun, you know, personal photographs."

"Good. At least you've done that. Facility with a camera is the rationale for your going with me. I'm a real klutz with those things."

"But I can't take pictures of the quality they will want."

"Sure, you can. Don't worry about it. I'll have one of the cameramen here give you a lesson before we leave."

Alistair had spent a couple of hours in the *Herald*'s dark room while an experienced photographer drilled him. "We're sending you with a Rolleiflex. You'll find it easy to use and the lenses are great. The key things to remember are that you have to work fast to get the best pictures and you can't crumble whatever the circumstances you're working under. Of course, sometimes you have to be patient and wait a long time for the perfect shot. Don't forget about the overall composition of your pictures and finding the right perspectives."

So, Peggy and Alistair had flown to Selma arriving shortly before the March 7 aborted protest and returning on the twentieth for the full march to Montgomery. Management was so pleased with their stories and photographs that the trips cemented their reputations at the *Herald* and augmented the readiness of the paper to send them together on other assignments. At the same time, Alistair's rising status in the world of journalism seemed to help him come to grips with losing Ginny. When Jonathan reported to him that she and Colin were engaged and getting married in the spring of 1967, he felt a mix of sadness and relief. "Well, I'm not surprised. I expected that would happen. I'm happy for her. It's what she has always wanted and from what you say I guess Colin is a good guy." A heavy lump formed in Alistair's throat. "She'll want a June wedding, I'm sure. She's sentimental and a traditionalist."

"That's what it is going to be."

A June wedding, how conventional! he convinced himself after hanging up. *That's not the kind of life I'm looking for.*

Over the weeks before the big day, wedding presents kept arriving at the Sloans' Etobicoke home, including one from Alistair. He felt he should send something but deliberated for a long time trying to decide what would be appropriate. He wanted to send a present that would reflect the love he still felt for her and had initially considered a necklace and matching earrings made from semi-precious stones, but when he mentioned this to Peggy over lunch, she killed the idea. "It's supposed to be a present for both the bride and groom, you flake. You can't send something intimate." In the end, he decided on an antique sterling silver sugar bowl and tongs along with a boxed set of eighteenth-century silver teaspoons. "Fine," Peggy concurred. "The perfect tchotchke. Expensive and pretty much useless."

When it came to the note he would enclose with the gift, Alistair decided not to discuss it with Peggy, but he laboured as hard over it as he had with the gift. He wanted somehow to communicate how bad he felt about breaking up and how much he still cared for her, but he realized he had to choose his words carefully, for there were others who might read the note, including her mother and Colin himself, nor did he want to upset Ginny and sow in her any doubts about the step she was taking. In the end, he kept it short: and, he hoped, his feelings were relatively enigmatic.

> *Dear Ginny,*
>
> *I'm so pleased that Colin came into your life at just the right moment. Jonathan tells me that he is a gentle, kind and considerate man, and if that is so, then he is hopefully worthy of the love of someone who deserves no less than complete devotion. I hope, and am confident, that you will have a long and happy life together, blessed one day with children you will dote over. I chose this little gift because I thought the sugar bowl in particular was appropriate for you to have as the sweetest person I will ever know.*

How to end the note was just as hard to decide. He wanted to close with "Love," but realized that was unacceptable. He almost signed it "As ever," but reconsidered, not wanting to leave the impression he hadn't agonized over the breakup and his unacceptable behaviour in the way that he actually had. So, in the end, he chose simply, "Fondly," though he felt that was pretty lame and did not express his real feelings about her.

Ginny had no difficulty discerning the true meaning of his words and her eyes welled as she read the note. She decided not to show it to her mother, only the gifts and the accompanying small card that Alistair had astutely included in the package which said simply, "Warm best wishes to you both, Alistair."

"Well, that's very nice, dear. Does Colin, in fact, ever drink tea?"

Jonathan was asked to be one of the four ushers at the wedding. It was a relatively large affair with some 150 guests attending, and the ceremony was at Colin's church, Timothy Eaton Memorial, rather than at the Sloans' because of its convenient location in the centre of the city and near the Granite Club where the reception was to be held. Ginny's mother had no objection to this arrangement; she was simply pleased that Colin was in the United Church and apparently attended services more often than Ginny did.

Alistair walked down from the apartment he had recently rented near Yonge and Davisville to observe the proceedings, standing across the road from the church as the wedding party and guests emerged after the ceremony. He had donned sunglasses and a broad-brimmed hat for protection, both from the sun and detection. Ginny, he thought, looked stunning in an ivory white satin dress with a long train; this time, he presumed, it was not her mother's handiwork.

Later, during the reception, he stood across the road from the Granite Club, wishing he could hear the speeches as he liked such presentations—observing how people managed important and stressful moments. Had he been able to, however, he would not have been particularly impressed. "No one was especially eloquent or witty," Jonathan told him the next day. "I thought the best moment came after the speeches when Ginny's mother went up to the groom and threw her arms around his neck. 'Oh, Colin, I'm so happy that Ginny went to that Beatles concert and met you! I didn't really like the Beatles then, but I do now!'" Jonathan started to chortle, "Aren't there already rumblings of discontent among the Fab Four?"

Eventually, Alistair felt embarrassed hanging around near the Granite Club as if he were a ghost observing the life he might have had if he hadn't chosen to kill himself off early in the drama, so he walked home, and called Peggy to go out for a drink to help him forget about the wedding. Her phone had only rung once when Alistair suddenly hung up. *Damn! I forgot she flew to Israel to cover the war. Well, it sounds as if this one is not going to last long. Peggy should be home soon.*

Alistair was right. In a surprise attack on Egyptian airfields on June 5, 1967, Israel virtually wiped out the Egyptian air force, gaining air supremacy that facilitated a quick assault into the Gaza Strip and the Sinai held by Egypt. The war was over within a week with Israel also seizing the West Bank and East Jerusalem from Jordan, and the Golan Heights from Syria. By the middle of the month, Peggy was back at the *Herald* and full of excitement as, over lunch, she reported to Alistair and other colleagues on her first experience as a war correspondent. "It was amazing, you guys. Israel really showed its military superiority. We lost less than a thousand lives, but twenty times as many Egyptians, Jordanians and Syrians were killed."

"We? Are we working for an Israeli newspaper or something?" Alistair asked sarcastically. "Isn't the *Herald* an objective, neutral observer?"

"Oh, back off, fuckhead! Of course, it is. I didn't put it like that in what I wrote."

"But it's how you feel."

"I can't help how I feel inside."

"What about the thousands of Palestinians who fled the West Bank and the Syrians displaced from the Golan Heights? The war has made the terrible refugee problem a whole lot worse."

"Let's drop the subject, eh," another reporter intervened. "Everyone is entitled to their personal opinions. They don't affect how we report."

"Thank you, Jack." Peggy glared at Alistair, and they didn't speak to each other again over lunch.

A few days later, however, Alistair sat down on a corner of her desk and apologized. "I know your reporting on the war was objective, and it was good, it really was. So, I'm sorry I goaded you."

"Thank you. I know you have strong views on this subject, too. But don't forget I'm a Jew and my family suffered in the Holocaust. Obviously, that affects how I feel about Israel."

"Of course, it does and it's understandable. I think this is a subject we'll have to avoid, or at least agree to disagree on."

"I'd prefer the latter. I can't see either of us not saying whatever is on our mind…So, are you okay now that the wedding is over? I wanted to ask the other day, but the conversation went in a different direction."

"Yeah, I'm okay. I want her to be happy, so this is for the best." Then Alistair confessed that he had stood outside the church at the end of the wedding and at the Granite Club for the reception.

"Oh, shit, no! You're meshuggeneh."

"You've got me there."

"Crazy. You're insane, ridiculous."

"I told you, I've always needed an analyst…So what are you doing for the centennial celebration? Any plans?

"Not really."

They agreed to meet at Nathan Phillips Square to watch a 40-float parade march past a reviewing stand with the mayor and other dignitaries upon it, and in the evening, they returned briefly to dance to go-go music before having dinner together. "I thought the most moving event of the year was at the beginning: the lighting by Lester Pearson of the eternal flame at midnight on New Year's Eve. It was such a beautiful evening, cold and crisp. Very Canadian."

"I missed it," Peggy rued. "And the opening of Expo."

"I wasn't there for that either. In fact, I still haven't gone."

"Nor have I… Hey, I have an idea! You know De Gaulle is coming later in the month and he is visiting Expo?"

"Yeah, there are rumours circulating that he's aiming to stir up trouble. He should be visiting Ottawa first, so this is a major breach of protocol."

So, he's sailing to Quebec City on a French naval vessel—"

"Retaking the Plains of Abraham, so to speak."

"Right. And then travelling by motorcade to Montreal. Why don't we ask to cover the event?"

"Wouldn't the Ottawa Bureau normally do that?"

"Probably if we were talking about Montreal alone, but I think I can persuade them to send us for the whole thing. No one knows when the sparks might start flying; that could happen in Quebec City. And, after all, I'm a Quebecer. My French isn't bad. Afterwards, we can visit Expo the same day as De Gaulle and then my parents. They'd love that. I haven't seen them since Hanukkah."

"But we'd stay in a hotel, right?"

"We would the first night, yes, because it will probably be late by the time everything is over, and we've filed our story. After De Gaulle visits Expo the next day, we'll stay with my parents."

"But we'll already have checked into a hotel somewhere. Why not just stay there?"

"Obviously you don't know my mother."

Chapter 16

ALISTAIR AND PEGGY were duly assigned to the De Gaulle story and flew to Quebec City on the evening of July 23 to be there for the French president's arrival the next day. They had dinner at the Chateau Frontenac on the terrace overlooking the St. Lawrence River, near where the French cruiser, *Colbert*, was to dock. "I don't know much about your parents and yet it seems I'm to meet them on the twenty-fifth." Alistair was quickly devouring his Coquilles St. Jacques appetizer. "I feel bad about that. We've spent most of the time talking reporter stuff and whenever it has been personal it's been about my relationship with Ginny. I know your parents are from Germany and that you were born in England during the war, but I don't know how you got there and to Canada."

"Well, after Kristallnacht in November of thirty-eight, my parents knew they had to get out or they would likely end up in a concentration camp. But it wasn't easy to find a country to go to. They all had restrictions on the number of Jews they would accept."

"I know. Canada was one of the least welcoming. Antisemitism was rampant in the media and in the Immigration Department."

"I'm impressed. You know your history."

"On this subject it helped going to Forest Hill."

"Anyway, Britain wasn't much better than Canada, but it did accept some refugees. Not long after Kristallnacht, in early nineteen thirty-nine, my mother was pretty sure she was pregnant with me, so she wanted to get out of Germany right away. Thanks to the British Quakers, she managed to leave that March. They put up fifty pounds as a guarantee she would not become a burden on the state if admitted and then they helped us get out. In fact, my mom did work as a nurse until just before I was born."

"What about the rest of your family?"

"My father and my two sisters stayed behind in Berlin until he learned about Kindertransport, a British transport program for children only. He got my sisters into it and, with the help of the Quakers, they managed to get to London in the summer of thirty-nine. Shortly after I was born in October, Mom went back to work since nurses were urgently needed, so my sisters looked after me. I'm sure they found me quite a handful."

"No doubt!"

Peggy stopped. Their main courses had arrived, and she took off the sunglasses she had been wearing as a shield against the setting sun so that her eager green eyes could feast on the succulent steak on her plate.

"What about your father?"

"That was the worst part. It looked at that point as if he was going to be trapped in Berlin when the war broke out and would die in a concentration camp. In the end, he did get out, but the whole thing was very traumatic. For our sake, he served in the British Army. I don't know much about his war experiences. He doesn't talk about them, not to any of us anyway. Maybe he will with you, but they certainly left some scars. Mm, this steak is delicious. Have a bite."

Alistair declined. He had been so absorbed in hearing her family's history that he hadn't taken more than a mouthful of his own dinner, but now he picked up his knife and fork again. "Geez, it must have been really awful. But it's amazing how you all got out and to the same country. I'm glad you told me these details. It might help me to shut up about Israel and the fate of the Palestinians."

"Oh, you don't need to worry about that—not talking to my mother at least."

• • •

"Oh, fuck no! Look how he's dressed—in full military uniform. What an asshole!"

Alistair and Peggy were standing in a flag-waving crowd as President De Gaulle stepped off his French navy vessel and was greeted by the governor-general, Roland Michener. "Yeah, I like that angle," Peggy said as Alistair crouched low to the ground. "We'll make the old boy look like Napoleon, only ridiculously tall…Look how he's avoiding talking to Michener now."

"I know. And did you hear the boos when the band played "'God Save the Queen?'"

Later, as De Gaulle's motorcade proceeded slowly to Montreal, with Peggy and Alistair following it, she asked him if he'd noticed the route they were following. "It's the old Chemin du Roy built before the conquest."

"I guess it's the Second World War and we're on our way to the liberation of Paris."

"Yeah, the shithead has extraordinary illusions of grandeur."

Later, standing on the open-air balcony of Montreal's City Hall along with the mayor and premier, De Gaulle waved to a joyful crowd, urging him to speak. "Hey, get this! They're plugging in that microphone. He wasn't scheduled to speak, but it looks like he asked the mayor to let him."

"Hmm. This could be really something."

And it was. The next day, following his infamous balcony cry, "Vive le Québec libre," the French president visited Expo 67 and hosted a dinner at the French pavilion. Alistair and Peggy covered the event and concluded their story by noting that De Gaulle was scheduled to continue to Ottawa the next day, but that speculation was rife that he would cut short his visit and, flouting protocol, not proceed to the nation's capital.

• • •

"MY SHAINA MAIDEL!" Peggy's mother flung open the door and threw her arms around her daughter later that evening. "Come in! Come in!" They were standing on the porch of an old, red brick duplex on Waverly Street in the Mile End district of Montreal. It had similar but smaller balconies on the second and third floors, each enclosed by wrought-iron railings. The Morgansteins had managed to buy the property shortly after arriving in Canada, although for the first few years they had occupied only the first two stories and rented the third.

"Mame, this is Alistair Parker."

"Shalom aleichem," Alistair greeted her.

"Ah!" She laughed heartily. "Very good. Aleichem Shalom. Welcome to our home."

"I'm afraid now I've used up a lot of my Yiddish."

"No matter. Come in! Come in." Alistair was struck right away by the physical features Peggy's mother shared with her youngest daughter. Her hair, though obviously dyed, was the same jet black and her eyes were similarly dark green and magnetic. She was about the same height as well, but plumper—too many meals of latkes and matzo balls, he figured.

"We brought you these." Alistair handed her a white cardboard pastry box. "They're rugelach. I hope I've pronounced that correctly."

"Why, thank you, Alistair, that is very kind. Peggy tells me you're a real mensch." She placed a hand on his back as she led him to the living-room.

Peggy had already gone ahead to greet her father who was standing in the middle of the room when Alistair walked in, a tall, stick of a man like a tree branch that had split and been knocked to the ground by a sudden gust of wind. He had bushy grey and white eyebrows and an unruly shock of white hair on the crown of his head. Deep lines were gouged into his cheeks as if, Alistair imagined, an SS officer had inflicted them for identification purposes. Watery , grey eyes, half hidden behind glasses with flimsy circular frames, studied him carefully. It seemed, however, to be a welcoming look, Alistair conjectured, engendered most likely by the pleasure of having his daughter home. Yet Alistair detected sadness and fatigue as well, perhaps even lingering anxiety. "Tate, this is my colleague and friend, Alistair."

They exchanged "shaloms" and then Alistair handed over the bottle of red wine that they had brought. It was Peggy's mother who thanked them first. "How thoughtful. But kosher wine! You didn't need to go to that expense. We're not orthodox."

"Oh, but I am," Alistair responded. Momentarily all of the Morgansteins looked startled. "I'm an orthodox atheist."

Peggy's mother laughed uproariously, and her father chuckled, "That's a good one. I like that."

"At least, I think I'm orthodox, and not just an agnostic. I'm not quite sure."

"Alistair is always full of doubt." Peggy uncorked the bottle and passed glasses of wine to everyone as they sat down. "He has trouble making up his mind."

Her father nodded in understanding.

Mrs. Morganstein disappeared briefly to the kitchen to check on the casserole she had in the oven. "Well, De Gaulle's visit has been quite the story for you to cover, hasn't it?" she remarked on return. "We listened to his address at City Hall last night." She motioned to the corner of the room where there was an old, wooden cabinet with a built-in radio that Alistair estimated dated from the 1940s. In fact, the whole room appeared to have been decorated and furnished in that era. There were lamps on brass stands with fringed and faded shades and couches with armrests rubbed bare of fabric. When Alistair and Peggy settled on one, he found that he sank in so deeply that it was hard to reach the wine glass he had placed on a chipped and scratched coffee table directly in front of him. On top of that, he had to keep shifting his position, seeking a place for his bottom free of jabs from the couch's springs. Alistair also detected what seemed like the smell of overripe apples mingling with the mellow aroma of pouch tobacco though neither was visible anywhere. Yet, somehow, despite all of this, Alistair liked the room. It exuded a quiet warmth that suggested it was not appearance that mattered but the animated conversation among family and friends gathered at any time. "De Gaulle is ridiculous," Mrs. Morganstein continued. "He should never have come back to office. To talk of French-Canadians needing to be liberated is absurd. And to interfere like that in our affairs. It was a dreadful thing to do."

"The separatists don't know what real repression is. They should appreciate the freedom they have in Canada and not try to break up the country."

"No. Leave that sort of talk to the Europeans," Peggy's mother interrupted her husband. "My, I like that man Trudeau, though. Did you hear what he said? How would De Gaulle like it if the Canadian prime minister went to Brittany and shouted, 'Freedom for the Bretons.' When Pearson steps down, that guy would make a good leader. He has chutzpah."

"Alistair's NDP, Mame. In fact, he grew up in David Lewis's riding of York South and is a big fan."

"Oh, that's okay. If we lived in Toronto, we would probably be NDP as well. And I like Lewis, but does this mean that you and Peggy don't agree on Israel and its borders?"

"No, we don't."

"Good for you, Alistair." she grinned at her daughter. "But Peggy is difficult to disagree with, isn't she? She's very persistent."

"So is Alistair. Oh, I forgot to mention, he's a fan of Mordecai Richler, too."

"Ah! So, you know about this neighbourhood then. We're just a couple of blocks from St. Urban Street."

"Yes. I think *The Apprenticeship of Duddy Kravitz* is one of the most authentic Canadian novels ever written."

Mrs. Morganstein beamed. "We do wish he'd come home, don't we Tate? This is where he should be living, not London." She stood up. "Sorry, I have been talking too much. Please come to the dining-room everybody; the casserole is ready. Bring your wine glasses and, Tate, please open another bottle. We're having bubbe's kugel and brisket. I hope that's okay with you, Alistair."

"It sounds perfect."

"And, of course, rugelach for dessert. Thank you again for bringing it."

They had almost finished their meal when Mrs. Morganstein reminded them that Prime Minister Pearson was about to deliver an address on national television in response to De Gaulle's address at City Hall, so they all rushed back to the living-room where Peggy turned on the Morganstein's small black-and-white television and adjusted the rabbit ears on top to improve the picture. "Certain statements by the President tend to encourage the small minority of our population whose aim is to destroy Canada," Pearson told his audience, "and as such they are unacceptable to the Canadian people and its government…Canadians do not need to be liberated. Indeed, many thousands of Canadians gave their lives in two world wars in the liberation of France and other European countries."

"Bravo!" Mrs. Morganstein shouted when the prime minister had finished. "That was perfect, and it should send the old man packing. Let's go and have dessert."

Afterwards, she insisted that Alistair and her husband return to the living-room and talk "man to man" while she and Peggy cleaned up. This was Alistair's opportunity to learn a little more about Mr. Morganstein's life and his wartime experiences, but he started obliquely by asking how he felt about the latest war in the Middle East and Israel's occupation of new territory.

There was no answer for two or three minutes while Peggy's father retrieved his pouch of tobacco from a cupboard drawer, cleaned out his pipe, and stuffed it. "I don't know. Not like them." He motioned towards the kitchen. "Their positions are firm. I just want peace. I'm glad to be in Canada and, I hope, to have left war behind me."

"Peggy mentioned to me that you were in the British army during the war."

"Yes, I was."

"That must have been very difficult."

"Yes…But I wasn't alone. There were about ten thousand German Jewish refugees who volunteered. It helped to make life easier for the rest of our families."

"Though certainly not for you."

"No."

It seemed as if that were all he was going to tell Alistair of his war experience, so he altered his line of questioning. "So, before that, how did you manage to get to England?"

"There was a place called the Kitchener Camp in Kent that was accepting Jewish men and arranging for their passages to England on the understanding they would not be eligible for British citizenship, nor allowed to work in the country. They were also to emigrate as soon as possible. So that is how I got out, but I was confined to the camp."

Mr. Morganstein stopped and puffed on his pipe, ruminating about the past. "Once the war started, my family was in constant fear of being interned as enemy aliens on the Isle of Man. But that risk disappeared when I volunteered for the Royal Pioneer Corps for refugees and was thrown into battle—into war against my own people… I don't like to talk about that time. I try to blot it from my mind."

"I understand. I'm sorry I brought the subject up."

"No, no. That's okay," he smiled. "But I'd rather talk about coming to Canada and being a tailor. I'm not very good, you know."

That night, Peggy insisted that Alistair sleep in her bedroom. "It's nicer than Gertrude's. I had it redecorated. I'll sleep in her room. Mom has turned Ruthie's into a sewing room."

"So, where are your sisters living?"

"Gertrude is in Winnipeg and Ruth in Halifax. They don't come home as often as I do. They have young kids to look after."

"So, you're Mame's shaina maidel." He poked Peggy gently in the stomach. "Her little girl, right?"

"Now, don't you start calling me that or you can sleep in a leaky tent in the backyard."

Alistair felt very strange lying in Peggy's bed trying to get to sleep. *Holy cow, this is weird. I never slept over at the Sloans' in the city, and here I am in Peggy's house and in her bed!*

In the morning they had bagels and lox for breakfast and then left. At the front door, Mrs. Morganstein gave Alistair a big hug and then turned to Peggy. "He's a nice boy. You should hold on to him."

"Mame, please!"

"No, I mean it. Don't let him get away."

They took a taxi to the airport about the same time that President De Gaulle left abruptly to fly home to France.

Chapter 17

Tʜᴇ ʀᴇsᴛ ᴏғ that summer and autumn, Alistair and Peggy were busy covering domestic Canadian stories, including alleged influence pedalling and bribery in Pearson's minority Liberal government and the work of the Royal Commission on the Status of Women. Then, in February 1968, Peggy read a wire story about the arrest of several students from South Carolina State University who had entered a segregated bowling alley in Orangeburg in a peaceful protest against discrimination. The arrests precipitated more disturbances on the university campus and Peggy calculated that the tension was escalating to the point where the *Herald* ought to cover the story. Having demonstrated already their ability to report effectively on racial protests, she readily obtained consent for them to fly to Charleston and drive to Orangeburg. Alistair's father had, however, suffered a heart attack that very week, so he didn't accompany her. While Peggy was away, he met up with his mother and Jonathan at the Toronto General Hospital for a visit with their father and afterwards went home for dinner with them. "Oh, I forgot to tell you, sorry," Jonathan said part way through the meal. "Ginny is pregnant."

"Really!" Alistair did his best to sound nonchalant. It was something he knew would eventually happen, but it was hard not to feel a pang of regret. "Well, that's great news. This is what she has always wanted. When is she expecting, do you know?"

"In April, I believe."

Alistair did a quick calculation. *Wow! That certainly didn't take them long!* He munched thoughtfully on his food. *I'm okay with this…I think… Yeah, I'm okay. Better that Colin is the father than me—for Ginny's sake.*

The evening that Peggy flew home, Alistair took a taxi out to the airport to meet her. Waiting for her to come out from the baggage hall, he contemplated how the nature of their relationship had changed somewhat. In the past, he would not have considered meeting her or any other colleague from the *Herald* and yet this time he had driven to the airport instinctively without any thought about it. *Why?* he wondered.

It was certainly partly because he had read her stories on the Orangeburg Massacre and realized that her experience of covering the event must have been traumatic and, indeed, risky to her own life. Peggy had been right about the situation there escalating to a crisis, and it had reached that point the day after she arrived. On the night of February 8, South Carolina State students set a bonfire ablaze on the campus and as firefighters attempted to put it out a wooden banister was hurled at a police officer injuring him. Shortly after that, state highway patrol officers fired their weapons into the largely black crowd of students, killing three and injuring many others. Peggy had been in the centre of the melee, one of very few reporters who covered the carnage. So, Alistair recognized that his presence for her arrival was partly prompted by his concern to learn if she had escaped the attack unscathed both physically and mentally. But then, there was another consideration. Alistair had got into the habit at work of confiding in Peggy about his relationship with Ginny and now there was this news about her pregnancy to pass on. Gradually, however, he realized that there was yet another factor influencing his decision to meet her. Ever since the preceding July when they had stayed at her parents' home, he had started to view her differently—not just as a colleague at the *Herald* whom he liked, but as a very close friend beyond their professional connection. He had enjoyed the atmosphere in her home; he had felt welcome there and comfortable in that unpretentious setting, talking with her and her parents. *I look up to her and I confide in her. But am I in love with her? I don't know, but I do enjoy her company and I miss her when she is away.*

Peggy came through the door, carrying the one packsack she had taken with her. She dropped it as she reached Alistair and threw her arms around him. Then, as their brief embrace ended, to his own surprise, Alistair kissed her lightly on the lips. "Oh! That felt nice," she said cheerily, her emerald eyes gluing on his. "Cheeky, but nice!"

"It sounded from your articles as if it was pretty awful," Alistair said walking to the taxi stand.

"Yes. A much smaller crowd than in Selma, but there were bullets flying everywhere for maybe fifteen seconds. The shooting was so random, I was afraid I might be hit."

"Geez. That must have been terrible."

"It was, but you know me. The horrible thing is that there was no evidence that any of the demonstrators were armed or had fired at the police, so it's clear the state patrolmen used excessive force. They ought to be charged."

When they got to Peggy's apartment near the Kensington Market, she suggested that they go out for dinner. "But first, I've got to have a bath. I feel so grubby."

"Okay, but why don't I order a pizza instead. It's getting late."

"Great! The number of the place I use is in the pad by the phone. Oh, and there is red wine in the rack in the kitchen and stuff for a salad in the fridge if you can be bothered to make one."

"Will do. What do you want on the pizza?"

"You choose. You know me. I'll eat anything and I'm fucking starving."

Alistair ordered the pizza with pepperoni, mushrooms, onions and mozzarella cheese, poured two glasses of wine and carried Peggy's to the bathroom door where he knocked. "Are you decent? I have a glass of wine for you."

"Decent? Me? Come in! I suspect you've seen tits before." Alistair slipped the door open and found Peggy in the bath largely covered in foam. She took a sip of wine and then carefully placed the glass on the shelf at the tap end of the tub. "See that stool? Take a seat and catch me up. How is your dad?"

"He's doing much better. He's going home tomorrow. He'll have to take it easy for a while and get more exercise, but the prognosis is positive."

"Good. So, Ginny is pregnant. Are you okay with that?"

"Yeah, better than I thought I might be, but then it was something I expected."

"So, are you're over her…ready to move on?"

"Yeah. A lot of time has gone by."

 "Good."

"You know as I was waiting for your plane, I found that more than anything else I was thinking about you…about your safety and whether it's worth the risks involved in covering these crises."

"It's a job that has to be done, Ally. The public needs to be informed intelligently and in detail about all the issues out there—and racial discrimination is one of the most endemic. Poverty and economic inequality, health care and education, women's rights, political repression, they all need media attention. It takes stories like ours that focus on the human dimension to influence public opinion and hopefully eventually government policy."

"You're right, I guess."

"I *know* I am. They're personal and moving. When I'm scared, I just think of Hitler and the Holocaust. That restores my chutzpah and makes me determined to carry on."

"That works for you, but you're much closer to that horror than I am."

"I'm not sure about that." Peggy laughed. "You're pretty Jewish after all—Jewish enough to satisfy my mother and that says a lot."

Alistair left to prepare a Caesar salad and by the time the pizza arrived, Peggy was out of the bath and sitting in her bathrobe at a small, circular, glass-topped table. She had, however, taken the time to blow dry and comb her hair. Alistair was conscious of never having noticed before how sleek it was and how brightly the black threads shone when exposed to light, this time from the candle he had found and placed in a dish on the table. Nor had he ever really appreciated the smooth texture of the skin on her hands and face. He replenished their wine glasses and retrieved the pizza and salad from the kitchen. "L'chayim," he toasted her.

"Well done," she responded. "L'chayim. Wow! This is delicious. How did you know that these are my favourite toppings?"

Alistair shrugged his shoulders. "Professional responsibility to see and remember details."

"Well, this reporter is certainly impressed. By the way, I meant to tell you, Charleston is really beautiful. I wasn't there for long, but I saw a bit of the centre. Lots of gorgeous ante-bellum homes with long balconies on their sides and pretty, little gardens. Of course, you don't have to walk too far north from the centre to see the poverty in which the African Americans live. Anyway, we should find an excuse to go there sometime, maybe as part of a series of stories on the connection between racial segregation and economic disparity."

"Good idea. Mix three parts pleasure with one part pain, the perfect cocktail."

After finishing the meal, they sat on the living room couch over another glass of wine, discussing Orangeburg again and pending stories they might cover. Eventually, Peggy leaned against Alistair. "So, are you planning on staying for the night, or are you going home?"

Under the circumstances, it wasn't an entirely unexpected question, but, uncharacteristically, Alistair had not given much thought as to how he would answer if the suggestion were made. "I don't know. How do you feel about it?"

"I'd love it if you stayed." Peggy snuggled closer to him and kissed him on the cheek. "You know that night in Montreal you slept in my bed? I felt so horny thinking of you there that I almost crept into my room to get in bed with you. I've wanted to fuck you ever since."

Their mouths joined for their first long kiss. Alistair had never before seen his relationship with Peggy as in any way sexual, but he did now. He was suddenly aroused and physically eager, something he had not experienced since the break-up with Ginny. He could feel an erection pressing against his pants, the first one he had had in a long time. As he slipped his hands inside her housecoat, she shrugged it off her back and kissed him again. Alistair ran his fingers over her breasts and felt her nipples grow harder and fuller.

"I think it's time we made a strategic retreat," Peggy said.

As they stood up to move to the bedroom, he gently restrained her with one hand. "There is something I ought to tell you first, though."

"What?" Peggy frowned anxiously.

"I'm still a virgin…well, sort of I guess."

"You are? Get real!"

"I kid you not."

Peggy laughed heartily. "You mean you and Ginny never—"

"Well, no…not exactly. We—"

"Never mind. I don't need to know the details. Well, you're having the real deal with me, kiddo." She tugged him by the hand, and they stepped into the bedroom. "It's that or nothing at all." As she lay down on the bed with her head on the pillow, she added, "Of course, you know I've had sex before."

"How many guys? You told me about someone you dated at McGill. That's all I know."

"There was one at Western as well. I'm sure I told you about him. A real hunk, but he couldn't write worth shit. Oh, and a reporter at the *Herald* I went out with before you arrived. So, three. That's all. Are you shocked by my promiscuity?"

"No, not really. It's a bit of a turn on actually."

"Well, then, climb on top of me, my cute, innocent goy, and I'll show you how it's done."

"Aah," she sighed afterwards. "That was wonderful. And you didn't need any teaching. Whatever you did with Ginny as a starter worked great with me."

Chapter 18

"**O**H, FUCK, NO time to hang around here. We've got to get going." Peggy and Alistair were in the *Herald*'s editorial room just two days after her return from Orangeburg. "The Yanks and the South Vietnamese army are pushing the North Vietnamese and the Vietcong back towards the DMZ. There has been some horrific fighting."

Peggy arranged a meeting with the paper's editors for later in the day, but they were doubtful about incurring the cost of sending them all the way to Vietnam when stories and pictures were flooding in by wire. "The Communist offensive has resulted in some of the biggest battles of the war so far, for shit's sake. We need our own angle on it."

Eventually, the editors yielded. "Okay, you can go, but for two weeks maximum, but not Alistair."

Peggy paced agitatedly around the conference room. "Oh, come off it! Be sensible. You know he takes great pictures; he's a natural. We need them to make our coverage stand out."

Still the editors wouldn't budge until Peggy threatened, "Do you want us both to resign? I'm sure the *Star* would be happy to have us back."

Two days later, they embarked on the long journey to Saigon where the U. S. Embassy itself had been attacked by the Viet Cong. Now there were only pockets of the city where the Communist forces were directing sniper fire at Americans and their South Vietnamese allies. Whenever an assailant was captured, reprisal by the southern army was swift and brutal.

"Jesus, I don't know if I can do this." They had spotted a young soldier in a Saigon street about to be executed. Alistair raised his newly issued single lens reflex camera to his eyes to capture the horrifying moment. Standing in the road in front of them was a barefoot member of the Viet Cong, handcuffed and stripped to the waist with a bandana around his black hair. A South Vietnamese soldier stood in front of him and raised his pistol to the head of the terrified youth.

Alistair snapped photos in rapid succession, not stopping until after the shots rang out and the youth lay dead on the pavement. Then he shuddered on the verge of vomiting until Peggy took his hand, and they walked away.

After that incident, they stumbled on little else that was particularly newsworthy, somewhat to Alistair's relief. "So, I guess we hang around the U. S. Public Affairs Office with other reporters and get our stories from the daily briefings."

"You mean, the 'five o'clock follies?' No way. We're going north to Huê to cover the battle for the city. The Marines and the South Vietnamese army are closing in on it, but the Communists are bound to make a real effort to hold on. It's symbolically significant for the South as the Imperial City."

Along with three other reporters, they hitched a ride north on a U. S. military truck. "You look like you're going into battle yourself." Peggy smiled at Alistair, dressed in a khaki shirt and pants and wearing a helmet. "Just as anxious as the troops as well." It was just a little later that a mortar shell hit the road in front of them. Bits of debris ricocheted off the windshield and hood of the truck and, as the driver swerved to avoid the crater in the road, he lost control and the truck spun into a ditch. It was at least two hours before assistance arrived, and, meanwhile, they felt like ducks squatting on a road, an easy target for a sniper shooting from a camouflaged blind. "I didn't volunteer for combat," Alistair said dryly.

"No, but you got good pics, and I think you've handled this very well."

Later, they spotted ahead of them a Buddhist monk walking serenely in their direction in the middle of the road. He was in saffron robes and shielding himself from the sun with a bright yellow umbrella. Behind him, a large cloud of black smoke was rising from another explosion. "This I've got to get." Alistair quickly changed films. "I don't know if we can get the *Herald* to use colour—it's so expensive—but we'll have to try to persuade them if this one is to stand out."

As they reached the outskirts of the city, they got off the truck to wander the sideroads on their own, finding other striking images to snap—Marines, knee deep in water in a rice paddy, carrying a wounded comrade to safety on a stretcher; a U. S. tank with a soldier in the turret scanning the thick jungle surrounding a bombed-out village, searching for survivors believed to be supporters of the Communists. *Are they really the enemy?* Alistair asked himself, *or are they just ordinary people whose loyalty depends on who can protect them best? Like Tate, I suspect all they really want is to live in peace.*

The nearer they got to the Citadel, an ancient walled enclosure in the centre of the city, the fiercer the fighting. "Holy fuck, Walter Cronkite was here on February tenth and the advance has hardly progressed since then. No wonder it's rumoured that in the footage he filmed he describes the conflict as a stalemate."

"Yeah, this Tet Offensive is going to be a great surprise to the American public. They had no idea the Communists had this kind of military capability and that, even though forced to retreat, they would put up such strong resistance. I think it will lead a lot of people to have doubts about what their government has fed them about winning the war."

"And what are they going to make of the executions of prisoners? It's a violation of the Geneva Conventions."

"True, but they've happened on both sides."

At the end, it required house-to-house fighting to drive the last of the North's snipers from the Citadel, and most of it was reduced to rubble. As they left, Peggy looked northward towards the DMZ. "I wish we could go to Hanoi and interview the Canadians there with the International Control Commission about our role in all of this."

"That would certainly be interesting. No one's hands are clean in this dirty war."

• • •

NOT LONG AFTER their return to Toronto, Jonathan called to find out how their trip had gone. "Sounds a lot scarier than risking an arrow strikinge you in the ass. You've come a long way."

"Not without some shoves in my posterior."

"Hen pecked and you're not even married," Jonathan kidded him. When they were about to hang up, he suddenly added, "Oh, I thought you might want to know that Colin Jameson told me last week that Ginny's baby has safely arrived."

"Oh, good. What gender?"

"A boy, I think, but you know me, I'm not very good about that sort of thing."

Alistair was unsure about sending Ginny a note of congratulations, but in the end, he decided that he would, since the issue of children had been an important one in their break-up. He chose, however, to keep it simple.

> *I was delighted to receive from Jonathan the news about the baby. You must be so happy and excited. I know that having a family was something you always wanted very much, and now you are on your way! My best wishes to the three of you.*

Ginny never responded to his note. *Well, it's been almost four years since that night at the Old Mill. I guess she decided it's best not to dwell on the past and try to sustain some sort of distant friendship. But I wonder if she ever contemplates how things might have turned out if we hadn't been so influenced by our parents and had gone ahead and had real sex? If I had got her pregnant, I'm sure I never would have left her for the sake of my career. I wonder if she realizes that.* He envisaged her looking down at her baby sound asleep in a bassinet, tiny fingers clutching the satin edge of a blanket. *I hope she never thinks this could be her baby and mine.*

In mid-August of 1968, Peggy's attention became focussed on Czechoslovakia. She had the gut feeling that the promising reforms introduced in April by Alexander Dubcek were about to be overturned by the Kremlin and that it was important that the *Herald* have a first-hand account of the situation in Prague. In the editorial room one afternoon, she broached the idea with Alistair. "All the changes that came with the Prague spring have raised public expectations. I think the Kremlin is anxious and may do something about it."

"But just a few days ago, Soviet and Czech leaders met, and the Czechs agreed to control the press better in return for the Soviets withdrawing forces that were on manoeuvres in the country. It seems unlikely they would bring them back right away."

"I'm not so sure. At the meeting, the Soviets made it clear they would intervene in any Warsaw Pact country moving towards a pluralist system of government. Whatever, I think we should go to Prague. It's a good time to see what's happening on the ground."

The editor-in-chief consented to Peggy's proposal and agreed to Alistair's going as well on the strength of his photographs from Vietnam. They flew to Prague arriving late on the morning of August 19, dead tired after an overnight flight that included a change of planes in Paris. They took a taxi to the Hotel Esplanade, a distinguished establishment near Wenceslas Square that was frequented by journalists because of its location and the presence of a telex booth and operator for filing stories.

As soon as they were shown to their room, Peggy flung her bag on the suitcase rack and stretched out on a bed, admiring the moulding on the ceiling and the classical prints on the elegantly papered walls. "Well, this is certainly an improvement over camping out in Alabama."

"Yes, but we're no better protected from snoring than we were then."

Peggy poked him in the ribs. "Come on, let's get some shuteye before we have a look around."

It was close to four in the afternoon before they awoke, showered, and got dressed. By then, they were starving, so they went to the hotel's marble and oak-panelled café for ham and cheese chlebicky—open-face sandwiches which they had with coffees. Afterwards, they peeked into the elegant dining-room with its glass cupola in the centre and large, Murano chandelier lighted by dozens of bulbs in little flutes. "Looks a bit grand for our per diem. I think tonight we should get a bite outside, assuming we can find somewhere half decent."

They went for a walk to Old Town Square, Prague's principal public space since the tenth century with its huge, contemplative Art Nouveau statue of Jan Hus, an early Christian reformer who was burned at the stake for refusing to recant his heretical views. "A reminder to Dubcek not to go too far," Alistair commented. From there, they followed several streets to the Charles Bridge, lingering on it for some time, admiring the ancient bridge towers at either end, and the eighteenth century statutes that lined the stone walls on both sides of the cobble stone walkway. At the far end, they continued to the steps leading to Prague Castle. "I had no idea the city was this lovely," Peggy remarked. "It doesn't seem like we're in a Communist country at all."

"No. None of those hideous apartment buildings that are all over East Berlin. The Communists haven't been around long enough to destroy its character—not yet anyway."

On the way back to the hotel, they stopped near the river for tankards of dark ale and pork sandwiches, cooked over a wood-burning fire in a basement tavern where they sat on a long bench. "Mm, delicious. But don't ever tell my parents I eat pork. They may not be orthodox, but that's still a no-no in their house."

"Where is everyone?" Alistair wondered as they walked home along largely deserted streets.

"Beats me. Looks like I got it wrong this time. Well, whatever, we can try to do some street interviews tomorrow, especially with students. Their views are important here."

"And members of the writers' union. Their journal is free of censorship now, and apparently plays a big role in shaping public opinion."

"We can even try to get an interview with Dubcek or at least someone in the presidium. None of this may be front-page stuff, but it may be enough to mollify our bosses."

That was not, however, the way things turned out. Early the next morning, Alistair heard a knock on their bedroom door and a voice call out, "Wake up, wake up! They've come." It was a member of the hotel staff, and he was hurrying down the corridor stopping at all the rooms where he knew journalists were staying; some had, in fact, been in the hotel for weeks. Peggy was in a deep sleep and Alistair shook her awake. "Looks like we've lucked out. Your hunch was right. Warsaw Pact forces have arrived in the city."

They dressed quickly, grabbed the camera bag, and without stopping even for a coffee, rushed to the street. A Russian tank was already parked in front of the hotel, the long barrel of its gun menacingly facing them. At the suggestion of another journalist, they followed him on foot to Wenceslas Square, one of the city's principal gathering places. A large crowd had already formed, surrounding several Russian tanks. Most of the people were young and they were shouting at the tank crews, "Why are you here? Go home." Some youths had climbed onto the tanks and on one they had painted a swastika. "Hey, you!" a young man shouted at Alistair after noticing his camera. "Are you American? Take my picture." He was sitting with his feet dangling over the long barrel of a gun and he inched along his perch to get closer to Alistair. "Spread your pictures and news of what's happening all around the world."

From Wenceslas Square, Alistair and Peggy hurried to the Prague radio station, passing Russian tanks at virtually every intersection as well as burned-out buses and trucks that the Czechs had tried to use to block the roads until they were rammed by tanks and set ablaze. "Fuck! That guy is dead," Peggy cried as they passed the body of a man, head skyward, eyes open in a vacant stare. "And nobody is moving his corpse."

Outside the radio station, there was a tank that the protesters had set on fire and several young people whom they assumed were students, were throwing Molotov cocktails at Russian troops fighting their way into the building to stop broadcasts about the invasion. Gunfire rang out around them, and they dropped flat on the ground in horror as a student a few feet away toppled over. To them it was as if the Russian who shot him viewed his victim as simply an object, knocking him over without any feelings of guilt or remorse—as if he were a mere bowling pin in an alien alley.

When the shooting stopped and they rose from the ground, Alistair spotted one of the Russian soldiers pointing his gun at him. "Press! We're press!" Alistair screamed at the soldier, waving his camera bag above his head. His palms and forehead were dripping sweat, and his heart was pounding like a power drill digging up a road. The Russian hesitated and for several seconds the two of them stared directly at each other with Alistair's life seemingly in the balance. Then, slowly the soldier lowered his rifle, and the frightening moment was over.

That evening, they filed their first-hand account of the invasion, and afterwards, they had their only meal of the day. Physically and emotionally exhausted by all that they had encountered, they chose to splurge and eat in the hotel's quiet, elegant dining-room that seemed half a continent away from the turmoil they had seen on the streets. They sank into plush, velvet seats while they studied the menu, eventually choosing to have svickova, a classic Czech dinner—beef stewed with cream, tomato paste, celery, carrots and other vegetables. "Just the ticket for an empty stomach." Peggy was delighted with their choice.

"Yeah, but I feel guilty being here after all we've seen. And if we ate like this every day, we'd soon be two more Russian tanks."

"Fuck, you. Don't go and spoil my meal. So, why do you think there was so little resistance? I just don't understand it."

"What would that have accomplished, faced by such overwhelming force? People knew the situation was hopeless as soon as the Russians took over the international airport and confined Czech forces to their barracks. Besides, they were under orders not to resist."

"But still, they could have tried."

"There was no point in being shot to death. Better to stay alive and hope for better days to come."

"Pacifist!"

"I don't know about you, but I was scared shitless out there myself. At the radio station, there were bullets flying all over the place. We could have easily been hit. And I thought that soldier who pointed his gun at me was going to pull the trigger."

"Well, he didn't, did he?"

"Fortunately, he decided that was risky... You know it's not that I'm particularly afraid of dying young. Whatever age you are—whether you're thirty or eighty—so long as you are healthy and enjoying life, I doubt you feel much different about how long you've been on this planet or any more ready to go. Time is like that. Pretty fuzzy. The main thing is that you don't want to die unnecessarily."

"Well, you didn't, and I don't think that soldier had any intention of shooting you. I also believe that the Czechs could have shown more balls and gotten away with it. Lots of them are going to regret their inaction the rest of their lives. They'll find it embarrassing and demoralising to be constantly reminded about it. Many Jews who survived the Holocaust feel that way."

"You call it cowardice. I call it realism."

Fortunately, the waiter returned to their table to refill their wine glasses, cutting short the argument.

Four days later, they filed their final story from Prague:

> Czech resistance to the invasion was light and as a result
> the number killed was little more than one hundred. One
> creative aspect of their passive response was the attempt
> to confuse the motorized divisions advancing on Prague
> and other cities by removing road signs or pointing them
> in the wrong direction and by posting false detours at
> important junctions. There were unverified rumours that
> one armoured column was totally lost most of the day,
> wandering aimlessly about the countryside. It was per-
> haps a story planted in an attempt to lift Czech spirits in
> a new atmosphere of hopelessness and depression.

The next day, Alistair and Peggy flew home, having unexpectedly borne witness to one of the major international events of the decade. It was early evening when they arrived in Toronto exhausted from the long hours of reporting as well as from the flight. "Let's take a taxi to my place," Peggy suggested. "You've got clothes and stuff with you so you can stay for the night. We'll sleep in tomorrow and take the rest of the day off. We deserve it."

"Fine with me, but I'll have to go home tomorrow to get clean stuff."

Around eleven the following morning, Alistair was awakened by a lock of hair falling across his face and lips pressed against his exposed cheek. He inhaled the warm, earthy smell of her nude body pressed against him. It was becoming familiar now and was different from the vaguely sweet aroma Ginny had emitted, but not unpleasant, a natural smell that suggested self-confidence and an open, spontaneous nature. He felt the weight of Peggy's torso and legs as she climbed on top of him. "Hmm. Nice tush, but roll over reporter, so I can read the worrisome headlines you are hiding from me." Alistair obliged and she kissed him on the forehead. Minutes later he was inside her, the lingering stress of the Prague experience dissolving in the pleasure of their lovemaking, and the security and reassurance he felt in the intimacy of their deepening relationship.

"Do you know what I was thinking while I waited for you to stir?" Peggy had just poured them a second cup of coffee at the end of a big breakfast of scrambled eggs, bacon, mushrooms, and toast. "I was thinking this is pretty stupid the way we are living. We have two different apartments miles apart and we're wasting so much time moving between them, fetching stuff and forgetting what we've left at each other's place. The sensible thing would be to move in together." Alistair didn't respond immediately, so Peggy added, "Now, don't go telling me you need several months to think this over while you weigh the pros and cons."

"No, no. I was thinking the same myself. But I didn't think you'd want to, not when preserving your independence is so important to you."

"For you, too, you big schmuck. But that wouldn't change. We'd both be free to come and go as we like, and the arrangement would last only so long as we both want it to. It would just be, you know, a more practical setup that way."

"Put like that, it doesn't sound very romantic."

"But it would be. Who knows, it could last as long as we live. The main thing, however, is that we'd have more time together…and more time in bed, too. I mean, shit, I'm not interested in climbing under the sheets with anyone else but, if for some reason that changes for either of us, then so be it. They're free to go. No hard feelings."

So, the deal was struck and at Alistair's suggestion—he had been privately thinking about it for several weeks—they decided to give up apartment-living and buy an old house in Cabbagetown that Alistair had spotted in the *Herald*'s advertisements and liked. It was dirt cheap because the neighbourhood was just starting to emerge from slum status and the house needed a lot of work on the interior.

"It's perfect! Rather like my parent's place." Peggy adored it from the moment she first saw it. "Their duplex needed a lot of renovations when they bought it."

"Yes, but our situation is different, right? We're not married and we're not heading in that direction either."

"Agreed. And no children out of wedlock. Thank you, science, for giving us the pill."

They both called their parents to pass on the news. They were all delighted although, not surprisingly, Peggy's mother said, "But why don't you get married? He's such a nice boy and Tate and I would much prefer that. No shanda."

"Mame, please! We don't want to, and there won't be any scandal. It's nineteen sixty-eight, not forty-eight."

The first time the Morgansteins visited their home, Peggy's mother exclaimed, "We love it! Don't we Tate? It's just like our place. I can't believe it. Even a front porch and a wrought-iron fence already. But why such an odd name for the area?"

"That's because the original settlers were Irish and Macedonian immigrants in the eighteen forties. They were very poor, so apparently they tore up their front lawns and grew cabbages."

"Ah! Just like our part of Montreal—only a century later, right Tate?"

"Yes, and I like cabbage," he answered, lighting his pipe. "Too bad that prosperity has led to their disappearance."

Alistair seized on his reference to the past to return to the inquiry he had politely dropped when they first met. As he passed him another glass of wine, he said, "I still don't know how you and your family got from England to Canada. Do you mind if I ask?"

"Not at all. As you know, Canada's immigration policy loosened after the war."

"Well, a little, yes."

"The important thing for us was that it started accepting some Holocaust survivors."

"So, that's how you got in?"

"It certainly helped. The Canadian government wanted to admit refugees who would work in labour-intensive industries that were short of manpower. Under that plan, The Tailor Project was set up in in Montreal. We came under it."

"Ah, yes, you mentioned before that you are a tailor."

"I wasn't really. I was a doctor by training, but Jews couldn't work in that profession either in Berlin or London even though both cities urgently needed doctors. When we came to Canada, Mame got a job as a nurse right away, so Gertrude and Ruth taught me the basics."

"You never returned to medicine?"

"No. It took me too long to learn English. I like tailoring anyway. It's less stressful, and I'm not that bad now."

What a tragic story! But what a man!

Chapter 19

OVER THE ENSUING year, Alistair and Peggy spent what spare time they had working on the house, painting the interior, and arranging for plumbers and electricians to come for needed repairs. At work, they were both busy reporting on the new initiatives of the Trudeau government, including the Official Languages Bill and the proposal to recognize the government of the People's Republic of China.

Throughout this period, they were also following closely the civil war in Biafra, an area of Nigeria where the Ibo tribe, a minority in the country as a whole, had formed a separate state which the federal government was now both fighting and trying to starve into submission. "Holy crap, we better get over there. The situation is looking increasingly desperate for the Ibos." Peggy was reading a wire story as she reached Alistair's desk. "The only food and other aid still reaching them is from non-governmental agencies, using dangerous night flights to avoid being shot down by Nigerian forces. If we don't go soon, Biafra is going to have fallen and it will be a case of genocide with the rest of the world having done little to prevent it."

In early October 1969, the *Herald's* management finally responded to Peggy's insistent pleas and sent her and Alistair to report on the plight of the Biafrans. They arrived late in the morning on the Portuguese island of Sao Tome off the coast of Africa, the departure point for flights to Uli Airport in Biafra. "Wow!" Alistair exclaimed, "this is such a beautiful, quiet place, it's hard to believe we're only an hour's flight away from the civil war. What did you say JCA stands for?"

"Joint Church Aid. It's a coalition of international and Canadian organizations, including the Presbyterian Church of Canada. That's why the air crews call the planes they fly Jesus Christ Air."

The next evening, they fastened themselves into bucket seats on one side of an aging Super Constellation aircraft that had been refitted as a cargo carrier with only room in the hold for themselves and the unloading crew. "This is weird," Alistair turned towards Peggy. "I feel like I'm a paratrooper about to be dropped into France."

"Don't kid yourself. You know you'd never have the nerve to jump out."

There was a tremendous roar as the heavily loaded plane lumbered down the runway gradually gaining speed until it climbed slowly into the darkening sky. About forty minutes later, as they neared the Nigerian coast, the cabin lights were suddenly extinguished. "That's it until our approach at Uli," the aid worker sitting next to them explained. "Only the pilot can use a penlight to read his maps. In fact, we're already under surveillance. There are Soviet fishing trawlers that monitor us."

"Now, you tell me!"

"Did you know that these Connies have a wingspan that is greater than the width of the landing strip at Uli? It's really only a stretch of undulating road in the wilderness with the trees removed on either side for our benefit. Yet, it is currently the second busiest airport in Africa."

"No kidding?" Peggy was busy taking notes as the aid worker talked. "It can't be easy to land one of these suckers there."

"It's not, especially without ground navigation lights and radar. Two months ago, a Canair plane flew into a ridge near the airport, killing all on board."

"Please, I don't need any more bad news…you know, I was just thinking about what Pierre Trudeau said in nineteen sixty-eight when he was asked about this crisis." Peggy sensed that Alistair was chattering away in an effort to dispel his anxiety. "He just gave one of his infamous shrugs and answered, 'Where's Biafra?' He should be here with us now to find out what it's really like."

They felt the plane begin to descend and sway as it dipped in uneven spasms. From their seats near the back of the hold, they could see the white traces of anti-aircraft shells arcing into the sky. "Don't worry." The aid worker noted their anxious looks. "Without our navigation lights on, those gunners can track us only by the sound of our engines, so their fire isn't very accurate."

"Worry is not the word I would use." Peggy patted Alistair on the knee. "I suppose to be honest I'm terrified myself, but I'm sure we'll be okay. All we need to do is focus on the task ahead, on the photos you're going to take, the articles we'll write and how we'll be helping to alert Canadians to the scope of the crisis and our pathetic response."

"I'd feel safer on Jesus Christ Air if I were a Presbyterian."

"Not really." It was the aid worker again. "None of us knows our destiny, only God."

That is supposed to be comforting?

Suddenly, below them, they could see the runway lights of Uli Airport go on. "We've reached an altitude of one thousand feet," Alistair and Peggy were told. "We're on our final approach." But moments later, there was a great roar from the engines as the pilot went to full throttle and the Constellation climbed steeply. "Looks like we've been waved off by ground control. There must be a bomber overhead."

Alistair gripped his armrest. *Come on JCA. You can do it. I'll sign on with the Presbyterians if you make it.*

Peggy was doing her best to stay calm, but she didn't feel that way either. Her mouth was dry, and her fingers were nervously strumming the back of Alistair's hand. Out the window, they could see a line of bombs chasing down one side of the runway. Then the airport lights went out and everything was black until, some twenty minutes later, the plane completed its circle and began its second attempt at landing. Once more the runway lights shone but this time the Constellation made it safely down, the engines were slammed into reverse, and the pilot radioed the control tower to extinguish the lights.

They taxied to a dimly lit unloading area and immediately the plane's doors flew open. "You've got to get off right away. It's very dangerous while we are on the ground." Alistair and Peggy, lugging their packsacks and camera gear, scrambled out as the aid workers on board began unloading the cargo to staff on the ground.

The moment they stepped onto the tarmac, however, they heard someone shout, "Bomb coming. Take cover!" They could hear the scream of an incoming shell above the airport and, following the lead of one of the workers, they sped to trenches dug into the ground close to the growing stack of unloaded supplies. The blast was deafening as the bomb exploded less than a hundred metres from them. Crouching, trembling in the shelter, they plugged their ears with their fingers and waited breathlessly for the next hit. That bomb struck the runway near the far end, so they knew that the plane was moving away. Nevertheless, it had gouged a large hole in the runway, preventing their Constellation from taking off to return to Sao Tome, and leaving it as an easy target on the ground. "Now, incoming planes will be stacked above Uli," the aid worker huddled next to them said. "That puts them in increased danger of being hit by artillery fire or Mig fighter planes."

Much to the reporters' surprise, however, a bulldozer soon arrived with a load of rubble and the crater was quickly filled by the airport's maintenance manager, enabling the flights to resume. "That will have to do until the morning when they'll repave that area." From the trench, Alistair and Peggy watched their plane take off and the airport lights go out. They rather wished they were on board and safely off to Sao Tome, but they also calculated rightly that the excitement was over for that night. "Did you get any good pics?"

"I doubt it. The light wasn't good."

"Well, I didn't see you lift your head very often to take one either."

When dawn arrived, they were driven in one of the delivery trucks to the nearest feeding station. "Jesus, this is terrible," Alistair exclaimed the moment he left the vehicle.

"It's so awful I can hardly bear it," Peggy agreed. She rarely flinched, but this time tears dripped from her eyes onto her cheeks.

Long rows of young children were sitting naked on hardback wooden chairs, a long, narrow table in front of them. Their exposed bellies were badly distended, the sockets of their dark eyes deep and their expressions a mix of fear and helplessness. Swarms of flies were circling them, yet they made no effort to swat them away. "They have given up hope. They have no conception of any life beyond their desperate struggle to stay alive." Alistair wrestled with his conscience as he reached for his camera. "It feels totally wrong to take photographs rather than help them in some substantive way."

"I know but we've got to arouse Canadians to action by showing them the enormity of this tragedy."

"But will they be? Or, safe on their patios at home, will they just throw some juicy steaks on the barbecue and carry on, indifferent to what's happening here?"

"That depends on how well we cover this. We've simply got to get the public and the feds to pay attention. Someone just told me that around two million people will have starved to death before this conflict is over. It's as if we are at Auschwitz at the end of the War."

Back at Uli Airport in the evening, Alistair and Peggy waited for their Constellation to arrive on its next flight from Sao Tome. It came in without incident and the moment the unloading was completed, they clamoured aboard. As the plane started down the runway and the airport lights went on, however, they came under attack by a bomber. From inside the cargo well, they could hear the clink of shrapnel embedding itself in the fuselage. Still the plane kept gathering speed, bumped over the repaved hole in the runway and at last lifted off climbing agonizingly slowly. But then, in the midst of the ascent, one of its four engines sputtered and died. "Looks like an engine got hit," the aid worker sitting next to them said. "Now it all depends on where."

Peggy leaned against Alistair, and they held hands tightly as the plane limped on. Neither spoke for some time until Peggy whispered softly in Alistair's ear. "I love you, you know. I don't want it to end, not now…maybe never and certainly not this way."

Alistair was taken by surprise. Peggy had never before said that she loved him, nor had he said that to her. But as he thought about it, he realized that probably he did—whatever love really was. He had lusted after her from the moment she first suggested he go to bed with her, but he realized that their relationship was much deeper than that now. He needed her as an anchor and relied on her advice as if the age difference between them were greater than it actually was. He appreciated the way she listened to his concerns and sought to help him, cajoled him even when necessary. He liked her frankness and the way no one intimidated her. He admired her intellect, her enormous energy, her idealism, and the courage she had to take on dangerous assignments. Yet, obviously it was more than that, for there was the physical side as well and the pleasure and release that flowed from it. Alistair kissed her on the cheek. "I feel the same way you do." It was an inadequate, cryptic response, but Peggy recognized that for Alistair, it was a lot to say.

At last, they were over the ocean and the Constellation began its descent. But then the second engine on the same side gave out, and they could see air streaming through holes in the fuselage. "Oh, shit, no!" Peggy cried out. "Surely, we're not going to crash this near to home!"

The remaining engines sounded rough as if the propellers were moving unevenly, and it was clear the pilot was having a hard time keeping the plane steady and aloft. During the final approach to the airport, there was no more talking; it seemed as if everyone was collectively holding their breath. Alistair noticed how the aid worker next to him had closed his eyes. The palms of his hands were clasped together, and his lips were moving. *Come on Jesus Christ! Do it for that guy's sake at least.*

Finally, the wheels touched the ground and, as the pilot reversed the engines, a loud cheer erupted from those on board. A fire engine and an ambulance came along side as the Constellation taxied to a halt at the terminal. "Home at last!" Peggy undid her seat buckle and threw her arms around Alistair.

That afternoon, they filed their story on the trip, ending it with these words.

> The Ibos have a proverb that they like to recite to those who assert that they are only protracting the war and adding to the starvation by fighting on in the face of impossible odds. "Only a tree," the Ibos say, "stands still when it knows it's being cut down."
>
> Will people and their governments around the world some day learn from that proverb? Or, like trees, will we remain impassive observers even in the face of genocide?

That night, nestled together in a double bed in their little hotel in the centre of Sao Tome, Alistair and Peggy found it difficult to get to sleep. When he finally did, Alistair dreamed that he was leaping over a deep, dark chasm out of which clouds of black smoke were rising. His feet , however, failed to touch down on the other side and now he was falling—falling without apparent end into the gaping hole. Unconsciously, he cried out, awakening Peggy who shook him out of his nightmare and then clutched him closely to her until he relaxed and fell asleep. But once more, he had a horrifying dream. He was at the door of an airplane enveloped in flames that was plunging steeply towards the ground. He had been ordered to leap out, but Alistair didn't budge until someone from behind gave him a shove and he tumbled through the open doorway, screaming. It was only Peggy awakening him by putting her arms around him and kissing his exposed cheek. This time Alistair rolled over, kissed her and they made love gently and slowly. It wasn't as good as it usually was—they were both too exhausted for that—but it was comforting and the tension they both were feeling flowed from their bodies. After that, they slept soundly until mid-morning when it was time for a quick breakfast before leaving for their real home.

Chapter 20

ALISTAIR AND PEGGY were embarrassed by the congratulations they received at the *Herald* for their vivid and disturbing reporting from Biafra. They were treated by their colleagues and superiors almost as if they were heroes who had accomplished an extraordinary deed. They did not , however, feel that way themselves, but rather as if they had carelessly intruded upon a tragedy that others had to live every day with no avenue of escape.

Over candlelit dinners at home, they spent a lot of time rehashing their experiences. The topic recurred in January 1970 when the Biafran resistance collapsed, and the war abruptly ended. "What was the point of all the risks and sacrifices everyone made, including us? Twenty-five JCA pilots alone were killed on missions. And as for the media reporting, we didn't push anyone out of inertia. It was all so futile. Nigeria is back where it was after the loss of close to two million people."

"I don't agree." Peggy finished her wine. "The media coverage had an impact on the public and NGOs, influencing them to get involved in relief."

"Maybe, but not on Canadians. We got there too late to have any effect. Besides, in the end, all the aid to Biafra did was prolong the fighting and the suffering."

"I don't see it as cynically as that. Even if we didn't personally make a difference this time, we might well in other crises."

Alistair patted Peggy on the knee. "The intent is noble, no question. I'm just not convinced the media can generate change. Maybe it would be better to get into politics."

"And make all the compromises those guys do? No, thank you."

They fell silent and reflective until Alistair said, "I've been thinking about how there were a lot of different motivations that drove the people we met in Biafra. The missionaries and some of the aid workers were, of course, acting on Christ's instruction to help heal the suffering. Still, it can't have been easy for them to face the dangers they did and make such sacrifices based on faith alone. Of course, a lot of the pilots and their crews were mercenaries, there to make money or because they had a thirst for adventure. But some of them—and some of the aid workers—were not driven by these considerations. They were in Biafra simply because there was a job that they believed had to be done; secular humanists, I guess you'd call them. That's the category where I'd slot you, and you all deserve praise."

Peggy kissed him on the cheek. "It includes you, goofball."

"I'm not sure. I am secular but unlike the rest of you I'm also skeptical. And I don't know how long we can go on dodging bullets without getting hit."

When they went to bed that night, they both lay restlessly awake, recalling yet again the most frightening moments of their trip. Eventually, Peggy rolled on top of Alistair, her hair falling in his face and her alluring green eyes close to his. "Biafra made me realize how close to death we always are. I've felt very vulnerable ever since…and it's changed my thinking."

"Oh, in what way?"

"About marriage."

"What?" Abruptly, Alistair sat up in bed with Peggy astride his waist. "What do you mean?"

"I mean I'd l like to get married despite what we've said before."

"You're joking."

"No. I'm not. I've been thinking a lot about it. I don't know about you, but now I feel I need more reassurance of permanence…for whatever length of time we have together. It would be a symbol of stability when, of course, there really isn't any in this crazy world."

"You're serious about this? I mean you've hit me completely out of the blue."

"I know and that's not fair … You'll need to think about it, but not for too long I hope."

"No, no. I'll put my brain in overdrive."

"It wouldn't really change anything. We'd still have an open, independent relationship with both of us free to come and go as we like, and we'd end it on good terms if one of us wanted out. And still, no kids to tie us down."

"But how would your parents feel if you married a goy? It wouldn't be what they're hoping for."

"No, of course, they'd prefer you were a Jew, and my mother would doubtless pressure me to get you to convert. But for her, it is more important that I marry."

"What about your father? He's more traditional."

"Yes, somewhat, but you know that on this he'd go along with whatever she says. She'd remind him that both of Richler's wives have been gentiles. The main thing, though, is that they really like you—love you, in fact. They see you as mishpocheh."

"Family?"

"Right. See you can talk like a Jew even. They like that."

"But I'm an agnostic, probably an atheist. It would be hypocritical to convert, and—"

"You wouldn't have to. I'm the same—a secular Jew anyway. So, we probably wouldn't be able even to find a rabbi liberal enough to marry us. That's a problem we'd have to work out and I imagine one without a solution my parents would like. How about yours?"

"They'd be okay with whatever we do."

"Nice. So, think it over and let me know your decision before the end of the decade."

"That's very generous!" While they had been talking, Alistair had contemplated what it would be like to be married to Peggy. *No different really from the way things are now. If she wants to do this, why not? I don't want to make the same mistake twice.* "Okay, I've thought it over and my answer is: I love you. Will you marry me?"

An enormous grin formed on Peggy's face. "Yippee!" What decisiveness! What chutzpah! I gladly accept."

After some research, Peggy uncovered information that she knew would unsettle her parents. While civil marriage in Quebec had been legalized in 1968, it was available only for residents of the province. "We'll have to get married here—at City Hall, I guess. But, if it's okay with you, we could go to Montreal afterwards and have another ceremony and reception there. We could include some Jewish traditions to appease my parents."

"Sounds like a good plan to me."

"I'll phone them tomorrow night—after a couple of scotches."

• • •

"THIS IS WONDERFUL news, shaina maidel!" Mrs. Morganstein put down the receiver and shouted, "Tate! Get on the other phone. It's Margaret. She and Alistair are going to get married. Isn't that marvellous?" Picking up the phone again, she added, "I'm overjoyed, I really am. All of my daughters married and to nice young men. What more could a mother ask for?"

"Mame, you're kvelling!"

"I know I am, and I don't care. Is Alistair there? Let me speak to him please." She congratulated her future son-in-law, and, after a brief exchange, she spoke to her daughter again. "So, you'll get married here, of course."

"We'd like to, but we can't have a Jewish wedding with Alistair being a gentile."

"But he will convert, won't he? That's very common in these situations."

"He can't do that. He's not religious."

There was silence while Mrs. Morganstein reflected on the dilemma. "Tate will talk to our rabbi and see what can be arranged. He's a nice young man and open-minded, too. I think he'll be okay performing a mixed marriage."

"Well, Mame, here's the snag." Peggy paused, giving her mother time to prepare herself for disappointment. "It won't be a Jewish wedding. It would be morally wrong when Alistair isn't a believer and I'm not a practicing Jew."

"But the rabbi doesn't need to know that! We can tell him simply that Alistair is a Protestant, and you are a secular Jew. I think he'll be okay with that."

"That wouldn't be right, Mame. It would be dishonest and deceitful. We're going to have a civil marriage."

Again, Peggy waited while this dissatisfying information was digested. "Alright, dear." Mrs. Morganstein's voice was sad and barely audible now. "Whatever you—"

"And it will be here in Toronto, since by law it can't be in Quebec."

"Oi, vey! This is too much. Tate, are you on the other phone? Did you hear this?"

"Wait! Here is the good part. We're going to pay for the two of you and for Gertrude and Ruth and their families to come to Toronto to attend, and then we'll all go to Montreal and have another ceremony there. We'll make it Jewish, but in our own way. We'll make it moving and a true expression of who we are…What do you think?"

"I don't know, dear. I'll have to discuss this with Tate."

Peggy was surprised when she was awakened by a call from her mother early the next morning. "Tate and I have discussed it. We'll come to Toronto and then have another ceremony here. If you're thinking of marrying this summer when the weather is likely to be good, we'll erect a tent in the backyard. Tate thinks it will be fun to make the ceremony different from the usual."

"Oh, thank you Mame. You're vunderlekh."

"I'm not. I'm a pushover already, you know that. Thank your father. The War liberated him more than I ever realized."

From the *Herald* later that morning, Alistair phoned his parents to pass on the news. Knowing from Jonathan that one of the reasons for the breakup with Ginny had been that Alistair didn't want the responsibility of raising children, they asked simply if he had changed his mind. To avoid disappointing them, he said only that they had not yet decided. Then he called his brother. "That's great. I don't know Peggy very well, but from what I've seen of her she seems very nice. Spunky, I'd say."

"She's that for sure. You know, I'm sorry we haven't got together more often. You haven't even been to our house for a meal yet. It's just that, like you, we've been very busy."

"Oh, that reminds me. We haven't talked on the phone for so long that I've never told you that Ginny has had another baby."

"No? Really? I wasn't even aware that she was pregnant."

"Sorry about that."

"Do you know this time if it's a boy or girl?"

Jonathan laughed. "If Colin told me, I'm afraid I've forgotten. No, wait, a boy. Yes, I'm pretty sure he said it was a boy... another one. They have other news, too. They're moving to Vancouver. Colin has been made a junior partner and he's going to head up our office there."

"Wow! That sounds like quite an honour at…what…thirty-three?"

"Something like that. Yeah, he's climbing fast. He's been made a Queen's Counsel as well. I think Ginny has been a real asset for him, but he's driven anyway."

"Is he an ex-footballer player or something? Still obsessed with scoring touchdowns?"

"Maybe, I don't know. Anyway, I'm going to miss them. Jennifer and I have become good friends with them both."

"Really!" Alistair was silent for a few seconds as he digested this ironic development. "Funny how life works out sometimes, isn't it?"

"You bet. So, when are you guys planning to tie the knot?"

"Probably in June"

"Seriously? You're going to be that traditional?" Jonathan needled him.

"We want to do it when the weather is nice, and the gardens will look good."

Jonathan laughed. "Is this really my unconventional brother talking? Anyway, Jennifer and I will clear the decks and rain or shine we'll all be there for both ceremonies. I'm really happy for you. It's been a long time coming. I hope it works out well."

Well, that's it, Alistair mused as he hung up. *Now, for sure, I won't run into Ginny again.* Yet, feeling the need for closure, he wrote her a note while he was at the paper and Peggy was out on assignment:

Dear Ginny,

> *I was talking to Jonathan on the phone today and he told me you have had another baby. I don't know just when and, once again, Jonathan didn't know for certain if it was a boy or girl. I can hear you muttering, "Grr. Men!" Anyway, I was delighted to receive the news. It will mean less fussing! Congratulations to both you and Colin.*
>
> *Jonathan told me as well that Colin has been made a partner and that you are moving to Vancouver where he will be in charge of the office. The first part of this is, I would imagine, good news. Colin is certainly rising fast in the firm and that must give you an added sense of security as you raise a family. Please pass on to him my congratulations.*
>
> *On the other hand, I was sorry to learn that you are mov-*

ing away. I had always hoped that, by chance, I might run into you on the street one day and have an opportunity for a chat, however brief. I have always wanted to say in person how sincerely sorry I am about the way that I treated you. It was unconscionable on my part to have sustained our relationship for so long without fully discussing with you my reservations about marriage and having children. It was behaviour I will always regret.

I remember well the wonderful times we had together as I assume you are now enjoying with your family, and I wish you every possible joy in life. You richly deserve it.

As ever (I guess!),
Alistair

I wonder how Ginny will react when she receives my note? Will she be touched, or will she just tear it up and throw it away? And if she happens to keep it, where will she hide it?. I know! She'll tuck it away in the middle of her copy of "Sense and Sensibility." That's one book she knows Colin is never likely to open.

Alistair's musings were at least partially answered when a letter arrived from Ginny a few days later.

Dear Alistair,

Thank you so very much for your letter. First off, I want you to know that I laughed very hard at your comment about fussing. It brought back such vivid memories of our conversations about parenting. And, yes, you are right, I am finding much less time for fussing now with two little ones always requiring attention. I don't know how people manage with three or more.

For some reason, you didn't mention in your letter, but left it for Jonathan to tell us, that you are getting married—and to Peggy Morganstein, that journalist at the Star you told me about and of whom I was once intensely jealous. You, naughty boy to have chosen her! Seriously, though, I was delighted to receive this news. For some time after that night at the Old Mill, I was angry with you and upset over what had happened to us, but, after Colin appeared, slowly my hurt turned to concern that you might never find someone else yourself. So, I am pleased to know that that will not be your fate. I hope that you will discover joy and comfort in the lasting company of someone you love.

Colin and I send you and Peggy our best wishes for every future happiness.

Fondly,
Ginny

Fondly. I think that's how I closed my note with their wedding present. Well, it could have been worse and at least she answered. But damn it, I still don't know for sure the genders of her kids. He found a research file that he had forgotten about in the bottom drawer of his desk. It was no longer relevant, so he slid the note into the middle of it and went back to work until Peggy returned from an editorial meeting and proposed that they go out for lunch. He squeezed her hand as they walked to the restaurant, his conscience now relatively free of guilt.

"You seem very happy today."

"I am. We're getting married!"

Chapter 21

THE CIVIL WEDDING was, as first proposed, in June with the lilacs at their peak and the roses coming into bloom in Peggy and Alistair's little garden. It was a simple affair at the new city hall and afterwards pictures of the couple were taken in Nathan Phillipps Square, with the curving walls of the mayoralty building and the arches over the pool and fountains as backdrops. Only the immediate families were present, with Peggy's older sister, Gertrude, and Jonathan signing the register.

The reciprocal gathering in Montreal the following Saturday was a much larger affair with friends and relations from Toronto and elsewhere attending as well. It started indoors at four when the guests began arriving at the Morganstein's Mile End home for the kabbalat panim, a period for greeting the couple before the actual ceremony. There was no set dress code, but most of the women wore new spring dresses and the men dark suits and ties, although some, influenced by the sartorial relaxation Prime Minister Trudeau had initiated, were in sports jackets with coloured shirts and bright flashy ties. Only wine, coffee and tea were served at this time, and Mrs. Morganstein kept the food simple as there was to be a dinner later for those who stayed after the wedding. Simple for Mrs. Morganstein was, however, a bountiful feast for most. Trays were passed loaded with foods to meet varied tastes: cheeses and fruit, matzo balls, gefilte fish, and lox . The centre piece, however, was her famous fresh baked challah, smothered in gooey Brie. In keeping with Jewish tradition, throughout the kabbalat panim, Peggy and Alistair refrained from drinking or eating, fasting until the ceremony was over.

Around five, everyone was asked to gather in the tent for the bedeken, the actual wedding. Then, Peggy appeared alone at the top of the porch steps leading to the garden, dressed in her cream-coloured wedding dress that touched the ground but had no train. This was the signal to her father, in a variant of the Jewish ketubah, to read out the marriage document that had been signed in Toronto. When he finished, Alistair emerged from inside the house and spread the diaphanous veil of the wedding dress over Peggy's face. They descended the steps to the tent and stood in the middle where they exchanged rings. In a line in front of them were their parents and three siblings, precisely the right number. As the eldest, Peggy's father stepped forward first and, holding a fluted crystal glass of red wine over the couple, began the recitation of a modern version of the sheva berakhot, or seven blessings. From there the readings continued through to the youngest, Jonathan, with each in turn holding the glass of wine over Peggy and Alistair. "May you be blessed by being part of a wider community. May you find it a blessing to be a link in a golden circle of family, friends, colleagues, and the people whom you serve through your work. May this circle be full of love, wisdom, support and joy, and may you long benefit from their presence in your lives."

Jonathan handed the small glass of wine to Alistair and he and Peggy swallowed mouthfuls after which Alistair wrapped the glass in a white linen napkin, placed it on the floor and crushed it with the heel of one shoe as the guests familiar with a traditional ceremony shouted, "Mazel Tov!" Alistair was aware that the breaking of the glass was a reminder of the destruction of the temple in Jerusalem, but also symbolized the fragility of relationships and the need for effort to preserve them. *We'll have to try our hardest to make this work. It won't be easy, since we don't always see things the same way. But we're making a big commitment and we want it to last.*

The speeches followed with Peggy's father up first. Despite his reserved nature, he spoke with a quiet, dry sense of humour. "Some of you may not know that I have spent most of my life in Canada as a tailor.

After much thought, however, I decided not to be the one to make Margaret's wedding dress." There were howls of laughter, led by his wife and daughters. "Isn't it lovely?" Everyone clapped. "Now, if I had sewn it, I would not have…well, never mind!" Alistair's father followed. He wasn't funny, but he hit the right notes, welcoming Peggy into his family, and sincerely thanking the Morgansteins for doing the same with his son and now with all of the Parkers.

As best man, Jonathan went next, choosing to gently roast his brother. "My most enduring image of Alistair is of him as *The Thinker* in Auguste Rodin's famous statue, only Alistair is not nude but wearing a pair of shorts and a t-shirt and he is not sitting on a rock but holding one in his hand—and in front of him is a glass greenhouse. This is what he is quietly thinking to himself in his characteristically analytical way: 'To throw, or not to throw, that is the question.'" Laughter among those in the audience familiar with the story. "'Whether 'tis better in the mind to suffer the taunts and jeers of an older brother, or to take aim against a shining pane and by striking end them.' Unfortunately, thanks to me, Alistair did in this case act and with predictable consequences; there was the rub. Today, he chose to act again, but I am sure that this time he made the right decision and one that will bring much joy to him and to Peggy."

Alistair followed and adjusted on the fly to Jonathan's remarks. "Friends, family and colleagues, hear my defence. I choose to clarify this view, not correct it.'" More guffaws. "Jonathan is right that I do often take a long time making up my mind, but in this case, it took only ten minutes and would have been still faster except that I had to satisfy myself first that Peggy was thinking straight in suggesting that we get married—that she was actually willing to take me on. She is after all an intelligent woman, capable of bold but not usually rash decisions."

Breaking with tradition, Peggy finished. "I want you all to know that I offered Alistair the whole decade of the seventies to make up his mind about marriage, so I was delighted that he took only a few minutes to agree to *my* proposal. The thing is that Alistair is way more than just a careful thinker. He's…well…" Peggy turned to face Alistair directly. "He's someone…someone I just love to bits."

Drinks and hors d'oeuvres were served until around 6.30 p.m. and then a traditional Jewish wedding dinner of roast chicken, potatoes, vegetables and, of course, more challah. Afterwards, everyone returned to the tent for coffee and dessert, large, rich slabs of rugelach to please Alistair, and then the tables were cleared and pushed to the side so that the hora could begin—circle dancing with, at one point Peggy and Alistair, seated on chairs, lifted into the air, holding napkins above their heads.

After that, there was more contemporary dancing and singing until well after midnight with Peggy and Alistair taking several turns together around the tent. "Hey, you're good," Peggy exclaimed as Alistair lifted her hand over his head and spun her. "I guess I know where that came from."

When only family was left, a weary, sweating, Jonathan stumbled up to his brother, "Holy crap! I never thought it would be this much fun. The Morgansteins' win the celebration trophy, hands down."

●　●　●

"OH GEEZ, NO! Did you see this?" Alistair handed Peggy a news report that had just come in by telex. "The British Trade Commissioner in Montreal—James Cross—has been kidnapped by two members of the FLQ. We better get back there."

It was just a few months after the wedding and they had not expected to return to Montreal so soon, but now it was urgent to do so. They flew there on October 10, arriving the day that Pierre Laporte, the deputy premier and Minister of Labour was kidnapped. "Fuck! Listen to this." Peggy had the radio on in her partents' home several evenings later. "Trudeau is invoking the War Measures Act. It goes into effect at four in the morning."

"No kidding?"

"Yeah, it's the first time a government has done that in peacetime. There will be troops patrolling the streets."

When they awoke, they hurried to the city centre where Alistair took photographs of the Van Doos regiment surrounding public buildings. "They're the most illustrious French-Canadian regiment in Canada's army. No wonder they were chosen for this sensitive job."

They also spotted a young man in jeans and a sweatshirt being bundled down the stairs of an apartment building and pushed into a police car. "A suspected member of the FLQ, I guess," Alistair said, clicking photographs in rapid succession."

"Yeah, and they'll probably hold him without charge."

● ● ●

"Holy fuck! Listen to this." Peggy raised the volume on their bedroom radio later that day. "Laporte has been killed. The police have found his body stuffed in the trunk of a car, owned by Paul Rose, an FLQ member."

"No! Where?"

"At a small airport a few miles from Montreal. The car was abandoned in the bush. He was strangled to death."

"That's terrible…. This is supposed to be 'the peaceable kingdom?' What bullshit." They rushed to the location but were too late to get any photographs that would be an improvement over those transmitted by Canadian Press.

Peggy and Alistair stayed for two more days, but the immediate crisis appeared to have ended, so they left for Toronto on the nineteenth. Over dinner on their last night in Montreal, there was an animated discussion of all that happened, ending in a debate over the appropriateness of imposing the War Measures Act. "I'm of two minds," Alistair admitted. "It looked like Quebec might be facing a major insurrection, but I'm also concerned about the government's trampling on civil rights."

"I just want peace everywhere," Mr. Morganstein asserted in his typical fashion.

"The feds went beyond what the situation called for," Peggy argued. "They're using the act to arrest, detain, and interrogate anyone who sympathizes with the FLQ whether or not they were involved in the kidnappings." Mrs. Morganstein, on the other hand, remained unwavering in her support of the Liberal government. "What Trudeau said to those reporters was perfect. 'Just watch me,' and then he acted decisively. He is the right person to have in charge."

"He's arrogant and authoritarian," Peggy countered.

Mr. Morganstein stood up and motioned to Alistair to do the same. "Come, we'll let the ladies do the arguing." He guided him to the living-room, got out his pipe and filled it with tobacco. "You don't smoke; that is wise. But I should buy you some chocolate cigars or something so that you can have one whenever we sit together."

Alistair laughed. "That would certainly take me back to my childhood."

Mr. Morganstein opened a cabinet, took out two crystal glasses and a bottle of cognac. "But you'll have some of this with me, won't you, meyn zun?" He pulled out the stopper and poured two hefty glasses.

His son! That's a first. "I will gladly, Tate." It seemed a good moment to learn more about his father-in-law's war experience. "Seeing troops on the streets of Montreal must be hard for you to watch after having served in the British army."

"It is. Fighting against your own people is a terrible thing to have to do. But we were very useful for the British after Normandy because we spoke German and knew the customs of the enemy. Still, we were terrified all the time."

"Who wouldn't be caught in that situation?"

"We knew that if we were captured, we would be executed right away as traitors of the fatherland. I still have nightmares about those years."

"Of course, you would."

"The rest of the family lived in a small flat in North London until I came home." Mr. Morganstein stopped and fell silent. "Well, you know the story from there." He drained his glass. "How about another cognac? I think I need one."

I would never turn down a snifter, thank you, Tate. Shalom."

Chapter 22

ON JANUARY 22, 1972, a protest march in Northern Ireland against the British practice of interning Irish nationalists without trial was stopped by paratroopers firing rubber bullets at close range and beating stone-throwing demonstrators with their batons. Allegations of brutality by the British army were widely reported in the media and the prospect of more unrest was clearly mounting. Peggy convinced the *Herald*'s management that it was time she and Alistair flew to Northern Ireland to report on the growing division between the Catholic and Protestant communities. Alistair, however, declined going. "I have a trip planned to Yellowknife. It's time we did some pieces on that area. The city is a boom town, thanks to gold mining, and I suspect before long they'll find other valuable minerals there."

"In the middle of winter? Why go now? The weather will be brutal, and there's no urgency."

"I have it almost all arranged—the people and places I want to visit. I'm not going to cancel the trip now."

Yet, when Peggy got home from Northern Ireland in early February, Alistair had not yet left for Yellowknife. "There were some screw-ups with the interviews, but I'm leaving next week. So how was your trip? It was obvious in your articles that things were bad in Derry…and you look whipped."

"I am." Dark circles drooped from her lower lids. "You would *not* have liked it. I got to Derry just before another march protesting internment without trial. It was the most violent of them all. They're calling it 'Bloody Sunday.' Bullets flying all around, some over my head. Thirteen civilians were killed, all Irish Catholics, and another so badly injured he may not survive. The soldiers gave no warning before opening fire, and in some cases, they shot people who were simply trying to get away. It's obvious what the consequence will be."

"More sectarian violence."

"Yeah, and a surge in support for the IRA." Peggy was gobbling down a bag of potato chips as she talked, hardly aware of what she was doing.

Comfort food, I guess. Alistair was watching her disapprovingly, she presumed.

"The meal on the plane was crap. I'm starving. What's for dinner?"

"Oh…I thought we'd eat out if that's okay. I've been busy all day getting ready for Yellowknife."

"Then let's get take-out. I don't want to wait that long. Sorry about that; God knows what you'll get to eat in Yellowknife."

"Simple fare, I imagine, but there is this one place I read about that I really want to try, Bullock's. It's just a log cabin with a notice that apparently says, 'Prices Subject to Change According to Customer's Attitude.'"

Peggy laughed. "You'll have to be on your best behaviour. None of your usual complaints about small napkins and plastic utensils."

Alistair's trip was a stark contrast with Peggy's. His story that garnered the most attention was about hiring a dogsled team so that he could pretend that he was an RCMP officer skimming quietly through the forest in pursuit of the Mad Trapper of Rat River, a notorious killer tracked by dogsleds for more than two weeks in the dead of winter until he eluded the RCMP by crossing the Richardson Mountain range on foot without climbing gear. In the Yukon on the other side, a monoplane was used to find him and the RCMP finally got their man. Alistair's own sled ride was a much tamer affair—in the forest outside Yellowknife with a guide on a snowmobile following him just out of view, and with the lead dog periodically glaring at him, put off by his poor handling of the sled.

It was night by the time Alistair and his team turned around to head back to the kennels, but a spectacular show of Northern Lights lit his surroundings. Blue, yellow and red streamers shimmered like magical dancers in long, flowing gowns as they traversed the enormous outdoor stage. They were like giant, swaying lamps lighting the track ahead of him to midday brightness. Alistair's photographs of the exploding sky with the sled and dogs in the foreground were the highlight of his coverage. *Colour again. It has to be.*

At the paper, Peggy followed his stories daily. *He's not the Mad Trapper. There are no mountains that Alistair is scaling. This is all fluff. It's good, but it's pablum.* She wondered when, if ever, Alistair was going to get to serious reporting on the gold mining industry, and more importantly on the welfare of the First Nations' people in Yellowknife and how they were managing in the midst of the growing intrusion of whites from outside. But those stories never came. Alistair was aware of this absence from his work, and it bothered him, but he already sensed that what he was writing were the kinds of stories his readers wanted and his photos the ones he should take to heighten their interest. For Peggy, this was a disturbing realization. *There's no passion in any of this, no concern for the welfare of humankind.*

In August 1972, Idi Amin, the brutal and dictatorial president of Uganda, ordered the expulsion of some 60,000 South Asians who had never been granted citizenship even though most had actually been born in Uganda. Aware of Amin's massacre the year before of soldiers loyal to his predecessor, Milton Obote, whom he had overthrown, Peggy proposed that they fly to Uganda to report on this latest attack on minorities. "He's not called the 'Butcher of Uganda' for nothing. The slaughter has been going on ever since he came to power. He's bent on eliminating anyone he thinks is disloyal, including journalists."

Once again, Alistair begged off going. "I'm making a trip to the Yukon. I want to go now while there's still twenty-four-hour daylight. It will make a nice contrast with Yellowknife."

This time Peggy didn't press him. "That's a pity. This is one of those times when pictures are likely to tell the story best."

Peggy did rue his absence, especially since the *Herald* balked at the cost of sending another photographer to replace him. "Fuck it! No photos exclusively our own of bodies floating ashore on the banks of the Nile," she reported to him on her return. "All I have are first-hand accounts of what it's been like. Really awful obviously. Thousands of fleeing refugees have never arrived in the countries accepting them." Peggy stretched her legs against the kitchen counter, glad to be on her feet after the long flight home.

Alistair handed her a beer from the refrigerator, and she guzzled it in less than a minute. "Your stories have been really shocking, even without our own pics."

"I'll do a wrap-up tomorrow." Peggy handed Alistair her empty bottle and asked for another. "So, what's there to eat around here? I'm fucking famished."

It wasn't until almost the end of dinner that Peggy said, "Oh, shit! I forgot to ask. How was the Yukon?"

"Way better than your trip, I have to say. I was amazed to learn that only about half the stampeders who started the journey actually made it all the way to Dawson City, and very few of them earned a fortune. The promising claims had already been staked. You remember that Pierre Berton was born in the Yukon, eh?"

"Yes, son of a stampeder, wasn't he?" Peggy yawned, worn out from the long trip home. She knew it was important that they share their journalistic experiences, so she tried hard to give her full attention to what Alistair was saying, but her mind kept wandering back to Uganda.

"I read his book on the gold rush before going. His explanation for the folly is that the stampeders tried to reach the Klondike River because it was their Everest."

"Pretty similar experiences, I guess."

"I think it was better going to the Klondike really. If you made it to Dawson at least there was lots of gambling, drinking and whoring. With only one per cent of the stampeders women, the saying went that, for them, the odds were good, but the goods were definitely odd! Oh, I got to Diamond Tooth Gertie's. I—"

"Really!" Peggy was all ears now. "And did you get into one of those 'dollar-a-dance girls' I've heard about?"

"No, I visited Pierre Berton's old home instead."

"Good for you."

"Oh, and I panned for gold on Hunker Creek, very near Gold Bottom where the first discovery was made. Geez, it's back-breaking work, but I actually recovered a few flakes of genuine placer gold in my last pan." Alistair chased off to their bedroom and returned with a little glass vial full of water that he held up near a ceiling light. "See?"

Peggy peered closely at the vial, but it took a while before she spotted four or five little, yellow flakes floating in the water. "Wow! A veritable fortune!"

Alistair sensed that he had gone on long enough describing his modest adventures. "Anyway, I've clipped my articles out of the *Herald* if you want to read any of them." He wasn't sure, however, that Peggy ever did.

In mid-September of that year, Alistair announced that he was flying to Newfoundland where an agreement had recently been signed between Ottawa and the province to establish Gros Morne National Park. "It's supposed to be stunningly beautiful with snow-capped mountain peaks and long, blue fjords like Norway. Interested in going?"

"What? And camp out?"

"Sure, but only for two or three days."

"No thank you."

"We need to do a feature on Joey Smallwood, too." Alistair tried to tempt her with a more serious subject. "It's nine months since he resigned as premier, but the *Herald* has never done a piece summing up his long career. I could meet you in St. John's after Gros Morne."

"You go to Newfoundland if you really think it's important. I'd rather hang around here and see if anything big pops up."

Alistair never did interview Smallwood and, flying home, he felt uncomfortable again about his absence of attention to important stories. *The state of the economy, the fishing industry, the changing nature of the outports, they all deserved coverage. What will Peggy think? What do I think? Am I becoming just another superficial hack?*

When he arrived home in early October, Peggy wasn't there, only a note on the kitchen counter. "Gone to Tel Aviv. War again! Will phone." It was signed "Love you, P," and below that, in lipstick, she had planted a bright, red kiss.

The next day, she phoned him at 6.00 a.m. "I didn't wake you, did I?"

"Oh, no, of course not. You know me. I'm always up at five, shaved, showered and ready for action."

"Sorry, it's hard to keep the time difference straight. Anyway, I've missed you so much I wanted to reach you as soon as I could. How was Newfoundland?"

"More importantly, how are you?"

"I'm fine but the war isn't. I'm not sure what you know since you've been away but on October sixth, in a surprise attack, the Egyptians crossed the Suez Canal ignoring the ceasefire line and rolled into the Sinai Peninsula. At the same time, the Syrians attacked the Golan Heights. This all started on Yom Kippur for God's sake. And it's Ramadan as well. So much for the Arabs showing respect for any religion."

"Not a concern for me."

"Now, don't you start to gloat about this setback. You can leave that to my mother."

"I'm not. Like Tate, I just want peace with both sides respecting the original borders and Israel abandoning occupied territories."

"Yeah, yeah. Capitulation you mean with Israel having to deal with undefendable borders."

Several days later, Peggy called again, this time at 8.00 a.m., and she was in a much more buoyant mood. "We've not only pushed the Syrians back to the old ceasefire line, we're advancing deeper into Syria, all the way to the outskirts of Damascus. On the other front we've driven forward as well. We're about to cross the canal into Egypt and maybe take the city of Suez."

"So, it's 'we' again, eh?"

"Yeah, we the good guys, the persecuted Jews who are loyal to the Western, democratic alliance."

"The persecuted Palestinians we can forget about."

"Fuck you, Ally. Go talk to my mother."

"I'd rather talk to you."

"Argue with me, you mean…So, one thing you'll be glad about, I've had a hell of a time getting near the front."

"So, no shrapnel bouncing off your helmet to enliven your stories?"

"No. If you read them, you'll notice that my accounts have been pretty tame."

The *Herald*'s editors were, nevertheless, pleased with her work, and regarded the restrictions she faced in getting to the front as a result of her not being a full-time international correspondent based in the region. That consideration, plus the enormous costs the paper was incurring sending her and often Alistair to hotspots around the world, led management to decide early in 1974 that it would be more productive and cost-effective to station Peggy permanently in the field. After much deliberation they chose Singapore as the location, calculating that Asia, even more than the Middle East, was likely to be the principal location for major, fast-breaking stories.

"You're going to accept their offer, aren't you"? Alistair asked over drinks at the end of the day the move was proposed.

"I don't know."

"But this is just what you've always wanted to be, a bona fide foreign correspondent. You can't turn down the chance."

"But that's what you want, too. You'll come with me, won't you?"

Alistair placed his scotch and soda on a coaster and retreated to the kitchen to check on a chicken he was roasting in the oven and to remove a pot of green beans from the stove. "What the *Herald* has in mind is a one-person show," he shouted to her. "I'd have to resign and rely on free-lance work. That would mean a substantial drop in our income."

"We could manage that."

Alistair returned to the living-room and his scotch, rolling the cubes in his glass as if they were dice. "The thing is it's not a good time for me to leave the *Herald*. My travel stories are starting to take off. They've increased the circulation of the Saturday paper, generated advertising revenue, and they have been syndicated to several other papers. If I can keep this streak going, I'll increase my value to the *Herald* and then I'll be able to write my own ticket."

"But is travel really the kind of journalism you want to build your career on?"

"Well, I enjoy doing it and the photography is a bonus that fits in well. I think I'm pretty good at it now, and I'm having an impact on readers as well, not in some big way, but at least in suggesting ideas for spending their leisure time."

Peggy stared at him in disbelief. Her green eyes appeared cloudy and without their usual spark—like melted candles sputtering at extinction. *Is this the same guy I met at the Star? Has he changed, or is this a side of him I simply ignored?*

Alistair caught her look of surprise and disappointment. "I know this sounds alien to you, and I understand your feelings...I...I certainly don't want to stand in the way of your accepting. I know it's what you want and it's perfect for you; it's just not for me... at least not right now.

If things go well, I can join you in Singapore and make a decent living freelancing. I just have to do my own thing, and not simply be the one who does the cooking and the dishes."

"I don't know, you're doing a pretty good job in the kitchen already." Peggy managed a small laugh, but inside she had the feeling that she was tugging on a rope and that the man at the other end might suddenly let go and knock her off her feet. Nevertheless, she had made her decision and she wasn't going to change it now. Only time, she figured, would tell if the rope was still strong enough to hold them together.

Chapter 23

Peggy flew to Singapore in May 1974 to open the office and find a place to live that was large and comfortable enough for Alistair as well if she could coax him to join her. A week later, she called him. "I've found a spot but it's only an apartment and it's eighteen stories up."

"Geez, that's a big change from our house."

"It's how everyone lives here. Nice view, though—over the sea."

"So why did the paper choose Singapore anyway? Wouldn't Hong Kong have been better?"

"Well, the war in Vietnam is still the biggest issue crying out for coverage and this puts me a little closer to Saigon. They also figured Singapore would be a cheaper place to locate the office. I'm not sure they were right about that, but it does also put me a little closer for covering South Asia and the Middle East."

"Either way, you're pretty much half-way around the world from me."

"So why don't you fly over and check the place out? The sea is only minutes from the apartment and there are lots of lovely islands offshore to explore. The food stalls in the old market are also fantastic. You might actually get to like it."

"I can't at the moment. I'm off to Pangnirtung on Baffin Island next week. I've arranged to do a hike from the end of the fjord there to the cairn that marks the Arctic Circle."

"How far?"

"It's an eight- to twelve-hour walk there and back but it can be rough going, especially in bad weather. There are several rivers to cross, and they can be deep and fast with run-off from the glaciers, so we'll camp out one night."

"We?"

"I'm going with a guide."

"Male, I hope. Isn't it dangerous, nevertheless? Lots of polar bears?"

"The guide will have a rifle."

"A cannon would be better. I hope he's a sharpshooter. All the same this doesn't sound like something you'll be comfortable doing."

"Well, I've been told what to do if a bear charges me: stand as tall as I can waving my arms and shouting."

"Oh, how clever! I'm sure that works every time."

"If it doesn't and the bear goes on attacking, I'm supposed to stick a finger in its nose."

"Ally! Come to Singapore. It's very safe here. I'd rather risk a random shot on assignment than wrestle with a polar bear."

Alistair's account of the hike was not his only absorbing story from Pangnirtung. The guide also took him by outboard from the fjord to Cumberland Sound to see the icebergs floating down from Greenland. Out beyond any sight of land, he cut the engine and they floated through a maze of pure white slabs of ice that looked like giant pieces of a jigsaw puzzle laid out for assembly. There was no sound except the gentle tinkle of the sea ice against the water. As they carefully sidled up to one iceberg with a flat area for landing, the water turned from sapphire to turquoise where the ice plunged deep beneath the surface. The guide threw his bow anchor onto the berg, chipped away loose snow and ice at its edge and invited Alistair to climb onto it.

This is surreal, he thought, as he walked up and down mounds of crusty snow and ice, snapping pictures. *There's nothing but ice and sea in every direction and it's awesomely silent. This is an experience that few people are lucky enough to have, yet it's quintessentially Canadian.*

It was that story more than any other that cemented Alistair's reputation as a travel writer and very quickly the number of papers buying his pieces doubled and then quadrupled. *I guess I can risk resigning to freelance in Singapore. I'll have a wider range of stories I can write about, and the paper might be able to syndicate them to still more outlets. Maybe I can mix travel and political reporting with Peggy.*

By the end of the summer, Alistair had tidied up his work at the office, organized their house and put it in the hands of a rental agency. He spent a couple of evenings with his parents knowing he wouldn't see them for some time and had dinner with Jonathan and Jennifer. "Singapore, eh? You guys sure get around! I haven't even been to Vancouver yet to see the Jamesons."

"How are they liking it, do you know?"

"Well, it's certainly been good for Colin at the firm."

"Is Ginny working?"

"I don't think so."

"I always thought she wanted to."

"I think it's reasonable to say they live a more conventional life than you and Peggy."

"But is she happy just being a stay-at-home mother?"

Jonathan shrugged. "There is always something else that women want. Usually, it's a more understanding and attentive husband."

"Who's the cynical one, you or me?"

"Touché. But remember, I have been married longer than you have."

In September, Alistair made a quick trip to Montreal to see Peggy's parents. After one of Mrs. Morganstein's roast chicken dinners, he sat in the living-room with his father-in-law while he smoked his pipe, and they drank cognac again. "I'm pleased you're going to Singapore, meyn zun. We both married strong women. It's important that we respect their wishes and follow them in whatever they choose to do."

"I think you're right about that Tate, as usual."

"But you two must be careful there. We live in a dangerous world."

From Montreal, Alistair flew to Singapore. It was the beginning of the monsoon season and the driving rain, accompanied by daily temperatures around thirty degrees, made for a torrid start to his time in the city state. "Holy cow, it's hot here. I feel like I'm in a sauna and someone has thrown a bucket of water on the coals. Then they left the place and locked the door."

Another day, he complained that Singapore was too claustrophobic and tight-assed for his tastes. He paced around their apartment like a caged tiger in the city's zoo. "You can't even drop a piece of paper on the street without getting a hefty fine. There are no stains on the sidewalks from people spitting out betel nuts. It's—"

"No spit on the sidewalks! Oh, that's a rich one."

Despite his grumbling, Peggy was delighted to have him back with her, and they made love every night the first week that they were back together again. Alistair's initial travel stories about Singapore and its environs did not, however, elicit much interest for syndication and he grew concerned that leaving the *Herald* to freelance had been a mistake. But that worry disappeared when he shifted his attention back to more serious issues in the spring of 1975. South Vietnam's long and hopeless battle against the determined Communist forces of the North was approaching its end as the People's Army of Vietnam, supported by Viet Cong guerillas, and no longer opposed by U.S. troops, was closing in on Saigon. "I guess we better get there right away."

"You're serious? You're willing to go with me?"

"I'm not sure I want a second tour of duty anymore than the GIs did, but I enlisted in order to be with you, so let's get going!"

Peggy hugged and kissed him. "That's my man talking!"

They arrived in the city in early April 1975 and went for a stroll along streets familiar to them from 1969. "Geez, you can hear bombs exploding in the outskirts and there's rocket fire lighting the sky. They'll be in the centre any day now."

"Yeah, and you know what I was just thinking. We never got to Hanoi to report on how our role in the International Control Commission helped the Americans. Fuck, I wish we'd been able to do that when we were in Huê."

"Actually, it would have been too early," Alistair answered. "A lot of the sordid details didn't come out until the publication of the Pentagon Papers in 1971—like the two Seaborn missions to Hanoi as a messenger boy warning the Communists of dire consequences if they didn't stop trying to overthrow the Saigon government."

"That smelled, considering we were supposed to be neutral. Of course, we never really were. We helped supply the American troops— ammunition, explosives, aircraft engines, napalm, and Agent Orange for defoliating jungles. Even the berets the U. S. Marines wore were manu- factured in Montreal, for fuck's sake."

Alistair nodded in agreement. "No, our hands are far from clean at the end of this thing."

On the morning of April 29, they awoke in their hotel room early, and turned the dial to U. S. Armed Forces Radio. "Hey, Bing Crosby is singing 'White Christmas!'" Peggy shouted.

"That's a stretch."

"No, no! The radio host just announced that it's one hundred and ten degrees and rising in Saigon. That's the signal that the American evacu- ation is beginning."

They dressed quickly, packed, and, hoping it wasn't too late to fly out to safety, had a driver take them to the airport. It was, however, already occupied by the North Vietnamese and closed to traffic. As they left, a bullet shattered their windshield and they ducked shielding their eyes. "That was a close one! Let's try the U. S. Embassy." All the way, the driver had to lean out the van window to see where they were on the road and the vehicle swerved several times into the oncoming lane.

"Holy shit! This is chaotic." When they reached the embassy, they encountered a screaming crowd, mostly Vietnamese, trying to scale the

14-foot-high outer wall to get to the evacuation helicopters inside the compound on the embassy roof. They were grabbing onto the clothing of people ahead of them to work their way up. Alistair managed to scramble to the top where he discovered that Marines were checking the papers of those who had made it that far. If their faces were white, the Marines were allowing them in without further questioning, but it appeared to Alistair that most of the people at the top of the wall didn't have identification and were being refused entry. *They're being forced down by the butt end of rifles. Peeled from the wall like annoying bugs. It's disgraceful.*

Alistair spotted Peggy at the bottom still struggling to climb the wall. "I'm coming down. We'll try again."

It was, however, hopeless. The crowd outside the embassy was even thicker now and people were fighting for positions to climb. "Let's try the harbour," Peggy suggested. But it was bedlam there as well with entire families struggling to get aboard fishing boats that were already so overcrowded that people were falling into the water. A kindly Vietnamese lifted Peggy over his shoulders as close as possible to the deck of a little boat while someone on board grabbed her arms and pulled her in. There was, however, no room for Alistair unless he shoved his way past Vietnamese who had been trying for much longer to get aboard and he couldn't bring himself to do that.

Minutes after Peggy was dropped onto the deck, the boat pulled out of the harbour. "Try another one!" she screamed at Alistair. Leaning precariously under the weight of its human catch, the little boat headed into the South China Sea. "I'll find you later," Peggy went on shouting long after Alistair could possibly hear her. "I love you, Ally. Don't give up."

Eventually, the little fishing boat reached the U. S. Seventh Fleet and along with several others deemed "acceptable," Peggy managed to transfer to an aircraft carrier. The scene there was frenzied as well, with dozens of South Vietnamese military helicopters hovering above the ship like a gaggle of over-sized geese, waiting to touch down. As soon as one on deck was unloaded, it was pushed into the ocean to make room for another. At the same time some pilots were ditching their helicopters in the sea.

Meanwhile, Alistair decided that his best chance of getting out was to return to the U. S. Embassy, so he had the driver take him there, paid him handsomely before he left and then managed to find a spot to climb the wall again. Because of the colour of his skin and his press identification papers, he was allowed in, and shortly afterwards, boarded a helicopter that headed to the Seventh Fleet and deposited him aboard a destroyer. Although he searched everywhere, there was no sign of his spouse.

A distraught Peggy did the same that evening aboard the aircraft carrier, but to no avail. Forcing herself, nevertheless, to remain calm and professional, the next day she found the aircraft's communications centre and got permission to file her story about their latest trauma and the end of the war. She finished her article by saying that "the long war, fought at tremendous human and material cost with cruelty and unimaginable deceit, has ended in a humiliating American defeat."

A day later, with the help of the communications centre, Peggy discovered that Alistair was safely out of Vietnam and aboard a U. S. destroyer, but it was not until their ships reached Manila that they were reunited. "Oh, God, that was terrible," Peggy cried, hugging and kissing Alistair. "I was afraid that you weren't going to make it out, that you might die in Saigon."

"Yeah, it was pretty bad. It felt like we were in Biafra again. So, I guess we're the first of what they are already calling the boat people, eh?"

"Sort of, I guess, but just think how much harder it is for the South Vietnamese to get out safely and to another country."

Alistair was chastened by their dangerous experience and briefly returned to travel writing. He made a trip to the island of Penang where the beach at Georgetown yielded some good pictures, especially one of robed and turbaned snake charmers playing mouth pipes for king cobras that were wriggling their bodies out of wicker baskets lying in the sand. Yet, to his surprise, he found he missed the excitement and the importance of covering major international stories and doing them side-by-side with Peggy.

For several months, Peggy followed the limited media reporting on the situation in Kampuchea where the Communist faction, led by Pol Pot, previously a bit player in the country's recent, turbulent affairs, had come to power in 1975. "There's something fishy going on. The new regime is getting very limited coverage, yet I've seen a few short pieces about Cambodians fleeing the country and surreptitiously crossing the border into Thailand. I'd better get over there and see what's going on."

"In that case, I'm going, too."

"Really? Good for you. Back in the fray."

They flew to Bangkok and travelled west to the heavily guarded border with Kampuchea, laced with minefields. Under cover of darkness, Cambodians were trickling across, and a few of them were ready to stop briefly to talk with Peggy and Alistair and a handful of other journalists. "He says there has been widespread torture by the Khmer Rouge," the interpreter they had hired told them. "Many people have been executed and their bodies dumped in mass graves. It's not just open opponents of Pol Pot but most of the country's middle and upper classes."

"This refugee says civil servants, businessmen, professionals and academics have all been targeted—anyone they think is an intellectual. They have also slaughtered ethnic minorities, Christians, and Buddhist monks."

Later, when they filed their stories and mailed their photos from Singapore, they were frustrated by how little attention they were given by the *Herald* and practically none by the syndicated papers Alistair had reached with the limited travel writing he had done. "No frontpage coverage at all," Peggy cried in despair. "Fuck! I just don't get it."

The following summer, the first outbreak of the Ebola virus any-where occurred in Africa. "Holy shit, am I seeing this right, or do I need glasses?" Alistair was absorbed in a report that appeared in the *Straits Times*. "I think it says that in one town the virus has virtually wiped out the population."

The outbreak lasted for only eleven weeks and the affected commu-nities were quickly quarantined, but by November 1976, Peggy decided that it was safe enough for them to go there and report on exactly what had happened. First, they visited the village of Yambukua, near the Ebola River in Zaire. "Yes, that's right. Eighty-eight per cent of the people who caught the virus here died," a local doctor told them. In Nazra in South Sudan, they learned that the fatality rate was fifty-three per cent.

Wearing masks, they interviewed several of those who had survived, including the families of some of the deceased. Alistair was concerned about the risk, but with Peggy courageously taking the lead, he soldiered on beside her. When they returned to Singapore, he complained of head-aches and muscle pain. "Oh, no! I've caught the virus! I'm going to die!"

Right away, they went to a specialist in tropical diseases but after two visits Alistair was declared fine. "It's probably a psychosomatic reaction," the doctor told him. "But you need to be more careful. You journalists are a rash bunch."

Chapter 24

In November 1978, Peggy's mother called them in the middle of the night in a hysterical state. "Tate died."

"Oh, Mame, no! Oh, shit, no. What happened?"

"He had a heart attack. Early this morning. An ambulance came. They rushed him to the hospital." She was trying to speak through sobs. "But he was dead… by the time they got there. I don't know what to do."

"Oh, Mame, I'm so sorry. This is awful." She turned to explain to Alistair what had happened, and then spoke to her mother again. "We'll fly over on the first plane we can."

"Oh, thank you, shaina maidel. I can't bear this without you."

"Are Gertrude and Ruth there?"

"Not yet. They will be soon. We shouldn't, but…we'll delay the funeral until you get here."

After the call, Alistair sat on the end of their bed holding his head in his hands and crying. "I guess that was the kind of call we knew would come one day. But it's Tate and that's a real blow."

When they arrived at the Morganstein home, Peggy's mother threw her arms around them, and they hugged while they all wept. "I am so glad you have come, too, Alistair. Tate would be honoured that you are here." She was gaining control of herself and patted him on the back as she guided him inside. "He was so fond of you. He saw you as his son. Come, give me your coats and bags. We'll go and sit in the parlour like you would do if he were here."

As soon as they entered the room, Alistair detected the old smell of rotting apples and pipe tobacco, forcing him to fight back another bout of tears. "You know that I really loved him, don't you, Mame? We talked together like two men who were close friends."

Mrs. Morganstein nodded appreciatively and rose from the couch where she had just sat down. "Here, let me get you a cognac. Strictly speaking we don't drink until after shiva, but—"

"Then I will respect that custom."

"Nonsense. We are not orthodox." Suddenly, she laughed looking more like her old self. "Remember that first time we met you and you told us you were an orthodox atheist? Tate loved that. He would want you to have a cognac now."

Alistair relented and when Mrs. Morganstein handed him the glass, she sat between him and Peggy without getting anything for herself or her daughter. "Well, then, here's to Tate." Alistair raised his glass. "Shalom!"

"Shalom, indeed." Mrs. Morganstein appraised them closely. "You both look well, perhaps a little older with those bits of grey but you"—she looked pointedly at Alistair—"you haven't put on any weight. That is good."

"It's probably because I haven't had any rugelach in a long time. You look well yourself, no older than when I last saw you and just as full of energy despite what you are suffering."

"Umzin!"

When Alistair looked puzzled, she switched to English. "That's nonsense. I am an old woman now… Oh, how I have missed you both and so did Tate. It has been so lonely without you here or nearby in Toronto."

"I'm sure it has been, Mame," Peggy said soothingly. "We wish we could have flown back to see you regularly. But it costs so much, and we have both been very busy."

"Well, I must say that you have been good about writing…well, at least Alistair has."

"We'll come as often as we possibly can."

"If you don't, you will find me in my grave."

Suddenly, Mrs. Morganstein jumped up again. "I'm sorry. You must be so tired and hungry after your long flight. I'm not supposed to cook until after shiva is over, but there is plenty in the kitchen for you. Margaret, you really shouldn't eat, but I suppose you will anyway."

"We only need a bissel, Mame." Alistair responded for them both. "Maybe some crackers and cheese, and then we'll go to bed. We're ready to plotz."

"Bissel and plotz. Good for you. You remember your Yiddish. Tate would be so pleased."

When they went to bed in Peggy's old room, she immediately pulled out a bag of Cheetos she had stuffed in her suitcase before they left Singapore and sat up in bed devouring them. "I was afraid it would be like this. That snack was bupkes."

The funeral service was held the next morning at the cemetery. It was brief with the reading of psalms and short eulogies by the three sons-in-law. Alistair focussed on the trials Mr. Morganstein had endured under the Nazis and the British when he was recruited to serve their war interests, and the challenge of shifting careers when he came to Canada. "He bore every burden in life with quiet grace and good humour and never sought vengeance, only peace and understanding."

At the end, all of the mourners came forward one by one to fill the grave with spades of earth, each of them placing the shovel back in the ground afterwards so as not to pass on their grief to the next mourner. That evening at the Morgansteins' home, they had the traditional post-burial meal of hard-boiled eggs and stewed lentils, prepared and served by friends and neighbours as the period of shiva formally began. "I wish I'd saved some of those Cheetos." Peggy lamented later when they went to bed. "I'm still starving."

Before a full week had passed, Peggy learned about the Jonestown mass murder and suicide on November 18 at the Peoples Temple in northern Guyana. "It's a remote cult settlement in northern Guyana," she explained to her mother, "led by the Reverend Jim Jones, a charismatic figure apparently but a real nut case. Over nine hundred people died there, most from drinking a concoction laced with cyanide."

Peggy immediately called the *Herald* and convinced the editors that she and Alistair should fly to Guyana right away for a post-facto on-the-spot report to be followed by interviews there and in the United States with the families of victims.

As they were preparing to leave, Alistair told his mother-in-law that he felt he had to accompany Peggy. "This is a story that needs in-depth coverage. These cults led by deranged people are becoming all too common. We need to understand what draws people to them and how best to combat their appeal." Later, at the door as they kissed goodbye, he repeated, "I'm sorry Mame, but Tate would expect me to go with her."

"Of course, you should already." She pressed a hand against his back. "Don't worry. I understand."

It was only two months later that Alistair had to fly to Canada again, this time following news of his own father's death—not from a heart attack as he had always expected but from a brain tumour. Peggy, however, did not go with him to Toronto. She was about to leave for Iran to cover the final collapse of the monarchy and its replacement by the Islamic republic led by the Ayatollah Khomeini. "Besides," she told Alistair, "I never knew your father as well as you knew mine."

There was no funeral this time; unlike his wife, Mr. Parker had become an agnostic and was not at all interested in organized religion. Instead, there was a gathering of family and friends at the family home for drinks, a buffet meal, and toasts of remembrance. Alistair made an impromptu one, recalling how reticent their father had been to punish his young sons whenever they got into trouble. "He was a kind, generous man who didn't push us in any particular career direction but supported us in whatever we chose to do."

Alistair stayed with his mother although one day he went down to

Cabbagetown to call on the people who were renting his and Peggy's home and to make sure that everything was in order. Several times, Jonathan came in the evenings to call on him and his mother and twice, after dinner, the brothers went for walks together. During the second one, suddenly remembering something he wanted to tell Alistair, Jonathan stopped. "Oh, given your experiences in Vietnam, this might interest you. The Jamesons have adopted a family of Vietnamese refugees."

"Really?"

"Yeah. Ginny mentioned it in their Christmas card. She's the one who writes them. Colin is way too busy for that sort of thing. I don't know if I ever told you, but he left our firm almost two years ago to establish his own group of partners. They have offices in several cities in the west. Apart from Christmas cards, I've pretty much lost touch with them since then, but they are still living in Vancouver. Anyway, helping the Vietnamese family to get settled in the city was Ginny's idea."

"Good for her. She hasn't lost her interest in the welfare of others."

"No, I guess not. Apparently, one of her kids was keen on the idea as well, and Colin agreed to it."

Well, that's probably the end of any news about Ginny, Alistair thought after the walk. *I just hope she is happy and has forgotten all about me.*

Alistair flew back to Singapore via Montreal so that he could see his mother-in-law briefly. A few months later, he was reading the *Straits Times* when suddenly he called to Peggy,. "Is it the small print or does this article actually say that in Kampuchea roughly two million people were slaughtered before the regime crumbled? That would be roughly a quarter of the total population at the time the genocide began. I just don't get it. Why so little media coverage, especially in North America?"

"War weariness after the fall of Vietnam maybe, but it makes me sick. I'd like to kick our own near-sighted editors in the balls."

"I think ideology may have been part of it." Alistair had been reflecting on his own question. "Those on the right, especially in the States, wanted everyone to forget about Cambodia. It was, after all, their government that was responsible for the Khmer Rouge coming to power. Parts of the Ho Chi Minh trail, used to infiltrate South Vietnam, ran through Cambodia. So, the Americans decided to kick the shit out of it; this article says it's the most heavily bombed country in history. That's what drove the Cambodians into the arms of Pol Pot."

"Yeah, but what about neutrals and those on the left?"

"That's harder to explain, but given American culpability, they were inclined to give the Khmer Rouge the benefit of the doubt and underestimated the extent of the torture and killing."

"Well, whatever, the lack of coverage was a fucking disgrace. This was a case of genocide, pure and simple."

On December 24, 1979, the Soviet Union launched an invasion of Afghanistan designed to end the factional rivalries in the Afghan Communist party which had taken control of the country in 1978. The goal of the Kremlin was to install quickly a new puppet government, pliant to the will of Moscow. "Geez," Alistair said to Peggy one day in late January from behind his newly prescribed glasses. "The Soviets are facing stiff resistance in the countryside from mujahideen freedom fighters. This could prove to be their Vietnam. We should go there, don't you think?"

"I'm certainly on if you are, my lion-hearted stud."

They flew to Kabul in February 1980 and made their way north to the mountains where they were greeted warmly by swarthy, moustached mujahideen, wearing pakols, soft, round woollen hats, and baggy pants and shirts. They had rifles slung over their shoulders and enormous grins on their faces. "Come, they will show you the cave where they have a shelter," their interpreter explained.

They scrambled for over an hour up a vaguely discernible path strewn with gravel and stones. Even though they wore sunglasses, they felt almost blinded by the glare of sunlight in the thin mountain air. The landscape surrounding them was so arid and barren that it seemed as if they had somehow alighted on another planet. The terrain appeared hostile as well since they could be sighted from miles away and there was no apparent place to rush for cover. Eventually, they reached a flat expanse of rock with a deep, dark cave behind it. "Protection at last!" Peggy cried panting hard as she collapsed on the ledge. "How long have these guys been living here?"

"Since the day of the invasion." The interpreter relayed the leader's response. "They have stored a lot of food and ammunition, but they have to go down to the valley now and then to get more water."

"No wonder they look so fit."

"And determined. Do they mind if I take some photographs?" Alistair asked. "I realize they may be sensitive about that."

There was an exchange between the interpreter and the mujahideen leader. "That is fine. They would like you to make news of their resistance to the Soviets known to people everywhere."

Another conversation ensued and then the interpreter reported, "They want to know if you would like to stay for the night. They have carpets and blankets, so you are welcome if you would like to. Otherwise, you need to leave now to get down to the valley before dark and find somewhere else safe to stay."

Peggy and Alistair looked at each other and nodded in agreement. "Thank you for the invitation. You are very kind. We would like to do that if it is not too much trouble."

After dark, they all gathered around a small fire outside the cave and had a dinner consisting of flatbreads, dipped in a bowl of yogurt mixed with spinach, handfuls of dried fruit and nuts, and tea, loaded with sugar. Afterwards, the mujahideen unrolled little handwoven mats and, kneeling in the direction of Mecca, said their evening prayers. Much as he wanted photographs of the scene, out of respect for their faith, Alistair refrained from taking any.

Early the next morning when Alistair and Peggy awoke, they could hear the coughing engine of a helicopter and the whir of its spinning blades. They threw off their blankets and rushed out of the cave. "No, no!" their interpreter shouted. "Get back in. It's a Soviet helicopter." The mujahideen gathered outside the cave were hurrying in and huddling deep inside. "I guess they haven't spotted us. The helicopter is moving away now."

The interpreter's relieved voice led Alistair to assume the threat was over. He grabbed his camera bag and stepped to the cave opening. "No, no! It isn't safe yet!"

Alistair, however, wasn't listening. He was taking pictures of the retreating helicopter as quickly as he could. Peggy moved outside to join him. But at that very moment, the helicopter wheeled and started towards the cave again. "Quick!" the interpreter shouted at them. "Inside! They've spotted you!"

It was , however, too late. There was a burst of gunfire from the helicopter, and then for Peggy and Alistair there was nothing. They were snuffed out like candles that left no trace of having ever flamed.

Chapter 25

"**W**HERE…WHERE AM I?" Alistair whispered. He had been in and out of consciousness for almost three days.

"You are in Peshawar."

"I'm where?"

"In Pakistan. You are in a hospital."

Heavily drugged, Alistair drifted off, but pain in one leg and his lower back awakened him again, and he repeated his question.

"Peshawar, near the Afghan border."

"Afghanistan! Peggy! Where is she?"

"We'll talk about that later," the nurse answered. "Right now, you need more sleep."

An hour later, he awakened once more, his leg throbbing and his throat burning in need of water, but with his memory more restored. "Afghanistan! We were there! In a cave in the mountains. Where is Peggy? Is she okay?"

The nurse bent over him and stroked his arm as she took his temperature. "The doctor will be in to see you later."

Alistair slept fitfully for another two hours, periodically moaning, "Peggy…Peggy. Where is she?"

Finally, the doctor arrived and standing beside him in a calm, professional manner, broke the news. "I am sorry to have to tell you that your wife is dead."

"Dead? Oh, Jesus no! No! That can't be true. We were safe inside a cave."

"That is not what I have been told. You were outside when a Soviet helicopter attacked the hiding. Your wife was struck by bullets several times. She would have died almost instantly."

"Oh, God almighty. No!"

"It is an unfortunate tragedy, and it's made worse for you by your present condition. You've had a concussion, and you have broken your collar bone. You also have shrapnel in both legs, and you've fractured three vertebrae in your back, but you were extraordinarily lucky. You should make a full recovery."

"I don't want to live. No! Not without Peggy." He felt a numbness in his hands and feet that he hadn't noticed before, as well as a headache pounding remorselessly in his skull. "She can't be dead. She's only forty-one. I can't go on without her."

"It won't be easy, but I am sure that in time you will be able to adjust. You must be a strong person to have been ready to be in that cave." Alistair didn't answer, but the doctor could see that he was weeping. "Well, I'll leave you now. We can talk again tomorrow. At some point, we will be flying you out to Lahore and then to Singapore."

A week later, he was taken on a stretcher to the Peshawar airport for the flights home and then he spent another six weeks in hospital in Singapore recovering. Towards the end of that time, his mother and Jonathan flew out to visit him. "It's all my fault," he repeated to them several times, crying whenever he mentioned that morning at the cave.

"Of course, it isn't, darling," his mother tried to console him. "Peggy wanted to cover the invasion just as much as you did. You both knew how dangerous the assignment was."

The day they moved him back into the apartment he had shared with Peggy, Alistair sat glumly in a wheelchair while his mother pleaded, "Why don't you come home, darling?" I'm sure you can go back to working for the *Herald* in Toronto."

"Maybe, Mom. But I'm not ready to do that yet. There are too many memories here."

"I thought you didn't really like Singapore," Jonathan interceded.

"It's not that. It's what I just said to Mom. It's too soon to contemplate a move. Besides, Singapore is not all that bad."

"You'd have a lot more space in Cabbagetown."

"But here, I know I have work. I should be able to get by freelancing…well, almost anyway."

As soon as he felt well enough to travel, Alistair flew to Montreal with Peggy's ashes. "Oh, Alistair, this is so terrible." At the front door, Mrs. Morganstein flung her arms around him the way she had the last time. "First, Tate, now my little girl. How can I go on without them?"

"You will Mame. You're a strong woman just like Peggy was. It will be hard for a while, but I know you will adjust and keep going."

"And no funeral even. Jews always have a funeral. Tate would not have approved." She looked at the box Alistair had placed on a table near the door. "And Margaret reduced to ashes! This is not right at all. Jews are never cremated."

"Peggy was a secular Jew only, Mame, you know that. Besides, under the circumstances, the only sensible thing to do was to have her cremated in Peshawar."

"Tate would have found that hard to accept. Poor man. I don't think he would ever have survived this tragedy."

Alistair slept in Peggy's room throughout his visit, but they were restless nights, for he kept mulling over the way that Peggy had died. *It was so stupid of me. I should never have left the cave. I should have realized that Peggy was bound to follow me.*

When Alistair left, his mother-in-law cried again, "Oh, Alistair why did this have to happen? I just don't understand why the two of you have always taken such risks. You must be more careful now. I love you like a son."

"I know, Mame, and I love you—just as I loved Peggy." He choked up as he spoke and had to stop to get control of himself. "I will go on loving you always, and I will visit you whenever I have the chance."

Several weeks later, Alistair felt well enough to return to work. *I think I'll try travel writing for now. I'm not ready yet for more risky assignments and travel will provide me with more steady income.*

He went first to Indonesia for stories and pictures from Java and Bali, then to North Africa and after that the Middle East. Jordan yielded one of the highlights of all his trips: Petra where he rode horseback through the narrow crevice in the red sandstone mountains on the Incense Road, used by the camel caravans of old. His destination was the famous Monastery, carved by the Naebateans two thousand years earlier into the ribbon candy-coloured rocks. Sitting at the edge of a cliff high above it, he was approached by Bedouins who invited him to spend the night in their encampment. He was touched, but thinking of the cave in Afghanistan, he politely declined. *This is incredible. I'm being paid for visiting places others spend their hard-earned savings to reach for just one big trip. If only Peggy were here, and willing to do this kind of work with me.*

His last expedition from Singapore was to Thailand which proved to be rich in stories his readers enjoyed because they were accompanied by vivid photographs, some of which appeared in colour in a handful of papers. One of his favourite shots was on Thailand's central plain where he found a bare-chested boy on a water buffalo in the middle of a flooded paddy, his gleaming black strands of hair like short lengths of fishing line. Another he took in a Meo tribal village near Chiang Mai: a line of barefoot boys in shorts smiling at his camera anticipating a handful of coins in payment for the only posed picture he ever dispatched. *Hmm, am I getting soft? Do I like these pics because the kids look similar to the way ours might have been if Peggy and I had chosen to have children?*

Back in Bangkok at the end of his trip, he visited the famous Oriental Hotel, including the author's lounge where he had a drink while he took photographs. Suddenly to his surprise, he had an image of Ginny Jameson, sitting in one of the fan-back wicker chairs. *If she were here, she would enjoy gazing at all the traffic on the Chao Phraya River and imagining that she is having daiquiris with Conrad or Somerset Maugham. It's sad to be doing all this travelling alone. Geez, I miss Peggy…Both of them, I guess.*

The stories Alistair's readers apparently enjoyed most, however, were his lurid accounts of the seamy side of Bangkok: the massage parlours and the dinner clubs where girls sat in rows in rectangular cubicles behind glass partitions waiting to be selected by the male patrons to ply them with food and drink and provide them with whatever else they might desire as a digestive. They were also titillated by his descriptions of the drive-in brothels on the notorious Sukhumvit Road with bedrooms above their discreetly curtained garages.

Peggy, he knew, would not have been at all entertained by these latter reports. *Where is my coverage of the victims of this horrendous exploitation? she would want to know. The young girls rounded up in villages of the north at thirteen and fourteen and sold by their parents to serve as virtual sexual slaves in these sordid places?* "It's not the function of journalists simply to give readers what they want," *she would have lectured me.* "It's to open their eyes to the truth."

That reflection led him to write yet another article discussing the issue of human rights violations in these establishments. *It's not what papers are looking for from me, but this piece will help at least to relieve my conscience.*"

Shortly after returning from Thailand, Alistair was surprised to receive a phone call from the *Sunday World* in London, England. The editors had been impressed by what they had read of his syndicated travel articles and were offering him a position as a fulltime travel writer. What's more, they wanted to base him in Paris to write stories principally about Western Europe, the focal point of the ever-expanding international travel industry. Alistair thanked them for the offer, said he would seriously consider it and call them with an answer as soon as possible.

Paris! That's not easy to turn down, he thought after hanging up. *It would be so much easier to send colour photographs from there. Here, if I don't dispatch them by air, but get them to a wire service, it takes hours to prepare them for transmission and then to have them sent. Besides, weeklies don't have tight deadlines especially for travel and they use more colour."*

The next evening, as he paced around the apartment considering the offer, the space he and Peggy had happily occupied together suddenly felt small and antiseptic again as it had when he first arrived. Even the objects he had purchased to personalize it no longer appealed to him either—the ebony elephants with ivory tusks from a market in Singapore, the brass temple bells and joss sticks he had picked up in Thailand, the contemporary-style batik painting of Balinese women from Jogjakarta, and the glass paperweight he had filled with brightly-coloured sand from Petra. Now as well, the little rattan rickshaw that he and Peggy had bought in Singapore, and which sat on the living-room coffee table looked as if it had just pulled up to carry him away.

The next day, he called the *Sunday World* and accepted the position in Paris.

Chapter 26

ALISTAIR FLEW FROM Singapore to London to visit the offices of the *Sunday World* and discuss his assignment with the editors. It was agreed that he would write a weekly column under the heading "Off the Beaten Track." He would have carte blanche to cover whatever subjects and specific places he chose as long as the emphasis was on locations that appealed to English readers and travellers, interested in making new discoveries. He was also to undertake whatever other assignments the paper requested, although most of his work was to be related to travel.

Three days later, he flew to Paris and quickly found a fourth-floor apartment in an old building in the Marais district on a side street just off Rue Bretagne, an area he was convinced Peggy would have liked. The Marais, once swampland that was a breeding ground for diseases, had become the city's Jewish quarter and was now a lively centre of narrow streets, museums, shops, and restaurants, including several good and inexpensive Middle Eastern ones.

Shortly after he moved into his apartment, he walked to one of them for dinner, installing himself at a small outdoor table with red and white checkered linen. From there, he watched the steady flow of young people walking along Rue des Rossiers, many of them munching on lamb kebabs, pita falafel and shawarmas that they had purchased at take-out windows along the street. He chose a selection of fried eggplant and tomato, chopped liver, falafel, hummus and pita bread as well as a carafe of red wine, the perfect accompaniment, he found, for the moderately spicy dishes. He knew right away that Peggy would have been ecstatic about the place. Sitting all alone and eating and drinking slowly to extend the meal beyond the brief time he was becoming accustomed to, he kept thinking of her. *Maybe I should have stayed in Singapore and carried on doing political reporting—stayed faithful to the values that led us both into journalism in the first place.*

From his corner table, he stared at the young couples parading along Rue des Rossiers arm-in-arm and at others who had stopped to hug and kiss, oblivious of everyone around them. *I'm forty now and I've lost the second woman I've loved. Where am I going? Nowhere in particular, it seems.*

He paid his bill and walked slowly back to his apartment in the cooler, less humid evening air. He took the old cage elevator up to his apartment, opened the shutters and looked down his street to the corner where a waiter in a café on Rue Bretagne was wiping down tables and sweeping the floor now that all the patrons had left. *This move makes no sense. I should have stayed in Singapore and carried on boldly at Peggy's level of commitment. Now, I'm in Paris and living a life that Ginny would have been delighted to have shared with me. What a screw-up!*

Alistair closed the shutters and went to the bathroom to brush his teeth. Afterwards, he studied himself in the mirror, examining the strands of grey that every year accumulated in larger numbers. *I feel so alone…But I guess that is the way it will be from now on.*

Little did he realize what lay ahead.

● ● ●

Much as Alistair liked Paris, the doldrums didn't leave him until the *Sunday World* passed on to him the first of the letters the paper received commending his earliest stories, all centred on Paris. Several of them were about his favourite out-of-the way art galleries and museums, including the Musée Jacquemart-André in the eighth district which contained a large wall fresco and a ceiling painting, both by the famed Giambattista Tiepolo, carefully removed from their locations in Venice and reinstalled at tremendous cost in Paris; the Musée Cernuschi, an excellent Asian art museum at the edge of Parc Monceaux; and the Musée Marmottan near the Bois de Boulogne, likely to be busier but, he told his readers, an absolute must with its huge water lily canvases by Claude Monet.

For a break from art and culture, Alistair suggested other diversions like walking through the famed cemetery, Père-Lachaise, that he had failed to persuade Ginny to visit in 1961; strolling along the tree-shaded St. Martin Canal and exploring Paris's famous glassed-in shopping arcades and bakeries where the heady aroma of croissants, baguettes and strawberry tarts fresh from the ovens floated irresistibly through their open doors.

From Paris, he moved on to articles about relatively near-by locations tourists often overlooked liked the historic Atlantic port of Honfleur from which Champlain had sailed to Canada, and the town of Cognac. He wrote a piece about the latter that he was confident would interest his readers, for it was there, in the chateau of the Baron Otard family, makers of fine cognac, that English prisoners captured during the Seven Years War had been held. Now, as visitors reflected on the conditions their predecessors had endured, they could taste and purchase the fine Otard cognacs of the chateau. Sipping a sample, Alistair mused, *Tate would certainly have enjoyed this place!*

Other columns took his readers to locales that were only moderately populated by tourists at that time: Saint-Rémy-de-Provence and the near-by asylum where Vincent Van Gough was hospitalized; Albi, birthplace of Toulouse-Lautrec; and the picturesque Mediterranean fishing village of Collioure. His final destination was Menton, "the pearl of France," situated on the Riviera at the Italian border. There, he went for a walk in the hills above the town. He was enjoying the glimpses to the Alpes-Maritimes to the north when suddenly he was hailed by two young, swarthy men simply dressed in short-sleeve white shirts, dark pants, and cheap running shoes. Over their shoulders, they had slung bundles that Alistair assumed contained the bulk of their worldly possessions. "Excuse me, how far to Nice?"

"I don't know exactly but it's over thirty kilometres. Why? You're not walking there, are you?"

"Yes."

"It won't be easy on foot. Where are you from?"

"Algeria."

They were refugees who had crossed in small boats from North Africa to Genoa and now they had slipped into France illegally, evading arrest by travelling on isolated mountain roads. Encountering the men troubled Alistair's conscience anew about the stories he had been filing. *This is the kind of situation Peggy would want me to write about, the perils of refugees fleeing from poverty and repression.* He knew he had to add it to the columns he would put together.

Back in Paris in early November of 1982, Alistair felt overdue for his first vacation. He decided to return to the French Riviera and spend two weeks in Nice which he had not covered in his previous visit to that area, but which he knew was worth several pieces that he could easily research while holidaying and, with luck, experiencing balmy weather at the same time.

On his third day there, he stopped for lunch on Nice's Cours Saleya, a picturesque street a short block from the seafront that even in winter in the late afternoon was bathed in sunlight that burnished the surrounding buildings in a golden wash. He had chosen Le Safari, a bistro that, like many others, had outside tables facing the morning market running along a wide boulevard. It was his second time there and he had discovered on the first visit that it was wise to choose a little table close to the entrance where the daily specials were chalked on a board since he could benefit from the extra warmth reflecting off Le Safari's exterior wall.

Half-way through a small carafe of Provençal rosé wine and an omelet embellished with chard, chopped parsley, and pine nuts, he noticed a blonde woman in white slacks, a blue and white-striped jersey, and a matching blue silk blouse glancing at him. Every time he looked her way, she shifted her head in another direction. She was wearing sunglasses, so he couldn't see her face until she tilted the frames up to her head to study the bill the waiter had handed her. It was only then that he realized that she was not only a blonde but a beautiful one with azure eyes that matched the colour of the sea a few metres from shore. Her skin was smooth and lightly tanned, and her hair reached several inches down her back. Periodically, she swept it from her face in what he found to be a sexy if practiced motion. She was, he guessed, like himself, in her early forties.

Alistair had been writing notes for his next article while he ate, but after he saw the woman more clearly, he found it difficult to concentrate and to keep from glancing at her attractive face even in profile. Eventually, she stood up—to go to the W. C., he presumed—and only then did he realize how tall and slim she was as well—close to five feet, nine inches, about his own height, and her stomach was almost flat, her hips and legs nicely proportioned. As she returned to the patio, her sunglasses in her hair, she looked at him and smiled. "D'où venez-vous?"

"Paris…uh, Toronto, Canada vraiement."

"Ah, English Canadian. That explains your accent. I heard you talking to the waiter, and you were easy to understand, not like your compatriots from Québec."

"You like to eavesdrop?"

She smiled, unembarrassed.

"I do, too. If I have my notebook out, people think I'm working when actually I'm trying to follow their conversation….Would you like to join me? Perhaps I can get you another coffee?"

"Thank you. That would be nice."

"Would you like a tarte with it, or maybe to split?"

"I'll take a bite or two of yours, thank you."

Alistair summoned the waiter and gave him their order as she sat down. "My name is Alistair Parker."

"Enchanté. Mine is Marianne Ste-Pierre."

"I must say you speak perfect English. That's nice for me with my fractured French."

"Pas de tout, you are easy to understand."

"Only because in high school, our French teachers spoke with Parisian accents. It was crazy really because I can't understand the Québecois and that's not good nowadays with the separatist movement so strong."

"Pfft, who cares? There are always agitators in every country. And I prefer your accent."

"So, how did you learn to speak English so well?"

"I work for the Lafayette department store chain, so I deal a lot with English-speaking people, mostly Americans. I am a buyer and I go to a lot of countries where English is the lingua franca."

"Have you always worked there?"

"No, before that I was a model."

"Ah, that explains your statuesque beauty."

Marianne didn't blush. It was obviously a compliment that she had heard often before. "I don't, however, have the figure for it anymore. I am not a Twiggy. I like too much to eat and drink. This tarte is delicious by the way. You were quick to find the best place for lunch on the Cours Saleya."

"That's because I asked around. It's my job to search out the best places."

"For whom are you a spy?"

"I'm a detective, I guess—for the *Sunday World* in London."

"I don't know it. I only read *Le Monde* and the fashion magazines. But you live in Paris, you said?"

"Yes, the paper wanted me there—to entice readers to visit the city and other great places in Western Europe, yet also find new experiences."

"So they can keep selling their product without boring their customers just like we do with fashion. I know all about that kind of motivation."

Marianne had taken only one bite of her half of the tarte and Alistair eyed the remainder longingly, but he resisted finishing it, knowing that over the last few years, unlike Marianne, he had begun to put on weight. "So, what brings you to Nice, then, and uncomfortable, rocky beaches? Why aren't you in St. Tropez lying on the sand, looking like Brigitte Bardot?" Alistair surprised himself by his brazen deployment of flattery; he couldn't remember ever doing that before.

Again, however, she didn't appear to notice. "It's not all about the sand." Marianne played with the glistening hair that floated sexily down her back. "There is more culture here, and better restaurants as well. Besides, my parents live in Menton most of the year and Nice is much closer to it."

"I know Menton a bit. I wrote a piece about the town. It's quite pretty and I liked the old squares back from the sea and near St. Michel Cathedral." Alistair didn't seek her opinion about the Algerian refugees he had encountered in the hills above it as his article about their plight had already been published.

"Ah, maybe when you were there, you passed my parents, parading along the waterfront with the other old Parisians, looking as sour as Menton's lemons."

"I might have," Alistair laughed. "There were certainly a lot of couples wrapped in coats who didn't seem to be particularly enjoying the warm sunshine."

When all the lunch crowd had left and Le Safari was almost empty, Alistair at last called for the bill. "Where are you staying?"

"At the Negresco. Lafayette gives me a generous per diem when I'm travelling."

"The Negresco, eh? Wow! If you're going there now, I'll walk with you." Alistair suddenly reined in his uncharacteristically forward behaviour. "I mean if that's okay."

"Bien sur," she laughed. "You are *so* polite! Where are you staying?"

"Oh, at a cheap little hotel by the railway station. I wanted to be near it as most days I plan to take the train to explore other places along the Riviera that I can write about."

"Then the Negresco is almost totally in the wrong direction for you."

Alistair shrugged. "Who cares? I often go the wrong way, and it's a lovely afternoon. I need the exercise."

They walked along the Cours Saleya first, stopping at some of the stalls where Alistair purchased Christmas presents to send to his mother and Jonathan's family: olive oil, Provençal spices, and lavender. Marianne slid her arm through Alistair's as they strolled. It felt good to him, but in France it was, he knew, a common practice that didn't really mean anything. When they reached the end of the pedestrian section of the Cours, they turned left to the sea, crossed the busy waterfront road, and started along the Promenade des Anglais. All of the restaurants directly on the beach had already closed for the season, their big straw mats rolled up and stored with the lounge chairs. The usual patrons were either sitting in the hardback metal chairs that lined the promenade facing the sea and the sun, or else they had retreated to the bars, restaurants and posh nineteenth century hotels on the other side of the broad avenue.

As soon as they reached the promenade, Marianne let go of Alistair's arm and set out at a brisk pace. *Just like I thought, holding on was nothing…No! Wait a minute! She knows I'm Canadian and might have considered that it did but that didn't stop her. Maybe now she simply wants to walk freely and quickly for a while? Bugger, here I go again, analyzing everything. I thought I was over that. Just fucking relax and enjoy the moment.* "So, where do you live in Paris?" he asked.

"I used to have an apartment in the sixteenth, but I let it go, so now, with my parents in Menton most of the year, I'm living in their flat on Ile St.-Louis."

"Oh, so you're not far from where I am. I'm just off Rue Bretagne in the Marais."

"Ah, maybe it is destiny that we have met!"

A twinge of excitement coursed through Alistair, but he didn't respond directly. "I like to walk down to the Seine and circle the islands. They are so beautiful and quaint. Do you go to Notre Dame for the Sunday service?"

"No, only when there is a concert. Even then, I prefer to go to Sainte-Chapelle."

"But you are a Catholic?"

"Badly lapsed. You?"

"A badly lapsed Anglican. You probably know it as the Church of England."

"Pfft! Badly lapsed anywhere. It doesn't matter."

Alistair found that it wasn't easy to keep up with Marianne. With her long, slim legs, she moved quickly yet lithely like a gazelle. Although he enjoyed walking quickly, he wasn't used to it. Wherever he had gone with Peggy, in the accustomed fashion of reporters, she had ordered taxis. "You've got to be fit to walk this fast all the way to the Negresco. What do you do to stay in such good shape?"

"In Paris, I go walking almost every day and sometimes jogging. I do stretches, too, every evening. And I play tennis in the Luxembourg Gardens, or when I am in Nice at the clay court club here. Do you play?"

"I did as a kid, but I haven't for a long time. I was always just a hacker."

"Well, you should start up again. We could play together."

The suggestion intrigued Alistair, even excited him, but his old caution kicked in. *I've only just met her. She could be a serial killer even for all I know! Maybe she's married or recently divorced and has affairs all the time. She's certainly too beautiful to be left on the shelf for long.* So, he chose to answer obliquely, "I've noticed the courts whenever I've walked through the gardens. It's such a beautiful place. I was there for the first time in 1961."

"Ah! So, you discovered Paris years ago. There is much about each other's past to learn."

When they reached the Negresco, Marianne said, "Why don't we meet tomorrow at Le Safari around eleven for coffee and croissant? If you are interested in visiting places near the coast for stories, I'll take you afterwards to St. Paul de Vence."

"Will you really? I'd love to do that, thank you."

They kissed three times on the cheek, simply a French custom, yet it made Alistair feel almost elated, an emotion he hadn't experienced since Peggy's death.

● ● ●

THE NEXT MORNING, as they seated themselves at Le Safari at the table Alistair had occupied the day before, the same waiter greeted them, "Ah! Vous êtes marié maintenant. Félicitation!"

They both laughed and then Alistair ordered them coffees and croissants. "Mm, this croissant is perfection, and the coffee is great." Since arriving in Paris, Alistair had largely given up tea because he found café au lait the perfect compliment for a croissant aux amandes. Now, however, he felt a little guilty about his choices because Marianne was having a plain croissant without butter and black coffee.

"Have you always been a travel writer?" she asked him.

"No. My wife—Peggy—and I both started as general reporters with the Toronto *Star*. When we switched to the *Herald* in Toronto, they sent us to cover hot spots everywhere. Peggy loved that kind of reporting. Major world problems really ate away at her. They concern me too, but she was braver than I am about covering stories in dangerous places. I have trouble risking my life for causes I don't believe I can really affect."

"So, you are divorced?"

"No, I am a widower. She was killed on an assignment."

Alistair explained what had happened in Afghanistan. "Oh, that is so awful, chéri." She squeezed his hand as he finished his account. "You must feel…feel completely be…bereft. That is the right word, no?" Alistair nodded. "But you are very brave as well to have been with her in that cave."

"Anyway, after Peggy was killed, I switched my focus to travel, which I had done earlier in Canada. I had enjoyed it and discovered a lot of places where Canadians rarely go. I was doing travel writing from Singapore when I got this offer to do the same in Paris."

"Ah, bien. So here you are! I would love to visit Canada one day. On a map it looks so vast."

"It is. Quebec alone is three times the size of France."

"Mais, non!" Her sparrow wing eyebrows, carefully pencilled, arched upwards. "C'est impossible."

"Si. C'est vrai."

"C'est incroyable."

"So, what about you? Are you married?"

"Non."

"Separated or divorced?"

"Non. Married life is not for me. But, of course, I have had lovers, several of them. I like men, but I would not want to be married to one. They are too spoiled and possessive."

"Did you like being a model?"

"Of course. I loved the attention. It is silly, I know, but I still do. I like to have men look at me and make a fuss to keep me happy. As a model, you are treated almost as if you are a movie star. I enjoyed that. I would have liked to get into acting, but I wasn't talented enough, so sometimes now I just pretend to be famous. That is egotistical, I suppose, but it is fun."

"You certainly have the bearing of a real star. I enjoy being with you. It makes me feel important, too."

"Thank you, darling." Marianne mimicked the voice of an actress as she shone her round, blue eyes at Alistair.

"So, why did you stop modelling if you enjoyed the attention?"

"I always knew it was false. And it's hard to go on doing it for very long. You have to maintain just the right figure. Besides, most of the time it was very boring and the other girls you had to spend so much time with could be pretty stupid and narrow in their interests. All they ever talked about was clothes, makeup, and hair. There is so much more to life that interests me. So, eventually I wanted a more normal existence. I wanted to eat and drink, and to party. I guess I am a hedonist. Maybe you are, too, and that's what brought you to Paris." Marianne glanced at her elegant wristwatch. "Speaking of pleasure—and work for you, I suppose you can call it—we should be on our way and not waste the day."

Later, in St. Paul de Vence, after they seated themselves for lunch at the Colombe d'Or, she told Alistair, "Yves Montand and Simone Signoret used to come here often. And Jean-Paul Sartre and Pablo Picasso were guests at the hotel once." Alistair got out his notebook to record the information, but then put it away to study the menu. "This is one of the oldest medieval towns on the Riviera."

"It's beautiful—like so much here. Easy to look at… and to remember."

Marianne ordered rainbow trout, served with potatoes that had been mashed with pine nuts and basil pistou, and Alistair a cassoulet that included duck confit and truffles from the region. "You realize, I hope," Marianne lectured him as he tucked into his meal, "that what you are having is full of fat."

"Yes, but I love a good cassoulet in the autumn and winter."

"Pfft! All you Americans eat too much fat."

"You mean North Americans."

She simply shrugged her shoulders and picked at the mashed potatoes she had barely touched until she changed the topic. "After lunch, I want to take you to the Fondation Maeght. It's not far away and it has an excellent collection of modern art."

At the gallery, Alistair was delighted to find hanging a painting by Jean-Paul Riopelle. "It's rare to see works by Canadians displayed any-where in Europe," he explained to her. "But, of course, Riopelle has lived in France a lot of his life."

"Do you like modern art?"

"Yes, but I'm a romantic at heart, so I guess I like the Impressionists best. How about you?"

"The same."

"So, what do you think of Riopelle?"

She winced. "There is so much colour splashed everywhere that if I had one of his paintings hanging in my apartment, I would have head-aches all the time…Mais, il peint bien, je crois."

Alistair wasn't convinced she meant it. *A diamond perhaps but cut in the rough wilds of an unimportant, far-off country.*

It was late by the time they returned to Nice, so they simply had a light meal of mussels dipped in a creamy brine at an outdoor table in Place Garibaldi and then parted for their respective hotels.

The next day, they toured the hill town of Grasse, famous for its perfume industry and, afterwards, Antibes on the coast where Picasso lived for many years. Touring the castle museum that honoured his work, Alistair stared for a long time at the artist's famous 1955 sketch of Don Quixote before he said to Marianne, "I like this one, but some of his later sketches seem almost fraudulent. Just a few simple lines scribbled quick-ly to make money." *Am I like that now, a fraud, rejecting serious journalism for the easy life of a travel writer?*

"I love doing things with you." Marianne grasped his arm as they left the museum. "You are not like other men who are interested only in sex."

Alistair's mood brightened right away. "I feel the same way about you. It is so much nicer travelling with you than doing all of my research on my own."

When they reached Nice, Marianne said, "I need a bath and I want to wash my hair, but why don't you come over to the Negresco later for dinner? I'd suggest going out somewhere less formal, but you really do need to see the hotel—all of it—if you're going to write an article about it."

"I'd love to have dinner with you, but only if you'll let me treat you."

"Non, non!" Her response was quick and definite, making it clear to Alistair that she was used to having things her way. "You paid at the Colombe d'Or and at Place Garibaldi last night. That is more than enough. Remember, I have an expense account. I don't usually stay at hotels as luxurious as the Negresco, only in Nice. It is a reward for visiting my parents."

Chapter 27

ALISTAIR ARRIVED AT the Negresco at eight o'clock sharp and had a clerk at the desk call Marianne's room before he sat down in an upholstered, antique chair in the Royal Lounge to wait for her. Eventually, she appeared in shimmering silver pants and a pink silk blouse that was unbuttoned at the top, revealing just a hint of cleavage. Her hair was curled at the ends and her locks were now brushed over the front of her shoulders. Her lips were painted in frosty pink and her nails polished in an identical hue, applied (Alistair assumed), by the hotel's resident manicurist. As he stood up, Marianne kissed him lightly. "Wow! You look lovely. Different than this afternoon, but just as stunning…more really."

"I try to change my appearance. It keeps men looking."

"Well, this one certainly is." Alistair handed her a dozen white roses that he had selected at a flower stand on his way to the hotel.

"Why, thank you, that was sweet of you." She seemed pleased, but it was apparent that his was a familiar gesture.

"I must say this is quite the room."

"Isn't it lovely? The Baccarat chandelier apparently has over sixteen thousand crystals. It was made for Czar Nicholas but, unfortunately, the revolution interrupted delivery, so the hotel purchased it." Marianne's comment prompted Alistair to get out his notebook. "Shall we go to the bar for a drink before dinner?" No answer was sought; she simply started in that direction. As they entered and Alistair was admiring the old walnut woodwork, she handed the flowers to a waiter and asked that he have them sent to her room. "The tapestry is seventeenth century." Alistair made a note of that as they seated themselves in comfortable chairs at a table for two by a window. Promptly, a smartly dressed waiter approached to take their orders. "What would you like?"

"I'll have a scotch and soda, please." Alistair closed his notebook. "Perhaps Johnnie Walker Red, but anything will do."

"How plebeian! I'll have a Campari and soda."

"So, is all the hotel this grand?"

"Oh, yes. Wait until you see the dining-room. It's really too much. Actually, I prefer to eat in La Rotonde which is much less grand, but you must experience Le Chantecler once at least. And wait until you see my bedroom. Did you notice the doorman when you came in? They are dressed like the staff of an eighteenth-century bourgeois family with postilion hats topped by red plumes."

"I was stupid. I should have brought my camera."

"Well, you'll be back, won't you?"

"Only if you invite me."

She smiled at him playfully. "That all depends…"

Alistair felt another stir of excitement. "So, when was the hotel built?"

"In 1912 by Henri Negresco, a Romanian who at the time was director of the municipal casino. It opened in 1913 and has had its ups and downs over the years, but it has always attracted distinguished guests, Salvador Dali, Grace Kelly, Liz Taylor, even the Beatles. You saw the pink dome at the entrance end when you arrived, I assume. It is one of Nice's best-known landmarks."

"You're making my research very easy."

"We should take the rest of our drinks to Le Chantecler. We're past our reservation time, not that they will mind." They stood up and a waiter rushed to their chairs. She instructed him to take their glasses to the dining-room and, placing them on a sterling silver tray, he led them in a small procession. A smiling Marianne swept through the restaurant doors like a movie star as curious eyes turned to view her, the clothes she was wearing, her hairdo and makeup and the person with whom she was dining that evening.

Le Chantecler, as Marianne had told him, was rather over the top. It was lavishly decorated with rococo furniture covered in pink, lime and lemon fabrics, ornate woodworking dating to the eighteenth century, and classical paintings from the hotel's extensive collection. For dinner, Marianne chose sea bass in a special sauce exclusive to Le Chantecler and Alistair, showing restraint this time, chose the same. "So, how did you come to choose an apartment in the Marais?" she asked him.

Alistair stowed his notebook again. "My wife was Jewish. So, I guess I chose it for sentimental reasons. It's a district I know she would have loved."

"That is very touching. But now you have been a widower for almost three years. You need a lover. But I keep forgetting you Canadians are so polite and proper. You don't just jump into bed like Frenchmen do with or without an invitation."

"No, but we are great lovers," Alistair joked.

"Ah, yes?"

"Oh, yes. We go crazily wild once we are under the sheets. Patient, but frenzied."

Marianne's eyebrows lifted in an inverted V the way they had at Le Safari. "The women always come?"

"For sure. Always."

"Ooh, la, la." Marianne realized he was kidding but played along. "Stop it! You are getting me all excited. Frenchmen aren't like that. They are only preoccupied with their own orgasms. They aren't great lovers."

Alistair laughed. "You're not volunteering to be mine, are you?"

Again, a coy, enigmatic smile.

When Marianne had finished all of the fish that she was going to eat, and had drained her second glass of wine, she said, "I don't want dessert, do you?" Alistair shook his head and Marianne nodded at the waiter standing alertly near their table. The bill arrived almost instantaneously.

"So, here we are together wanting above all to have pleasure." She signed the chit and rose from the table as a bussboy pulled out her chair. "Shall we go to my bedroom?"

Right away, Marianne went to the bathroom while Alistair sat in a comfortable chair by the French doors that opened onto a private balcony overlooking the sea. All of the bedrooms at the Negresco were individually decorated and furnished with pieces from the contemporary, baroque and classic periods. Marianne's was at the lower end of the price scale, so it was contemporary and less grand than many—especially those that she had told him boasted mink bedspreads. He got out his notebook to record more of his impressions but found that he was too distracted to concentrate by what seemed about to happen.

Marianne reappeared wrapped in a soft white bathrobe and lay down on her bed with her head propped on a pillow, looking at Alistair who was still struggling to update his notes. She undid the tie and wriggled the robe open, revealing her nude body to Alistair. "Well, are you going to ravish me?"

He dropped his notebook and gawked. To him, she was like a marble statue of a reclining goddess with smooth, rose-tinted skin and breasts that whispered:, "Ttouch me." An erection formed instantaneously in a body that had gone without sex for so long. "You are a Parisian now, chéri," Marianne said soothingly as she slid the robe off her shoulders and dropped it in a heap beside her. She ran a hand up her thigh and let it come to rest between her legs. "It is time to live like one."

Alistair trembled with anticipation, any reservations shattered. He rose from the chair, hurriedly removed his clothes and lay down on the bed beside her drawing in the enticing fragrance of her expensive French perfume. He rolled on top of her, and their tongues played together until Alistair dropped his face to Marianne's breasts and kissed them before sucking on her rigid nipples. He moved from there to her flat stomach and soon his tongue was licking at the entrance to her body. He could feel Marianne's legs stir involuntarily and then her whole self writhe in expectation. Her responses to his touch seemed authentic, but it was hard for Alistair to be sure, given her theatrical nature.

Soon after he moved inside her, he could feel her come, but he went on pressing as deeply as he could until he felt warm fluid flowing from her again. When it was all over, she sat up in bed and stroked his thighs. "That was lovely, chéri. You were true to your word. You are a great lover."

Alistair laughed. "You know when I was twenty-one, I had this really nice girl friend. We went to Europe together that summer, but we were such innocents that during that trip, and throughout our relationship, we never had real sex.

"Non! I can't believe it."

"Neither can I now."

"No one in France would ever be that inhibited. You certainly wouldn't have gotten away with that in bed with me."

"I seem to have changed a lot since I was in my twenties…especially since moving to Paris."

"Good, but to me you are just my sweet and innocent lover."

Her North American sauvage more likely, though perhaps salvageable with a little French instruction.

"Maintenant, tu es mon amant bien sur." It was the first time that Marianne had used that term of endearment, and he recognized that she had deliberately chosen that moment, intending it to be meaningful.

The next day, they went by bus to Beaulieu-sur-Mer, and from there they walked along the coastal path to St. Jean-Cap-Ferrat, pausing while Alistair took pictures of the mansion owned by the British actor, David Niven. That night they dined together again at the Negresco, but this time in the much more casual La Rotonde. After the meal, they went hand-in-hand to Marianne's bedroom and made love again, although Alistair sensed that for Marianne it was a little different this time. She seemed to let herself go without any dramatic flourishes, signalling that her commitment to him had now taken on more meaning.

Following that night, they went to Cannes, home of the famous film festival, where, with Alistair on her arm, Marianne paraded happily along the promenade, perhaps hoping to be mistaken for a star herself. The colour of her hair was different that day and when she realized that Alistair had noticed the slightly darker shade, she said alluringly, "For Cannes, I am a dirty blonde."

"That's fine with me."

After that, it was the casino at Monte Carlo where Marianne used her reputation as a former model to get them into the Salle Privée as well as a peek at the one-room Super Privée where gambling didn't start until late at night. On the last day before Alistair was to return to Paris, they took the train to Ventimiglia across the border in Italy for the Saturday outdoor market, and afterwards to Menton to meet her parents at their apartment. He found them much younger than he had expected—in their mid-sixties perhaps—and not at all sour, as Marianne had described them. They smiled readily and helpfully spoke slowly so that Alistair could follow their French without difficulty. When they left, her father put his arm around Alistair's back the same way that Tate had. He sensed that the couple liked him and that they were pleased that Marianne had met him. *How many other lovers has she taken to meet them?* he wondered as they left for the railway station. *I don't think I can ask her and, anyway, I'm not sure I want to know.*

The next morning, Alistair took the train to Paris, and the day that Marianne arrived home, he phoned her flat early in the evening. "Can I come over to your apartment and spend the night?"

"Oooh, la, la. Avec plaisir, mon amant! But hurry, or I'll come before you get here."

Chapter 28

Over the ensuing two years, Alistair and Marianne spent virtually every weekend together at her parents' Ile St. Louis apartment. It was in stark contrast with Alistair's Spartan quarters, lavishly furnished in reproductions of Louis XV furniture with ornate, grey and gold-gilded stuffed chairs. They often explored areas of Paris that Alistair had not yet discovered and that were worthy of stories for "Off the Beaten Track." As in Provence, Marianne continued to give him ideas on how to cover well-trod places. His article on Sainte Chapelle, for instance, recommended doing the standard tour on a sunny day when the stained-glass windows were at their most brilliant and then returning for an evening concert to enjoy the chapel as it should be seen—in a calm and dignified atmosphere. On weekdays, Alistair moved back to his own apartment, but they frequently got together for dinner at one of the many restaurants scattered between their two homes and after he walked her to her apartment, they would sometimes climb into bed together.

They also flew on trips that for both of them combined business with pleasure. Milan, the fashion capital of Europe, was an important one for Marianne to visit regularly. In its case, rather than recommending out-of-the way places to see, Alistair proposed that his readers amuse themselves by having a shot at what he described as the city's "trifecta": visits to the chapel containing Da Vinci's "The Last Supper"; La Scala Opera house; and the pinkish white marble Milan Cathedral where one could walk along the roof top, admiring from close range the elegant Gothic arches, filigree pinnacles, towers, and statues that adorned it.

In stylish but crowded Florence, to escape after the exhaustion of doing the usual sites, Alistair suggested something totally off the wall: crossing the Arno River and climbing to the Michelangelo Piazza for a panoramic view of Florence and then continuing higher still to the Saint Miniato church. There, a shrine had been erected in the fourth century in memory of this Armenian prince who served in the Roman army until he became a Christian hermit. During the persecutions of A. D. 250, he had been thrown to the beasts in the Amphitheatre where a panther refused to eat him, so the emperor had him decapitated instead in Florence. Yet, undaunted by his dire situation, Saint Miniato allegedly picked up his head, tucked it under his arm, crossed the Arno and climbed to the spot where the church now stood. Only then, did he lie down and die.

Standing outside the church after they had taken the same walk, Alistair glanced at his watch. "Moving at admittedly a fairly leisurely pace, it has taken us an hour and a half to get here, and we weren't burdened by having to carry our heads."

"Ah, true," Marianne laughed. "But, of course, the good saint would have been in a terrible hurry!"

Rome was another city Marianne went to regularly on business and one Alistair knew he should cover but where, like Milan, it might be hard to find out-of-the way places to write about. The Borghese Museum was a must to mention, but how to recommend doing the gallery differently? It was Marianne who came up with the idea of reaching it at least from off the beaten path by renting bicycles at the far end of the extensive gardens and arriving at the museum as if by horse-drawn carriage in an earlier era. Alistair much admired the gallery's sculptures by the famed Bernini, but what particularly took his fancy was the nude work by Antonio Canova of a voluptuous Pauline Bonaparte, sensual and wayward sister of Napoleon, depicted as Venus. It had been commissioned by her second husband, Prince Camillo Borghese and carved in white marble that was polished so smoothly that the torso, arms, and legs had the appearance of actual skin. To Alistair the sculpture captured perfectly the vanity and pretentiousness of the great families of Rome, but it also gave him pause. *Marianne certainly looks the way Pauline does—irresistible. But is she also fickle, and, if so, how long will our relationship last?*

On all these visits, they slept and made love in the same bedroom and yet when they got back to Paris, they returned to their own apartments. When Alistair commented on the oddity of this arrangement and suggested that perhaps they should move in together, she kissed him and said gently but firmly, "Ah, non, mon amant. Look what happened to you and Peggy when you did that, but I am your sex kitten. That is enough."

"No, you're a full-grown cat and beautifully sleek. I'd like to spend nine lives with you."

Marianne looked pleased but did not respond.

In the summer of 1983, Jonathan and his family came to Europe on a three-week vacation that included five days in Paris with Alistair's mother accompanying them for the Paris portion. On arrival, Jonathan put on a performance that utterly baffled Marianne. He was dressed in a Toronto Maple Leaf hockey jersey with a matching, woollen tuque, and he spoke in a language she could barely follow, talking of hosers, two-fours, and telling Alistair to "takeoff, eh." He also emitted a mysterious cry that Marianne assumed must be the call of a rare bird. "Hey, we brought you some maple syrup, pancake mix and back bacon. But save it until after we've left, eh. If you open it now, the kids will scarf it all, know what I mean?"

"Oh, Jonathan, enough," his mother ordered. "Do grow up. You're boring everyone. I'm sorry Marianne."

"Pas de tout," she answered, smiling weakly.

Alone later with Alistair, Jonathan asked, "Where did you steal her from, a Parisian fashion show? You could get a hard-on just looking at her. But I doubt she knows one end of a hockey stick from the other."

After they had all departed, for breakfast, Alistair served Marianne pancakes that were swimming in butter and maple syrup. She politely ate half of one, emitting a deep-pitched guttural sound. "Well, what do you think?" he asked. When she hesitated answering, he added, "Of course, they would be much better sprinkled with wild blueberries."

"Perhaps. But the butter and maple syrup, they are simply too much. I prefer crepes. They only need a dusting of powdered sugar."

"In that case I don't think you are going to like poutine either."

"Perhaps not, mon amant, but I will certainly try it."

A notable change in their Paris lives came that August when Marianne's parents arrived from Menton and settled into their Isle St. Louis apartment. As a result, she moved into Alistair's. He was delighted by this, hoping that it presaged a change in their relationship, but, to his disappointment, she insisted it was just until mid-September.

Adding to his chagrin was the fact that she brought with her a young and frisky French poodle that her parents had acquired some months earlier, but which was not permitted in the apartment on Isle St. Louis. Alistair found Frederique irritating. He smelled, bounced around the small apartment as if on a pogo stick, and barked for food and attention. Marianne, however, was smitten by the dog and seemed to derive enormous pleasure from walking him on a long leash. On outings with Alistair, he pranced in front of them, drawing attention to her as if he were a horse, pulling her carriage past admirers. Every so often, they would have to stop while Frederique relieved himself, contributing bountifully to the gooey and slippery excrement all over the streets of Paris. Alistair tolerated the dog as best he could, viewing him as a small price to pay for the pleasure of living with Marianne and reminding himself that it was a short-term annoyance. In the autumn, however, when Marianne's parents were preparing to return to Menton, she begged them to leave Frederique in Paris and they relented. Pleasing their strong-willed daughter was a paramount concern. Now, however, since she was returning to the Isle St. Louis apartment where pets were not allowed, the dog was going to have to remain in Alistair's flat.

That Christmas, they were sitting on the floor by their tree, with Marianne wearing a long red nightie that he had never seen before. Frederique was in her lap, enjoying the gentle strokes of her soft, warm hands and looking at her expectantly. She rose spilling Frederique onto the floor where, in his typical fashion, he abruptly knocked a decoration off the tree. She moved close enough to Alistair for him to smell her delicious new perfume lightly applied, and to admire her glossy red lips. "I think we should find a larger apartment, maybe near St. Paul, somewhere closer to the Seine."

"What? You mean…give up mine and… and live there together?"

"Why, yes, mon amour!" Marianne's smile was mischievous but her affirmation definitive.

"But that is something that you said you'd never want?"

"Well, I do now."

"You mean permanently?"

"Maybe. Why not? You are a widower, and now you are not my amant. You are l'amour de ma vie."

Alistair was delighted by her change in attitude, but also a little confused. *Did she think I wasn't really ready for this before? That seems unlikely. Is this something entirely new and, if so, why did it happen just now?* There was no obvious answer and for some reason Alistair didn't feel he should pry. Sometimes, Marianne was an enigma and she seemed to enjoy having it that way.

Chapter 29

FOR SEVERAL MONTHS, Alistair and Marianne lived happily together in a new apartment near the St. Paul metro station. It was spaciously furnished in a stylishly contemporary fashion to which Marianne immediately added touches of her own. On one wall she hung a series of blow-ups from her modelling days. In several of them, she was scantily clad and reclined on couches in seductive poses. Yet, there was also a very ordinary one of her and Alistair in t-shirts and jeans sitting on a bench overlooking the Seine. The sweet scent of lilac sometimes wafted through the apartment, leading Alistair to conclude that Marianne periodically sprayed everything lightly with an eau de toilette.

All was fine apart from the fact that that Frederique remained with them. He crashed around their quarters, knocking over freshly filled wine glasses and vases of flowers and scratching the expensive silk fabrics on couches and chairs. Alistair was, however, more used to his presence now and tolerated the nuisance in their larger space. Whenever the dog released particularly noxious wind, he was able to retreat to the second bedroom with a pine spray and shut the door. Each time a major international story broke, he thought of Peggy and how it was another crisis that she would have wanted to cover. *But how many times could she have done that and safely survived?* He kept these musings to himself, however, not wanting Marianne to know that Peggy was still on his mind and that he had bouts of guilt over her death, especially in light of his own pleasurable life in Paris.

Everything might well have gone on in this comfortable and enjoyable state had it not been for a report from London in October 1984 about a famine of "biblical proportions" in Ethiopia. From that origin, the news had spread to media around the world and pictures appeared on French television and in the press of hundreds of thousands of villagers near starvation, especially in the north of the country where the autocratic Ethiopian government was also engaged in a bloody struggle against secessionist forces. Donations for relief assistance started to fill the coffers of non-governmental organizations in many countries.

"You know the humanitarian organization, Médecins Sans Frontières, don't you?" Marianne asked Alistair one evening after they had both watched television coverage of the famine.

"Of course. I'm sure I told you they were in Biafara when Peggy and I reported on the starvation there in sixty-nine. MSF had just come into existence. As I recall, that was its first formal mission."

"Yes. It was formed by several young French doctors. I have been supporting them from the start."

"Really?"

"Why do you sound so surprised, mon amour?"

"I didn't mean to. It's just that I didn't realize that you got involved in that sort of thing."

"Well, they are non-political. That is part of what I like about them. They provide medical assistance and don't care about national boundaries, people's race, religion, or ideological views. I send them financial donations regularly, and a few years ago I did some work for them." Marianne stood up and paraded theatrically across the room as if on a catwalk. "I did appeals for donations. Now they want me to go to Ethiopia for another campaign. MSF is running a nutritional program there." She sat down close to Alistair and squeezed his hand. "Will you come with me?"

"You mean you've already agreed to go?"

"Yes. I feel compelled. Besides, I want to have some new and exciting experiences like you have already had. I've told MSF about you."

"About me? What have you said?"

"That you are a very experienced journalist and that you are wonderful with a camera. We could shoot some appeals in the field, surrounded by children who are suffering and close to death."

Alistair shuddered involuntarily, recalling what he and Peggy had seen in Biafra. *It would be like that all over again and probably just as dangerous.* At the same time, he was dumbfounded. It was not a proposal that he had ever expected to hear from Marianne. "But I don't have any experience with film other than still photography."

"It can't be that different. You could learn very quickly, couldn't you?"

"I…I don't know." *Geez, this sounds like Peggy talking.* "Maybe… I suppose."

After the experience he had had in Africa with Peggy, the notion of going back to the continent and being exposed to innumerable diseases or perhaps contracting malaria or dengue fever did not appeal to Alistair, but he was reluctant to say no, and see a divide open between them. So, he telegraphed the *Sunday World* and got their consent to a two-week unpaid leave. The paper also agreed to pay his travel costs and living expenses for the first week he was away on the understanding that he would file several stories about the famine along with photographs that would be exclusively for the *World.* Marianne managed to obtain better terms from Lafayette because the department store wanted to demonstrate its support for MSF and famine relief; she was given three weeks paid leave with all her expenses covered and permitted to stay longer at her own expense. Just before leaving, she made a quick trip to Menton to see her parents and to return Frederique to them, expressing the hope that they wouldn't find the dog too spoiled by all the attention she had lavished on him.

Despite his reservations about going to Ethiopia, Alistair hoped that he might actually experience a high from doing this kind of reporting again, but that never happened. Even though he was there during one of the coolest periods of the year, he found it unbearably hot, especially in the arid north when they were not in the mountains and that was most of the time. On top of that, they were constantly surrounded by poor, undernourished Africans whom he imagined were carrying every conceivable disease from AIDS to yellow fever. "Stand back!" he was constantly shouting at Marianne as he was filming the children surrounding her, clutching at her pantlegs. "You mustn't touch or hold them."

"Don't be silly, darling. They are just desperately hungry, that's all. Look at them. They are *so* adorable."

Just at that moment, a little boy, barefoot and naked to the waist, coughed practically in Alistair's face and he jumped back in alarm, almost losing hold of his camera.

Alistair didn't catch anything in Ethiopia other than a bad case of diarrhea, but he found the experience stressful and too much like his worrisome African experience with Peggy. He stayed for the two weeks the *Sunday World* had agreed to and, at Marianne's urging, one week more that he would somehow have to justify to the paper. After that, he flew back to Paris leaving her to return a little later.

But she never came. After four months, she phoned him to say that she had moved in with a French doctor working for MSF. Alistair was bitterly disappointed, but not entirely surprised because it was a scenario he had considered might have happened when she didn't return within the timeframe promised. "Does this mean it's all over between us?"

"I'm not sure, chéri. You know me."

"Well, do you still love me?"

"Of course, I do. But I love Phillipe as well."

Some months later, in 1985, MSF was expelled after denouncing Ethiopia's abuse of international aid, much of which was being channelled to government militias in the north while being withheld from insurgent areas in the same region where the need was greatest. Just before the mission ended, Marianne called Alistair again. "I'm going with Phillipe on his next assignment. We're getting married and we are adopting an Ethiopian orphan. He is a year old and *so* cute."

"But…But…I don't understand. What has happened? This isn't like you at all. It's not what you ever wanted."

"I know, chéri. But you changed me. Living with you has made me a different woman."

Alistair was dumbfounded and depressed for weeks after he received the news. It struck him as an almost inconceivable change in personality and he felt even worse realizing that, if Marianne had wanted to marry him, he would have agreed right away; and if she had wanted to adopt a child he would also have concurred. The last thing he wanted at his age was for the relationship to fail. Alistair was ready to do almost anything to hold onto Marianne, but now he was forced to conclude that she didn't feel the same way about him; that really hurt, and he couldn't fathom how it had happened. *Is it because deep down she was thirsting for adventures she felt I was no longer up to? Maybe at first, she was just flirting with Philippe the way she did with me, but then, because I went back to Paris, it grew more serious.* He could hear Peggy castigating him, "You should have left the paper and stayed with her in Ethiopia, you dumb fuck. Her conscience was awakened by a worthy cause."

Alistair reluctantly gave up their spacious St. Paul apartment as it was too expensive for him to afford on his own, and he moved into a much smaller one near his original location off Rue Bretagnnge. He had gone back to his usual travel writing for the *Sunday World* as soon as he had returned from Ethiopia, throwing himself into his work with intense vigour to take his mind off Marianne's absence. He found, however, that he kept unsettling himself with the thought that he should have stuck with hard news reporting all along but then rejecteding that notion. When the Chernobyl nuclear disaster struck in 1986, for instance, he envisaged Peggy going there as soon as journalists were allowed to enter the restricted zone. *But am I prepared to abandon my self-indulgent life in*

Paris to do that, after Peggy's death and all the close calls we had together? No, I don't think I am. In the same manner, he wondered where Marianne was now with her doctor husband, attending, he assumed, to the needs of the sick and poor in some other African country. It hurt him to think of her with another man, yet he recognized that the path she had chosen was not one that he wanted to follow.

Abruptly, in 1988, the *News of the World* informed him that, due to declining sales and rising production costs, they were closing the Paris bureau and moving him back to London where he would become an assistant editor. He hated the idea of leaving Paris, a city he had come to know well and to love. Further, he wasn't at all sure that he liked the nature of the assignment he was to assume. *Bugger, I won't be in the field writing my own stories. That really sucks.*

Before leaving, he made a brief trip to Nice, and took the train to Menton to call on Marianne's parents. They greeted him warmly as did Frederique, raising his paws onto Alistair's chest, whimpering and licking him on the cheek. Strangely, he suddenly realised that he was going to miss the dog, and that led another thought to strike him. *Marianne always said that Frederique was adorable, the same way she referred to the Ethiopian baby. Was that a factor in her decision to stay and to leave me— Phillipe's willingness to adopt the boy as if he were a pet? Or was it really something much bigger than that? Did her exposure to the tragedy totally transform her?* "She's like the doctors now, you fucking idiot." Alistair didn't really know the answer but deep down he suspected that the voice that wouldn't leave him was right.

In French, Marianne's parents explained how sorry they were about what had happened because they liked him and saw him as a son. For Alistair, however, the ironic comparison with Peggy's parents was painful. At the door, as they were saying their farewells, Marianne's father put an arm around his shoulder and offered softly another explanation of his daughter's action. "C'est Marianne, un oiseau toujours en vol."

A bird always in flight, eh?

"Peut-être qu'au printemps elle te reviendra."

Maybe in the spring she'll come back to me? Well, it's spring now and she isn't here!

A week later, feeling old and discarded, he winged his way to London not particularly looking forward to what awaited him.

Chapter 30
Toronto

• • • •

The Present in September

IT IS FIVE o'clock on a warm evening and the residents are gathered on the top-floor deck of the long-term care home for a pre-dinner performance by an aging guitarist and singer in the waning stages of his career. They are sitting on folded chairs set up by staff so worn out by the years of pandemic that they find it difficult to hide their sense of strain and weariness. Some of the residents are wrapped in blankets that look as old and tattered as the stooped and shrinking bodies they are covering. Yet, despite these signs of wear, there is also an atmosphere of relief riding on the light breeze—relief borne by the likelihood that the worst of the pandemic is behind them and that things are returning to normal.

The performer's gig is comprised largely of old folk songs that many in the audience know by heart or once did—everything from "This Train is Bound for Glory" to "Where Have All the Flowers Gone?" He is a favourite at the residence and those who remember him from one appearance to another are always urging Angela to invite him back. But his circuit of nursing homes and seniors' residences is a large one, so he is not easy to book, especially now when the Covid-19 restrictions have eased.

Even the woman beside Alistair brightens when the performer starts strumming, sitting upright in her chair, eyes focussed steadily on him. Her lips begin moving in approximate time with the lyrics as he sings

"Blowin' in the Wind."

When the concert is over, the residents are ushered to the elevator and take it down to the dining-room floor, some managing quite well on their own, others assisted by the staff. Alistair lifts his charge into a wheelchair and pushes her to the elevator. This is a new development but one that seems necessary, particularly in the evenings when she is often exhausted, as she is now after the excitement of the performance.

The décor in the dining-room is simpler than in the lounge. There are no paintings on the walls apart from a large portrait in oil of the home's founder and chief benefactor hanging at one end. There are simple translucent plastic curtains that can be pulled back in daytime to let in more light and heavier, beige ones that are always shut in the evening. A small vase of flowers adorns every table, and the residents eat using porcelain crockery, stainless steel utensils and glass tumblers filled with water and ice.

The women who are the most alert sit at tables that are exclusively for them. Their conversation is animated if repetitive and frequently factually inaccurate, yet they always seem to enjoy the evening meal together. The others are guided to their designated places with their positions altered every few weeks in an effort to stimulate interaction. Usually, however, their exchanges are sporadic to non-existent; the residents sit silently, slowly chewing their way through their meals. Several of them are easily distracted and stop eating altogether unless fed by spoon. The vanishing shadow that Alistair is feeding—her real self lost in a thickening fog—has slipped into this latter category and he has to wait patiently while she munches endlessly on a piece of chicken. Then he wipes her mouth with a napkin before coaxing her to take some more. Almost always, part way through the meal, one of the male residents bolts from the dining-room certain that he is expected somewhere else. This time it is George who is afraid he'll be late getting to the Blue Jays' game and Angela has to chase after him to reassure him that it is not now, but

Sunday afternoon and that his brother is coming to pick him up. "After dinner, I'll show you your calendar. So, don't worry about it. Just come and finish your dinner."

The incident provides entertainment for the chatty ladies and afterwards one of them waves her hand in the air and calls to Alistair, "Yoo-hoo! Come and join us. We'd like to have your company."

He nods and smiles at them. "Thank you, but I can't." He looks at the silent diner beside him, "She needs me right now."

"Oh, she won't even notice that you are out on the town."

The table erupts in laughter. Alistair is stung by their comment but accepts that they don't really mean to be cruel and that sadly their observation is accurate. After dinner, he wheels his charge to her room, gets her into a nightie and tucks her into bed. He kisses her on the lips but there is no response, for almost right away she has fallen asleep. So, he tiptoes out the door, hoping that Angela will find him in the living-room as she usually does when she notices that the bedroom door is shut. He contemplates preparing coffee and tea for them but decides he shouldn't appear presumptuous about her staying at the end of her shift and that, in any event, he doesn't really have the authority to go into the kitchen and raid the supplies.

"Poor George, I feel so sorry for him,." Angela says when she arrives later. "He's not going to the Rogers Centre, only to his brother-in-law's to watch the game on television. He could see it here but no one else is interested and on his own he'd lose focus and wander away. He might come back but by then someone would have switched the television to another channel."

"A guy issue everywhere."

Angela laughs. "Tea?"

"Love some, thanks."

"It was a good performance, I thought." Angela returns with the cups. "Everyone seemed to enjoy it. Even your gal was mouthing some of the words."

"I noticed. She likes folk music, and protest songs even." Alistair pauses reflecting. "'Blowin' in the Wind' … You know when I went by boat up Pangnirtung Fjord to do the hike to the cairn marking the Arctic Circle, the guide I hired told me there used to be the nose of a glacier that you could see beyond the fjord. In eighteen eighty-three, an anthropologist recorded it as about two hundred feet high. There is nothing there now. It has all washed to the sea as in Bob Dylan's lyrics."

"Terrible!" Angela shakes her head.

"And what have we done about the issue in all the years since? Nothing really except talk about it. We've set goals for reducing carbon emissions and then never come close to reaching them. We need to reduce drastically our consumption of material goods, but is anyone talking seriously about doing that? As it stands, it takes over one and a half of our planet's ecosystem to support our demands on Mother Earth each year. Where is the plan to persuade the public that our present behaviour is unsustainable? And so far, we've just watched the ice caps melt away, the sea level rise, and the oceans become choked with plastic and other waste. We keep dancing around all these issues and never attack them boldly because the commitment that it would require would mean enormous economic and other sacrifices."

"Can I get you a cookie?" Angela interrupts. "I think I'm going to have one."

"No thanks," Alistair laughs. "You're not stuffing one in my mouth to shut me up. It feels like we're waiting for a specific day that will be so calamitous and things will suddenly be so obviously bad that the public will acknowledge that radical measures are necessary right away. But it probably won't happen like that. Things will just get worse at an accelerating rate and by then it will be too late."

"I'm just going to get that cookie."

Alistair sips his tea, quietly contemplating his own lifetime record until Angela returns. "I bet I could have eaten one of those and gone on talking without choking. Anyway, what have I ever done about these environmental issues myself beyond complaining about inaction for years? Yes, I made sure they were covered in the *Sunday World,* and I've written the odd letter-to-the-editor and gone to a few demonstrations, but I've done zipola that is really substantive, and all of my flying has been a contribution to the problem."

"Oh, dear. Here you go again, knocking yourself as if it is all your fault when everyone is to blame."

"Of course, most of the big issues we face have been in the public eye way longer than the state of the environment. The Selma marches that Peggy and I covered were in nineteen sixty-five. The concern then was registration of black voters. That's still a problem. And, in addition to that, these days, Blacks are regularly gunned down by the police on the slightest provocation and subjected to all sorts of indignities. Our own treatment of racial minorities, especially Indigenous peoples, isn't much better."

Angela waits patiently for Alistair to finish his rant, certain of how it will end. "It was in January nineteen-eighty that Peggy and I went to Afghanistan to cover the Soviet invasion. The Russians thought that war would be over quickly. They made the same mistake in Ukraine with a terrible cost in lives once again. It's almost forty years since Marianne and I were in Ethiopia because of widespread famine, yet that remains a recurring problem there. And the disparities in wealth between the richest and poorest countries are greater than ever. But what have I done to help eliminate these terrible injustices? Nothing of real import. I've just been blowing in the wind."

Angela finishes her coffee and slings her purse over one shoulder. "Why do you always torture yourself with these thoughts? We are who we are, and no one is perfect. We all have regrets and wish we could do better."

"I'm a nut case. You know that."

"Would you like to come with me? I can drop you off at a psychiatric ward."

"No thanks. Not there. I'd rather go on torturing myself with dark thoughts."

Chapter 31

Working as an editor at the *Sunday World* required considerable adjustment for Alistair. He regretted no longer being a reporter and a cameraman and having the freedom he had in Paris to choose his own stories. *Still, I have to admit I don't know enough about Britain and what is going on to be effective in the field. So, I'd better just get on with what they want me to do.* That was to assign journalists to stories, suggest improvements in their drafts, and edit their final copy.

There was another unmentioned feature of his position that he had not anticipated—mentoring young reporters. This entailed advising them on what to look for to add colour, imagery, and a sense of place to their articles, how to conduct interviews as well as tricks for getting the most out of them, how to deal with difficult colleagues and senior staff, and how to deport themselves in public and around the newsroom. It was a sort of fatherly role that he had never experienced before, and it surprised him how much he liked it even though it was a responsibility that affirmed he was aging.

Quite quickly, Alistair installed himself in an affordable flat in Fulham on a street that emptied into Bishop's Park which in turn stretched along the Thames from Putney Bridge to Craven Cottage, the quaint, redbrick home of Fulham Football Club, the oldest professional team in London. In 1988, flats in his area were still affordable, so with pleasant surroundings, good pubs and restaurants, and easy connections to central London by underground and bus, he was happy with his neighbourhood discovery.

Settling into life in London and at the *Sunday World* was also facilitated by his becoming acquainted on his very first day at work with Cynthia Cartwright, the receptionist who sat at a desk just outside the paper's editorial offices. "So, *you* are Alistair Parker! I'm delighted to meet you. I was a fan of all the travel articles you wrote from Paris. I loved them and your vivid descriptions of the fascinating places you have been. They made me envious and yearning to get out of here and have some experiences like yours."

"Well, thank you. It's nice of you to say that. It's not often you get positive feedback from readers. Usually, they only dwell on your short-comings and factual errors. And, yes, I do feel that I have been very lucky to have travelled widely, and on someone else's ticket, but there have been some nasty thorns in that proverbial bed of roses." Alistair didn't elaborate and walked through the door to the editorial offices.

This became a regular occurrence when he arrived at work. Cynthia always stopped him to chat, asking if he had had a pleasant evening and what he had done the preceding night. Several times, she inquired as to how well he was settling into London and getting to know the city and if she could help him in any way. And at lunchtime she would phone to see if he would like her to fetch him a sandwich or a drink, and at 3.30 p.m. a tea or a coffee. *Is she flirting with me?* he eventually asked himself. *Surely not. She can't be more than thirty-five…forty tops.*

Cynthia was relatively tall, perhaps five feet, seven, Alistair estimat-ed. She had large bones as well that gave her the appearance of being somewhat overweight, but she wasn't really. "I'm a bit of a fitness fanatic," she confessed to him. "I go jogging regularly in the city and horseback riding at my parents' farm. We go for long country walks there as well." Compared to Marianne, she was not what he would have described as "bowl you over beautiful," but she was certainly attractive: large, dark brown eyes, wavy chestnut-coloured hair, cut mid-length with tints of rusty red at the roots. Her fulsome lips were always painted to com-plement the colour of her hair, and her mouth turned readily into a big smile. For some reason, Cynthia conjured in his mind a figurehead on the prow of an old sailing ship—confident and serene, the bearing of a woman who believed she could plough unphased through whatever seas confronted her. He appreciated as well the fact that her conversation was cheery—unless she happened to get on to the subject of Margaret Thatcher who, by the time of Alistair's arrival, had already been in power for the longest, uninterrupted stretch of any prime minister since 1812.

Alistair found that the more he saw of Cynthia and listened to her talk, the more he was attracted to her despite the obvious difference in their ages. *Maybe it's just that I'm lonely, it's hard to tell.* Whatever the explanation, one day, when she phoned him at noon to ask if she could fetch him a sandwich, he answered, "Thanks, but I think that today, because it is so beautiful, I'll go out for lunch. You get an hour off at one, don't you? Would you like to join me?"

"I was beginning to think that you would never ask. Of course, I'd love to."

They went to a café near the office where Alistair bought them prepared sandwiches, coffees, and bran muffins. As they seated themselves at an outdoor table in the May sunshine, Cynthia unwrapped her avocado and Ccamembert selection and Alistair his roast beef sandwich with mustard, lettuce, and tomatoes. *At least I chose whole wheat bread and requested tomatoes,* he comforted himself before asking Cynthia if she were a vegetarian.

"Yes…well, sort of at least." "I do eat fish regularly and I have chicken occasionally. It's for health reasons mainly, but I don't like killing animals either. I'm not fanatical, though. How can I be when I go fox hunting at the farm?"

"You have a flat in Chelsea and also a farm in Surrey. Amazing."

"Yes…well, no. My parents have the farm actually. Daddy and Mummy live there fulltime now that he is retired."

"And you ride to hounds. How brave!"

"You sound sarcastic. Are you opposed to blood sports?"

"Actually, I've never been asked that question. It is not a subject that ever comes up in my circles. So do your parents hunt as well?"

"They used to, but not any longer. Still, we stage one of the hunts every autumn. You should come and watch when we host the ride in the autumn."

Does she mean it or is she getting carried away talking about it? "I wouldn't want to watch a horse break a leg going over a fence…or you for that matter, not one of your long, slim limbs." Alistair surprised himself with his boldness as he had when he first met Marianne.

Cynthia put down her half-eaten sandwich. "Are you teasing me? Or are you flirting?"

Was I? Surely not. The age gap is ten years maybe. "May I ask you a question a man is never supposed to put to a woman?"

"Try me."

"Obviously, you don't have to answer but I'm wondering how old you are?"

"I'm thirty-four."

Holy crap. It's thirteen years!

"You're frowning. Why? Do I look older than that?"

"No, no! I was just hoping that you were."

"I guess I'm flattered. But why, for heaven's sake? You like older women?"

"No, because maybe I was sort of flirting with you, and I shouldn't be when I'm forty-seven."

Cynthia grabbed his hand and squeezed it. "There is nothing wrong with that. I've wanted you to from the day I met you. I felt I already knew you and you turned out to be just the person I was hoping you would be. So why don't you come to dinner at my flat tonight?"

"Thank you, that is very kind of you, but I'm afraid I can't."

"Why not?"

"Because you're so much younger and I've experienced a lot of—"

"Well, I have some history, too, and I suppose it's time you knew about it. I got married when I was twenty and I have two sons."

"You're married? You never told me that."

"No, it's okay. I'm divorced."

"Divorced with two sons and you're only thirty-four? It does sound like we have a lot to talk about. On second thought, I'd love to have dinner with you if you mean it seriously."

"Of course, I do."

"So where in Chelsea do you live?"

"In a mews off King's Road." Cynthia pulled a notepad and pen from her purse and wrote down the address and her phone number.

"You mean to say that you are one of those Sloane Rangers I read about, those wealthy young women who parade the King's Road in the latest fashions and get drunk at the private clubs?"

"No, I'm most certainly not one of them. I only live in Chelsea because Daddy pays the rent. It's sort of compensation for introducing me to my erstwhile husband. You'll find that it's easy to get to my place from Fulham."

"I know, and our real-world clubs are fairly close neighbours, even though they are on opposite sides of the social divide: mine is impoverished and struggling to stay afloat while yours is thriving and well financed." Cynthia looked bewildered and he realized right away that she was not a fan. "Chelsea Football Club, I mean."

"Oh…oh, yes…Them! I thought you were talking about a dance club or something. As you might guess, it's all rugby in my family, I'm afraid." Cynthia stood up. "But don't get me talking about the disadvantaged and Margaret Thatcher now or I'll be late getting back."

Alistair arrived at Cynthia's flat at 7.30 p.m., carrying a bottle of white wine from New Zealand and a dozen tulips that were a blend of orange and white. "I'd have brought roses, but, hell, it's springtime and the season to honour the Dutch and their resilience during the War."

"They're lovely, thank you, and I agree; here's to resistance to tyrants everywhere! So, what can I get you to drink? It looks like a delicious wine that you brought but would you like a cocktail first?."

"I'm really partial to whisky if you have some. A whisky and soda."

"With ice?"

"Please."

"And not just one cube like my inflexible countrymen, I assume. I'm going to have a gin and tonic, of course, because I am so predictably English." She seated Alistair in the living-room and brought their drinks in from the kitchen through a hatch at one end of a counter that divided the two rooms.

"Why is it that the English are so partial to gin?" Alistair asked. "After all, it's cold and damp here so much of the time you'd think whisky would be more popular."

"Well, some say it's because of the quinine. It's supposed to be the healthiest of all liquors."

"Yes. Churchill claimed that gin and tonic had saved more lives and minds than all the doctors in the Empire."

"You have quite a memory. I didn't know he said that. Anyway, I think we love gin because we are always yearning for warm weather that never comes, so we have to pretend that it is fine outside. G and Ts are a prop in that illusion."

"I like that explanation. Of course, it could be because they think the Scots are inferior. Cheers in any case."

Cynthia seated herself beside Alistair on a white leather couch with throw cushions covered in a material with a heather hue that matched the curtains on the room's large windows, designed to let in a stream of sunlight from the mews on one side and from a little garden on the opposite. The frames of the windows and the living-room walls were also painted white; on them Cynthia had hung several large limited-edition prints—by contemporary painters, Alistair assumed, judging from the *avant garde* nature of their work. "Wow, it's a beautiful flat. Not at all like mine. I mean my digs are comfortable but they're pretty ordinary. This is high fashion. You *are* a Sloane Ranger!"

"No, those girls are mostly Tory snobs and I vote Labour—with extra zeal ever since Thatcher came to power. I absolutely despise her. Even the Church of England has blamed her for the decay of inner cities and is calling for fairer income distribution."

"I've noticed how much the parks in London have deteriorated since I was first here. They look unkempt and the facilities run down."

"It's been dreadful and there is no stopping her now that she has won her third election in a row. The lady's not for turning. Anyway, let's get off the topic of politics." Cynthia kicked off her sandals and lifted her bare feet onto the couch. At first, she tucked them in against her thighs, rubbing her ankles with her long, slender fingers and setting the gold bangles on her wrists tinkling softly. But then she stretched her legs across Alistair's thighs, moving them gently in a form of massage that had the effect of emphasizing what she was saying. "Do let's talk about something else—something innocuous—like, how are you enjoying living in London?"

"Very much…Meeting you has, of course, helped enormously." Cynthia pressed her legs a little harder into Alistair. "But really, I'd like to learn more about you. What happened to your marriage that it ended in divorce, and when?"

"Oh, dear. That is to risk getting back onto politics. I married Rupert in 1974. I was only twenty and pretty impetuous. It was a stupid thing to do, but I thought at the time that I really did love him. Daddy had introduced us just the year before. He was a portfolio manager at the investment firm in London where Daddy was a vice-president. He saw Rupert as one of their rising stars and thought that he would be a good catch. I suppose at first I was drawn to the prospect of our living comfortably together in the green belt outside London."

"So, you, too, had a home in the Surrey countryside?"

"We lived in Guildford actually. Not as large a home as Hazelnut Farm, but very nice and spacious."

"But no horses, no fox hunts?"

"No, although we weren't very far from the farm and went there often."

"So, what went wrong?"

"What went wrong was Margaret Thatcher came to power. Like Daddy, Rupert was an ardent Conservative and they both thought she was just what the country needed. I totally disagreed with them, and we started arguing all the time."

"Surely, political differences alone couldn't have been enough to drive you to divorce. You could simply have made a pact not to discuss how she governed. Presumably, lots of other couples have had to do that."

"Maybe, but I just couldn't. I finally realized that our values were just too different for our marriage to work. Besides, he was commuting to London every day and getting home late, so we didn't really have much of a life together. And he didn't want me to work, so I felt frustrated and unfulfilled, a kept woman alone all day looking after two little boys. It was not what I wanted. I suppose I've always been a bit of a rebel and unconventional, so I did what I wasn't supposed to do in our circle. I left him and moved to London to find a job with only my A level certificate and a few months of university completed. The receptionist job at the *Sunday World* was all I could get. My parents were humiliated. Daddy is not fond of journalists, especially ones with papers that criticize Thatcher. So, they've been vague with their friends about what I do. I love them, I really do, and they have been very good to me. But it's not easy having a father with a very strong personality. Mummy isn't really like that. But he rules the roost on the farm. Gracious, I've blathered on far too long about myself. You are such a good listener." Cynthia lifted her legs off

Alistair and stood up. "I must check the roast potatoes and get the other vegetables cooking. We're having poached salmon. I hope that is okay with you."

"Sure, I love it. I'm a Canuck after all."

Over the meal at a table in a small room overlooking the garden, Alistair asked Cynthia about her sons. "They are thirteen and eleven."

He did a quick calculation. "So, the older one must have been conceived almost right after you were married?"

"Yes. That's Charlie. The younger one, Jeffery, was just a toddler when Thatcher came to power, poor love. He hardly knew his father when we moved out. To be fair, Rupert didn't contest my wish to have the boys and, in return, I'm generous about giving him time with them."

"So, where are they now?"

"They're in boarding school."

"Boarding school? So, they're not with you very much?"

"No. Only at holidays. But I go to Windsor every few weeks as well to see them for an afternoon."

"They are at Eton?" Alistair was non-plussed.

"Charlie is. He is finishing his first year. Jeffery is at preparatory school—St. George's at Windsor Castle. But he'll go to Eton, too, when he is thirteen. Daddy has insisted on it. That was his school, and he is paying the tuition, room and board—everything, in fact. I could hardly have said no. He wouldn't have listened anyway, and I didn't want to upset him further after leaving Rupert. Of course, he wants them both to go to Oxford—to his college, Balliol—and he will pay for that as well."

"And then it will be the Guards, I suppose."

"No. That I will not tolerate. I'm not going to have them go off to get killed in another senseless war in some Godforsaken country. There is a limit to what I will put up with to please Daddy."

"Oh, good for you!"

"Stop it! I know what you're implying."

"Sorry, I didn't mean to sound sarcastic." He did, of course, but not to the point of upsetting her. In fact, he was thinking how deliciously contradictory Cynthia was. *She's all over the map. She's a hypocrite just like me!*

Chapter 32

Two weeks later Cynthia invited Alistair for dinner again, and this time she suggested that he stay overnight. "That way, if it gets late, we don't have to worry about bus or Uunderground schedules."

"Okay, I'll sleep in the boys' room."

"You don't have to. It has twin beds so it's not very comfortable."

For dinner that night, Cynthia prepared a salad that included chunks of fresh tuna, tomatoes, diced red onion, and hard-boiled eggs. It was rather like a Salade Niçoise only simpler and it reminded Alistair of his time with Marianne. *Cynthia is another hedonist, but hopefully consistent about it. Maybe things will turn out better this time.*

When they went to bed, Cynthia repeated her invitation to sleep in her room, but Alistair politely declined. "Thank you, but I'll be fine in the boys' room unless I get nightmares about being in a boarding school." But this time, before retiring, he kissed her on the lips and felt a tingling sensation, the first since parting from Marianne.

After breakfast and coffee, they went for a long walk along King's Road window-shopping and stopping in one fashionable establishment while Cynthia bought an expensive pair of tight pale blue jeans with glittering fragments of costume jewellery sewn on the pockets. "Courtesy of Daddy?" Alistair asked. She didn't answer, but as they left the shop, she took his hand and said, "You'll like them. They'll be tight across my ass. You'll want to claw them off me."

For lunch, they stopped at the Antelope on Eaton Terrace in Belgravia: a pint of bitter for Alistair and a half for Cynthia along with crab sandwiches. Alistair's treat. Afterwards, they strolled up Sloane Street to

Knightsbridge and went to Harrods for tea and a single scone each with strawberry jam, but no clotted cream. Cynthia's turn, but Daddy's largesse. This was followed by a long walk around the Serpentine in Hyde Park and a short stop at the Albert Hall to buy concert tickets for the coming weekend.

When Alistair arrived that Friday, Cynthia kissed him at the door as she took his overnight bag. "May I put it in my room this time?" She studied him intently, fiddling with the chain of her gold necklace and drawing Alistair's attention to her white silk blouse and its little buttons that looked ready to burst from the pressure of what lay beneath them. "Mine is a large Queen."

It was what he expected her to say but he evaded a direct answer. "I haven't been in a house in Britain that had a king. Once, I saw pictures of the state rooms on the Britannia and I noticed that, when they are on board, the Queen and Prince Phillip sleep in single beds and in different rooms."

"I know it's just too English. I'm going to assume your answer is yes," and Cynthia dropped Alistair's little bag in her bedroom, leading his aging neglected groin to stir once again.

Sitting on the living-room couch with a scotch and soda that Cynthia brought him automatically, he asked her again about her past. "You were so young when your sons were born. How did you feel about having them at the time?"

"Oh, I wanted them. I was anxious to get on with life."

"And how do you feel about it now?"

"I'm so happy I had them when I did. It's not easy, of course, having them away so much of the time, but I'd probably never have been a mother if I hadn't got pregnant when I did…Why do you look so sad when I say that?"

Alistair was wondering where Ginny was at that very moment. *Probably home alone getting lunch. After all, the kids are pretty grown up now.*

What? Eighteen and twenty, I think. Maybe the younger one is over at the Vietnamese family they helped. A caring person like Ginny. If we had married in sixty-two, how many kids might we have had and what would their personalities have been like?

"Hello? Where did you go? I asked you a question."

"Sorry … Oh … it's nothing."

"Yes, it is. Tell me, but first I better check on the casserole we're having."

Alistair as well rose from the couch and followed Cynthia into the kitchen. "Is there anything I can do to help?"

"Yes, there is, in fact." She put their glasses down on a counter. "You can kiss me better than you did at the door." Alistair took her in his arms and planted his lips on hers for their first extended kiss. "Good." She suddenly broke away. "That will do as an appetizer but if we don't stop there, we'll never have dinner."

It wasn't until they were sitting on the couch after the meal that Cynthia asked him again what it was that had caused him to look so sad talking about having children.

"Just something that happened in the distant past—when I was determined not to be tied down. It's irrelevant now."

"I'm not at all sure it is." Cynthia got up from the table, and sat in Alistair's lap, peering intently into his eyes. It was only then that it occurred to him that the three women with whom he had had serious relationships had all had striking, inquisitive eyes. And now this was true of Cynthia as well. Was it their eyes, he wondered, that initially drew him to them? "You mean you wish now you had had children then?" When Alistair didn't answer right away, she ran her hand over the bulge in his pants. "We could go to bed now and make a baby of our own."

"What? At forty-seven?"

"That's not too old."

"Not too old to do it, but too old to have kids."

"Well…there are always mine."

"Two boys who are at elite schools and destined for Oxford? I can hear Peggy screaming in my ears just at the thought of my having any kind of connection with that sort of establishment upbringing."

"You could talk to Daddy. You might be able to get him to agree to their going to state schools. He's more likely to be persuaded by a man than by me."

"Cynthia, I like the idea of going to bed with you, but that's all… You're moving much too fast for me."

"Oh, but I want to …I'm not that young anymore either." Cynthia kissed him on the neck, her soft, sleek hair falling across his face. "Besides…I know already that you are the man for me, and I'm hoping you feel that way about me, or that you will soon … if you'll just let it happen." She unzipped his fly and placed a hand inside his underpants. "Anyway, let's go to bed and see where our relationship is in the morning."

When Alistair first opened his eyes, he spotted Cynthia in her bra and panties on the bedroom floor doing yoga. She was sitting cross-legged, her palms lightly cupped in front of her chest with her fingers pointing upward. Since she didn't notice him, he rolled over to get more sleep; he needed it as they had been up late. A half hour later, however, he was wide awake and gave up trying, but when he sat up in bed, there was Cynthia still on her mat kneeling with her arms at her side beginning the Reclined Hero's pose. He slipped out of bed and tiptoed to the kitchen to make tea. When the kettle whistled, Cynthia heard it and called out, "Good morning, sweetie. I'll be finished in a couple of minutes. Did you sleep well?"

"No, but the hours before made up for it. How about you?"

"Oh, I slept like a log. I always do."

"Are you on the floor like this every morning?"

"Only on weekends. It's too hard to fit in before work."

When the tea was ready, Alistair carried the pot and two cups on a tray to the bedroom and lay down on top of the rumpled sheets, his head propped against a pillow. "How about the hours before you slept?"

Cynthia finished her routine and joined him on the bed with a kiss. "They were like devouring a box of very special chocolates. It was wonderful."

Early that evening, before going to the Albert Hall for the concert, they had cocktails at the Basel Hotel, a fashionable old landmark favoured by country gentry and located on a back street not far from Harrods. They climbed the carpeted staircase past pale green walls to the glassed-in lounge on the second floor where, before you entered, you could study the guests. "This is where my parents used to stay when they came to London. But not any longer. It's too close to Harrod's, so it is overrun with American tourists now. Look, you can see a couple of them—in New York Yankees' jackets and baseball caps. How simply awful. It didn't used to be like that. There was a strict dress code."

Alistair imagined how in the past, when you opened the door, the patrons in their tweed jackets or skirts looked up to scrutinize you and to signal to their companions their approval or displeasure. *What if we were coming for a drink with Cynthia's parents? What would they make of me? Yet another dishevelled foreigner and a journalist to boot.*

When they got back to the flat, Cynthia yawned. "I don't know about you, but I don't need any dinner—just a few more chocolates in bed."

"That sounds enticing to me."

Before he left early Sunday afternoon to return to his own flat, Cynthia asked him, "Well, do you think we can make it work?"

"What?" Alistair pretended not to follow, but he knew what she wanted him to say. *I like her. She is fun to be with. She's bright and lively and we've had some good times together. But she's so much younger and obviously impetuous. Does she really want this to be permanent or is it just an infatuation? Maybe she is just looking for a surrogate father for her kids. Do I love her? ... I'm not sure.*

"You know what I'm asking about. Our relationship. Will it work?"

"Well, yes, I do…I mean I—"

"Good." Cynthia hugged and kissed him and then broke away. "Actually, the I do's come later, and only if we have a church wedding which, of course, is what my parents will want. Now, all you have to do is propose."

"Wait. No! That's not what I meant. As I said last night, this is moving far too quickly. We need to wait a while."

Cynthia looked totally taken aback. She pouted like a teenager who had just been told by her parents that they wouldn't buy her the revealing dress she wanted because it was too mature for her age. "I don't understand. You just said we could make it work. I thought you meant you were ready to marry me."

Alistair kissed her to soften her disappointment. "I…I just think we need some time to get to know each other better. What you're talking about would be a very big step."

"I don't need anymore time, sweetie. I know that I love you and I want to be with you always."

"I don't know yet for sure… but I think I may feel the same way." Alistair was being as bold as he could, and he hugged her again to show her that his affection was genuine. "But I need to get to know you better and your family as well, your boys and your parents. It's important that they like me and are okay with this if we…we stay together."

"But they *will* like you, and they will be delighted that we are marrying." Alistair didn't respond, and after waiting impatiently for him to say something more, Cynthia yielded, "Well alright if you are adamant. We'll see the boys first. I'll check their schedules and find out when they are free to meet you."

• • •

THE EARLIEST TIME turned out to be a Saturday afternoon in mid-June after Charlie had finished his weekly cricket match, so they took a morning train to Windsor, met Jeffery at St. George's, and walked with him to Eton, crossing the Thames by an ancient footbridge. They had a light lunch on the High Street during which Jeffery talked almost exclusively to his mother, nattering on about school, all the homework they were assigned, the meals he liked and hated, and the boys with whom he had become acquainted. Alistair didn't know what to make of him—whether Jeffery had taken an instant dislike to him or was simply too shy to talk to someone he had just met, yet who might be destined to play a significant role in his life. He did, however, think that the boy was rather cute with his flushed and freckled face, earnest brown eyes and reddish hair that was almost as messy as his own.

They arrived at the college in time to watch Eton bat last in the second inning. Now, Jeffery was so intent on watching the match that he barely looked at either his mother or Alistair, although he chattered constantly about the rules of the game and the various terms exclusive to cricket automatically assuming that they needed instruction. In fact, Alistair was familiar with both. "Did you know, Jeffery, that being able to describe both a no-ball and a googly is a distinguishing attribute of citizens of the Commonwealth, excluding most Canadians." The boy stared at him and then went silent.

At the end of the match, Cynthia introduced Alistair to Charlie who greeted him politely but formally in the manner that he had obviously been taught at the college. Then the three of them waited on a bench outside while Charlie showered and changed in his dorm. "So, how do you like St. George's?" Alistair seized the moment to build on his promising intervention about cricket.

"Oh, it's a jjjolly fine school," Jeffery stammered. "I wouldn't want to be at a ppreparatory school anywhere else, but I do look forward to going to Eton."

When Charlie arrived, they headed off to the High Street for tea—

supper really for the boys. They were dressed in their school uniforms which for Charlie meant a black tailcoat, matching waistcoat, pin-striped trousers, white shirt with a false-collar and white bow tie. There were other boys walking into town as well, all on the narrow sidewalk on the same side of the road. To Alistair, they looked rather like penguins but not entirely. They weren't strutting ostentatiously, chests out proudly as if in a formal parade. Rather, they were moving slowly and casually, indifferent to their appearance and to the eyes of tourists and even locals staring at them curiously—so used to the prestige of being at Eton that they took their privileged status for granted. After all, they were the best in breed, and everyone already knew that. It was an antiquarian view of themselves, but Alistair found it not just amusing but informative, reflecting the enduring strength of the class system in England.

The boys chose to have full afternoon teas comprised of sandwiches cut in quarters, two scones each with pots of jam and clotted cream, all served on a silver, tiered tray. Cynthia ordered one scone with jam and Alistair, while tempted to have two and with cream, felt obliged to follow her disciplined lead. "So, I understand you are planning to go to Oxford," Alistair said to Charlie. "I know it's a way off yet, but have you thought at all about what you plan to study?"

"I…I should have thought that what you mean is wead. That's what we say here."

"Oh, shut up, Jeffery. It's perfectly fine to say 'study.' It's a term that is widely used. And I wish you'd grow up and stop lisping and stuttering. It's a terrible school-boy affectation."

"You do yourself. I've heard you."

"Not anymore."

"Oh, yes you do. I heard you jjjust the other day."

"Boys stop it! What has happened to your manners? Don't they stress that any longer?"

"Well, Charlie is always bwullying me."

"See, there you go again. Lisping like a little boy."

"Boys! Stop it at once! Charlie, just answer Alistair's question."

"Perhaps bullying is an old tradition at Eton,." Alistair intervened. "It is at many of the private schools in Canada, or, before Jeffery corrects me, what you rather oddly call public schools although why escapes me. The practice of bullying is one of the reasons—only one of them, mind you— why, if I had had children, I would have sent them to public schools in Canada rather than private. They are actually very good as they are here, I believe, especially in prosperous neighbourhoods. Anyway, back to my question if anyone remembers what it was."

Charlie turned as polite as possible. "I haven't decided yet what I will study, sir, but—'"

"Please call me Alistair, or just 'hey, you.' The boys both laughed, easing the tension. "But in what 'fields' would you like to 'take' courses?" Alistair gave Jeffery a gentle nudge on the arm. "I realize I've now employed other terms of which you may not approve." Jeffery grinned good naturedly.

"The arts and social sciences. After my first degree I would like to study business."

"And follow in your grandfather's footsteps?"

"Yes, *rather*."

"Is he also why you have your heart set on Balliol College? Your mother tells me that that is where you want to go."

"Yes, and I do, too." Jeffery was trying his hardest not to stutter and stammer and to alter the opinion he assumed Alistair had formed of him. At the same time, Charlie didn't complain that Jeffery was too young even to have an opinion about what university or college to attend.

"Good for you, Jeffery," Alistair risked patting him on the shoulder. "And Charlie, if you're keen on going to business school, you might even want to consider Canada. We have some excellent ones and a major change in your environment might be a good idea before you settle down to a career in England—in your grandfather's firm perhaps?"

"Yes, that is what I am planning."

"Well, in that case, I think you might find it helpful to have some international experience first. It would help you broaden your knowledge of the business world and corporate practices."

"I should like to do that very much. Thank you for the suggestion, sir."

"You mean 'old fart.' Please, don't call me sir."

The rest of the tea passed amicably in a discussion about Canada and Alistair formed the opinion that gradually the boys had come to like him. On the way back to London, Cynthia expressed the same view and kissed him for finding a way to reach them. "I have an idea," he told her in the taxi to her flat. "Why don't we take a trip to Canada with the boys sometime in August. I really should see my mother and Peggy's in Montreal. In her last letter, she sounded lonely and depressed."

"Oh, sweetie, that would be wonderful! I am dying to and I'm sure the boys would be overjoyed to go."

• • •

ALISTAIR MANAGED TO arrange a three-week absence from the *Sunday World* based on his accumulated vacation time from Paris and the strength of his argument that he needed to see his ailing mother and mother-in-law. He spent what spare time he had in June and July planning their trip, and in the second week of August they flew to Montreal. They stayed at a *manoir* on Sherbrooke Street and on their first full day he visited his mother-in-law while the others took a carriage ride up Mount Royal.

"Oh, Alistair, I've missed you," she cried as they settled in the unchanged living-room. "It's been so long. And look at me. I'm a frail old lady now." Alistair was, indeed, shocked by how elderly she looked. Her face was like a washcloth rung out to dry, but still discoloured and spotted with grime from overuse, and strands of grey hair were escaping from her bun and trailing down her face. She walked stooped over and used a cane. "I'm a shmatte."

"A what?"

"You know, just an old rag. I don't think I can live much longer in this house even with the help I get every day. The girls both want me to live with them. But I don't want to leave Montreal."

"No, I don't think you should. This is where you have always been in Canada. Why not a seniors' home here?"

"I hate the idea."

"But I'm sure you could find one with a lot of Jewish residents where they would treat you well. You'd be everyone's bubbe."

She laughed. "Good for you. Maybe you are right; I'll think about it. Anyway, enough about me. How are you and how is it in London?" Alistair gave her a summary of his brief time there and finished by telling her he had a girlfriend. "Ah! That is good," she said to his relief. "You are much too young to spend the rest of your life on your own. What is her name?"

"Cynthia Cartwright."

His mother-in-law frowned. "She is Anglo Saxon?"

"Yes."

"And Church of England?"

Alistair nodded.

"Oi, vey! Why couldn't you have found a nice Jewish girl already?"

Alistair smiled and then hugged her, moved by what she had unintentionally implied. "Sorry, Mame.,"

After two days in Montreal, Alistair took Cynthia and her sons by train to Quebec City and to dinner at the Chateau Frontenac where they ate on the terrace looking down on the St. Lawrence River, not far from the spot where President De Gaulle had arrived on his notorious visit to Canada. Then they flew to Toronto for several days, staying in an inexpensive hotel on Avenue Road on the edge of Yorkville. They visited Alistair's mother and Jonathan and his family several times and one evening he and Jonathan went for a walk alone together. "You sure know how to pick them. She's not as beautiful as Marianne, nor as Ginny, but she's certainly very attractive. I've got to hand it to you. You're quite the Don Juan. I never expected that."

They spent the rest of their time entertaining the boys, including taking them, along with Jonathan, to a Blue Jays' game at the SkyDdome. Everything they were taken to see, the boys politely said they enjoyed, but Alistair knew that they were impatient to get to what they anticipated would be the highlight of the visit: canoe tripping in Algonquin Park.

And so it proved to be. In a rented car, they drove to the southwest entry point and started their trip on Canoe Lake, famous as the one on which the painter, Tom Thomson, mysteriously disappeared. From there they paddled northward on a five-day circular route that entailed a number of portages, but none of them particularly long. Alistair and Charlie managed to carry the canoes without much difficulty although Alistair was conscious of how the weight on his shoulders dug painfully into his bones in a way he could not recall having happened as a C. I. T. at Camp Comak. It was the same problem sleeping; the pre-Cambrian shield seemed much harder now, especially compared to the fields of Alabama where rain not rocks had been the issue. The boys, however, loved every minute of the trip and Cynthia as well—if only because of their enthusiasm. They caught fish and pan-fried them on an open fire; they gathered wild blueberries and had pancakes using the batter mix and syrup that they had brought in their supplies; they sang songs and told scary stories around their fire at night; and during the days they swam in several different lakes as well as in what Alistair described to the boys' amusement as "piss ponds." They grew accustomed to informal Canadian ways and in no time were at ease addressing Alistair by his first name.

"You see!" Cynthia was gleeful at the end of the canoe trip. "You're a natural. You'll get on famously with them."

Chapter 33

CYNTHIA'S SONS RETURNED to England full of stories to tell their friends and grandparents. Alistair, however, was plunged back into work right away on issues like Thatcher's opposition to economic sanctions and disinvestment in South Africa, and her rejection of greater centralization in decision-making in Brussels that revealed an emerging deep divide in the Conservative Party over future ties with the continent. As a result, it was not until October that Alistair could fit in the long-delayed visit to the farm of Cynthia's parents.

Several days ahead, she asked him, "What colour are your wellies?"

"Black."

"And the jacket you plan to wear?"

"Blue. It is the only one I have."

"Right, we need to go shopping. We're beagling on Saturday and those colours simply won't do."

"Why? Too easy for the antis to spot me or is it because I might alert the hare to our presence?"

"It is custom, sweetie. Everyone *always* wears green. I want my parents to like you. Do you drink port?"

"Rarely."

"Well, Daddy is bound to serve it at least one night, so I'd better explain to you certain traditions in passing port."

They arrived on the Friday evening at the train station in Stoke d'Abernon where they were met by Cynthia's father for the short drive in his Land Rover to the farm. "Come in, come in!" Cynthia's mother, Mary, greeted them at the door. "It is so nice to meet you at last, Alistair.

Cynthia has told us all about you."

"Oh, dear, nothing too shocking I hope?"

"No, no. It has all been very positive, I assure you."

Alistair handed them the gifts that they had brought, pancake mix and maple syrup for Cynthia's mother and a bottle of Crown Royal for her father. "Oh, how sweet of you both to have brought presents all the way from Canada. Thank you so very much." Right away, Alistair liked her open, effervescent personality, so similar to Cynthia's. Indeed, they even looked alike. She was tall with a moderately large frame, but not overweight and obviously in good physical condition. While he assumed that she dyed her hair, it , too, was the same chestnut shade although cut much shorter. "Please, do come into the study. It is much cozier than the living-room when there are only four of us. Tony will fix us drinks, won't you dear? I'll have some of the Crown Royal you brought. That will be something totally new for me."

As they crossed through the living-room to the den, Alistair got his first good view of how beautiful and "olde England" the farmhouse was. There was a large inglenook fireplace at one end and an enormous oakwood cupboard with glass doors at the other, stuffed with old bone porcelain dinnerware. A large green leather sofa in front of the fireplace beckoned guests to sit and a polished oak coffee table rested in front of it with easy chairs at both ends that matched the sofa. The floor was grey slate, cheered by several Oriental scatter rugs, and the room had large windows with small lead-lined panes; Alistair presumed they looked out on a well-manicured garden and added light to the room during the day. In one corner, a small cherrywood table with folding leaves had been opened and set for four.

As they seated themselves in the den, Anthony stood in front of them rubbing his hands vigorously. "Now, what can I get the two of you?" Cynthia requested her usual gin and tonic and Alistair a whisky and soda, explaining that he didn't want to deplete the bottle of rye that they had brought. "Well, I'm certainly going to try the Crown Royal myself. How do you drink it?"

"Neat or with a little ice and water."

"Ah, that suits me perfectly."

When he returned with the drinks, he stood momentarily in front of them, a broad man with a square face, prominent chin, and ruddy complexion from spending as much time as he could outside with his employees managing the farm. His hair was white but still covered all his head and he had bushy eyebrows that were a mix of white and black. His mouth turned slightly down as if he were deep in thought but when something amused him, he smiled readily. Cynthia had told Alistair that he was seventy and only recently retired. He found it easy to imagine her father in a red jacket perched on a horse having a sherry before a hunt, or as a rather portly major in front of his troops, barking commands. "Well, cheers everybody," he said and he took a sip of his Crown Royal which he had chosen to have neat with no ice. "Hmmm. Not bad…Not bad at all."

After twenty minutes of conversation, mostly about the trip to Canada, Mary excused herself to warm her casserole in the AGA in the kitchen. "It contains wild hare which Cynthia will have to pick out, but there are lots of vegetables as well."

"I'll help you get ready, Mummy." and Cynthia, too, got up.

"Yes, well I should fetch a bottle or two of wine from the cellar. I think a claret would go well with this meal if that would suit you and Cindy."

"That sounds just fine. Is there anything I can do to help?"

"No, no. Just sit and enjoy the rest of your drink or help yourself to another from the bar." As he left the room he suddenly stopped as if the idea had just come to him. "Oh, yes, as a matter of fact there is something. We're going to eat at that little table by the fireplace. With just the four of us that will be nicer than using the big one in the dining-room.

Would you be good enough to light us a fire? You'll find everything you need in boxes there."

"I'd be happy to." It was an assignment—a test, in fact—that Cynthia had warned him to expect. Alistair rummaged through the pile of paper beside the fireplace. It was mostly old copies of *The Times,* but he did spot two *Sunday Observers* near the bottom. *I guess the World is too liberal for their tastes but at least they get some change in diet once a week.* He crumpled up several sheets of paper, placed the kindling at odd angles on top, added several logs, and lighted the fire. It blazed quickly just a few minutes before the casserole and wine arrived at the table. "I say, well done. That fireplace isn't always easy to manage."

"Thank you, sir. Of course, as a Canadian I have had lots of experience. Your—"

"Please, call me Tony. No need to be formal. After all, we're not all that far apart in age." It was meant as a friendly statement, Alistair assumed, but it struck him like a horse's kick. He glanced at Cynthia, but her face was expressionless as if she hadn't heard her father or was pretending not to have. "You were about to say?"

"Oh, simply that I think you will find your grandsons adept at making fires now."

"Yes, I'm sure I will. I'm delighted that they have had some exposure to the Commonwealth." As Alistair pulled out Mary's chair and they all sat down, he lifted his glass of wine, "Well, here's to the Queen, Britain and the dominions," and everyone dutifully responded, "To the Queen."

"You know when I asked Cynthia's Rupert to lay a fire, he botched it completely."

"Oh, the poor man," Mary cried as she ladled out the casserole. "He was so embarrassed."

"Was he *really*? I should have thought he would have been a man about it."

"Yes, he was…*really,* Daddy. He was mortified. I wish you wouldn't play these little games the first time…someone is at Hazelnut."

"It's not a game, Cindy darling. It's simply a polite ask. I'm sure that is how Alistair understood it. Didn't you?"

"Of course." *Someone? Boyfriends obviously. How many others have been tested?* Alistair didn't let that thought bother him. He was feeling chuffed about passing the fire drill with flying colours, so he simply waited patiently for Cynthia's exchange with her father to end and his host and hostess to lift their forks.

For breakfast on the Saturday, they had pancakes made with the batter and syrup from Canada. The Cartwrights were game about eating them but neither Cynthia nor Alistair was able to persuade them to use enough maple syrup. "It's not like Marmite. You need to smother it on."

"Mms," mumbled doubtfully by both of them.

After breakfast, it was time to go to a neighbour's farm for the start of the beagling expedition, an English pastime about which Alistair knew nothing. He quickly discovered, however, that it bore some resemblance to a fox hunt, although one designed for commoners and gentry without active riding stables. Rather than a fox, a hare was pursued by a pack of beagles followed by a party of walkers, trying desperately to keep up with the dogs. There was also some familiarity in the clothes worn by the truly committed, for they were dressed in black riding caps, green jackets with red trim on the collars, white breeches, and brown leather walking shoes. *A curious choice for trudging through farmers' sodden fields,* Alistair mused. The rest of the party, however, including the Cartwrights and Alistair, were attired in forest green overcoats, trousers of subdued shades, and green Wellingtons. Hats varied from none to cloth caps and, in the case of Anthony Cartwright and several other aging gentlemen, plaid deer stalkers.

When Anthony and Mary first saw how Alistair and Cynthia were dressed, they smiled approvingly. It was the same when her parents observed that Alistair had equipped himself with a stick forked at one end with which he could lift barbed wire, helping others to move safely through fences from field to field. They were also impressed at how Alistair walked at a pace that matched Cynthia's, and that he did not stop the way some others did to rest under a tree, hang over a fence talking to locals, or to consult a bird guide for the name of a warbler singing on an apple bough. All such diversions were of course possible and generously tolerated because usually the hare, in an effort to put the beagles off the scent, would reverse directions and circle back close to where the pursuit had started. That Alistair refrained from submitting to these temptations was, however, to the Cartwrights a sign of solid character. Thus, the outing passed agreeably for all, even though the beagles never succeeded in running a hare to ground and the antis never appeared to add a note of excitement.

That night the Cartwrights decided to have drinks in the living-room around another fire that Alistair laid and lit. He noticed that, while Mary had another Crown Royal, Anthony reverted to his customary single malt whisky. "Well, that was certainly an enjoyable outing. "Maybe I can get you back here, Alistair, the next time we have a shoot."

"I'm afraid I'm not much good with a rifle."

"*Really*? I should have thought you would be, coming from Canada. Perhaps we could use you as a beater then?"

Alistair evaded answering directly the offer of a lower status position. "Your grandsons are keen on going back to Canada to go hunting for deer or moose, even bear."

"I'm not surprised. I should like that myself. I shot a tiger once in India but that was some years ago."

For dinner they had the roast beef and Yorkshire pudding that Mary would normally have served on a Sunday night, but with Cynthia and Alistair leaving that day, Saturday seemed the time to have a joint. After the table was cleared, Cartwright fetched an old bottle of port from his cellar and placed it on the table to his right. As he poured the port into a decanter, Mary brought in a tray of cheeses and crackers. Once she was seated, Anthony passed the decanter to his right to Cynthia who poured a tumbler and then passed the port to Alistair on her left. From there it went to Mary before returning to the host. Sometime later, after cheese and much amicable conversation, the port was launched on another circle of the table, but Alistair deliberately let the decanter stall in front of him pretending to be distracted discussing his work as a newspaper editor. "I say, old chap," Cartwright asked mischievously, "do you happen to know the Bishop of Norwich?"

"Oh, I'm most dreadfully sorry," Alistair apologized profusely as he quickly set the decanter in motion again. "Yes, the poor absent-minded Bishop of Norwich. But he was in his nineties at the time, wasn't he? I have no such excuse for my forgetfulness."

The Cartwrights fell completely for the ruse, delighting in Alistair's understanding of English tradition and never suspecting that he had been coached on the arcane etiquette for passing and drinking port. Later, Mary caught her husband's raised eyebrows and rose from the table. Let's leave the gentlemen to their tumblers, shall we Cynthia? There is some fabric I want to show you in my sewing-room."

The weekend had gone so well that Alistair decided it was the moment to make a suggestion to the man who might become his father-in-law. "I wonder if you have ever considered the possibility of your grandsons going abroad for their university education—to Canada, for instance."

"No, I haven't. They are going to Oxford and, I hope, to my college, Balliol. That's a family tradition and as you know we are big on that in England."

"Perhaps for graduate school then?" Alistair plunged bravely on. "Charlie in particular seems keen on a business career—on following in your footsteps. In that case, he might find it helpful—a broadening experience that would expose him to rather different corporate case studies."

"Perhaps. How about you? Did you ever consider coming to England for graduate school?"

"Not really."

"No. I suppose that isn't something you need…when you are a journalist."

"If I had gone further, I would have stayed in Canada or chosen a university in the States because both countries focus more on course work than in England where research is central. That's also why graduate studies in business in North America would be good for Charlie. He'd have to take a wider selection of courses."

"We'll see." Cartwright put down his tumbler and rose. Alistair did the same, immediately sensing that he had perhaps said too much. "After all, that decision is still a long way off. I've committed myself to financing my grandsons' education for as long as they stay in school and it's an obligation that I intend to keep, so I suppose ultimately where they go is my decision." He put his arm around Alistair's shoulder and steered him towards the sewing room. "Let's rejoin the ladies and see what they have been up to, shall we?"

* * *

"Well, that went famously," Cynthia said jubilantly the next afternoon the moment their train left the station and they had finished waving to her parents. "You were brilliant, sweetu 'ems, absolutely brilliant. Mummy adored you, she even told me so, and I could tell that Daddy really liked you. That is as far as he'll ever go. After all, to him, I am still the little girl he doesn't want to lose."

"I sensed that."

They held hands sitting close together until finally Cynthia said, "Well, now do you feel you know me and my family well enough to propose?"

"You…you don't mean right here, do you? On a train?"

"Yes, why not? Before the Tories get around to privatizing them."

"But…but we haven't even bought a wedding ring yet."

"That doesn't matter. We can go shopping for one next week."

Alistair sensed that he could not delay any longer without upsetting Cynthia and perhaps jeopardizing the continuation of their relationship. *I think I love her, and I've grown very fond of the boys. Cynthia needs me for their sake at least. And I think I need her. Life all on my own is a dismal prospect.* "Well, okay… if you are really sure you want to do this?"

"Yes, sweetie, I am, surer than I have been about anything."

"And right here on the train?"

"Yes."

Alistair leaned over and kissed her. "Then will you take this decrepit old man to be your husband and put up with him for better or worse so long as we both shall live?"

"Oh, yes, I do with all my heart."

Chapter 34

ON THEIR RETURN to London, Alistair arranged to sublet his Fulham flat and moved into Cynthia's. Shortly afterwards, they went to Windsor to tell the boys about the engagement. They were both delighted. "Does this mean we'll get to spend more time in Canada?" Jeffery asked.

"Yes, probably, but we'll still live in England."

"Have you told Daddy about this?" Charlie wanted to know.

"Not yet, sweetie. I will shortly but first we need to tell your grandparents. So, please don't breathe a word to anyone until we can get back to Hazelnut."

As it turned out, that was not possible for some time because Alistair found himself swamped with work. There were journalists to assign and copy to be edited on a number of major international stories, including the beginning of perestroika in the Soviet Union, the impact of the termination of the Pinochet dictatorship in Chile, and the election of George H. W. Bush as U.S. president. On the domestic front, there were on-going issues to deal with related to the economy and the early stages of construction of the Channel Tunnel to France. It became clear that he would not be able to get to the farm with Cynthia before Christmas, but then their holiday plans were disrupted on December 21 by the downing of Pan Am Flight 103 over Lockerbie, Scotland. Alistair was so busy at the *Sunday World* that he was able to go to Hazelnut only on Christmas Eve, returning to London very early on Boxing Day. Cynthia arrived a day earlier with the boys with the intent of staying until some time after New Year's. With Alistair there so briefly and the mood sombre because of the crash, they decided at the last moment that Cynthia alone would break their news on New Year's Eve by which time hopefully the atmosphere would have lightened.

Alistair had just returned from the office on New Year's Day, showered and changed when he heard the door open, and Cynthia burst into their flat in tears. "Daddy says I can't marry you!" She threw her arms around Alistair's neck and clung to him tightly.

"What? Say that again." Alistair gently pushed her away so that he could see the distraught and confused look on her face.

"He says I can't marry you."

"I can't believe it!"

"Neither can I."

"I thought he liked me."

"He does. That's what is so stupid."

"Then what's his problem?"

Cynthia was struggling to explain through sobs and spasms in her chest that were affecting her breathing. "He thinks you are too old for me—that you are closer to his generation than mine."

"That's absurd."

"Of course, it is. He's almost a quarter century older than you are." Cynthia was recovering a little. She took off her coat, hung it on the newel post and sat down on a couch.

"Well then what is the real reason for God's sake?"

"I'm not positive, but I think it is the boys. He is afraid that you will be a big influence on them."

"You mean that I'll encourage them to resist, persuade them to go to university in Canada?"

"Yes. That sort of thing. Whatever, I think he's afraid of losing control over them to you…and of me for that matter—that I'll be your little girl, not his."

"Well, the hell with what he thinks." Alistair kissed her on the cheek.

"Let's go ahead and get married anyway. He'll probably change his outlook when he realizes there's no ugly plot to undermine his authority."

"We can't." Cynthia began to sob again. "I told him precisely that and he said that, if we married without his consent, he'd cut off my allowance. Then we would lose everything: the flat, money for entertainment, shopping, dining out, travelling. We wouldn't even be able to go to Canada for holidays."

"We can get by alright. We'll just have to downsize that's all. We'll move into my flat, for instance."

"It's far too small for two of us, let alone the boys when they are home. We'd have to move into a council flat way out in the suburbs. It would be miserable."

"I don't think our circumstances will be as bleak as you're portraying them."

"No, hopefully they won't because I have a different plan." Cynthia's eyes were drying as she laid out her scheme. "We'll wait a bit and let Mummy work on him. She was delighted to learn we are engaged. I think she can turn him around. It may take a little time, but in her own way she can be very persuasive."

So, they waited, living the life they already had in Cynthia's flat, enjoying their weekends together and all that Chelsea had to offer. At work, Alistair was distracted from their personal dilemma by being very busy, especially with international stories like the fall of the Berlin Wall, the collapse of the Soviet bloc, and the Tiananmen Square Massacre. He could imagine Peggy racing off to cover them all and rather wished that he were back in the field doing the same.

They visited the boys in Windsor several times and they kept asking when the wedding was going to be—and Jeffery whether or not they were going to Canada for the summer holidays. They even returned to Hazelnut for a weekend in May. Cynthia wore her engagement ring; at New Year's, her mother had declared it "simply lovely," but her father never noticed it on either occasion or at least pretended that he hadn't. Their conversations over the weekend were amicable, but nothing was said about their relationship. In the kitchen, cleaning up after dinner the first night, Mary quietly reported to Cynthia that her father had not yet budged about marriage, while over port alone with Alistair, Anthony avoided any personal subjects. Their conversation was pleasant, warm even, Alistair felt, but it was as if they were simply old friends chatting happily together after a long time apart.

Alistair and Cynthia grew increasingly impatient waiting for a change of heart. "Maybe you should tell him if he doesn't change his mind, we're going to move to Canada with the boys and get married there." Cynthia agreed to go to the farm and try that approach in the presence of both her parents, but when she returned, she reported to Alistair, "If we do that, he says he will not only cut off my allowance but remove me as a beneficiary in his will."

"He'll go that far? That's incredible."

Alistair was troubled by Cynthia's unreadiness to sacrifice wealth for love, but he kept this concern to himself, and they simply went on waiting for a change in Cartwright's attitude. In 1990, however, their circumstances altered. The Intergovernmental Panel on Climate Change issued its first report, concluding that human activities were substantially increasing the atmospheric concentrations of various greenhouse gases. Without remedial action, the report asserted that over the twenty-first century the Earth's surface was likely to warm more than it had over the preceding 10,000 years and that the mean global sea level would rise by 65 centimetres. Then, in November, facing probable defeat in second round voting in a leadership challenge, Margaret Thatcher withdrew from the ballot and, after John Major was selected the new leader, she formally resigned as Prime Minister.

Cynthia had lost her political nemesis but at almost the same time she had found a new cause to champion, and she threw herself into it with vigour. In early 1991, she started working part time as a volunteer for the environmental lobby group, Greenpeace, and in 1992 she resigned from the *Sunday World* to accept a full-time administrative position in the organization's London office. She urged Alistair to do the same and now he was conscious of two voices cajoling him from within: "Do it, you dumb fuck. You can't be afraid of getting shot for protesting, not in England; and, "Oh, chéri, make her happy. I don't want you to be miserable pining for me. You're too young not to have a happy sex kitten." But he didn't heed them. He had grown to like and better understand the importance of his job as an editor, dealing as he had been recently with such major issues as Operation Desert Storm in Iraq and genocide in Bosnia. Besides, his position offered financial security that he knew he wouldn't have with a non-governmental organization. "What influence would we actually have on the environment?" Alistair argued in defence of staying at the *World*. "None really. I don't think there are any democratic governments willing to take the financial and political risks that major initiatives to deal with climate change require. It's a sure-fire way to be turfed from office."

Cynthia didn't agree at all and was increasingly frustrated by Alistair's lack of commitment. It began to show in their relationship. She was often late getting home from her new office and the name of a co-worker kept coming up in their conversations. "You really should meet Vincent Samuels. He's from Jamaica and he's very bright. He will convince you of the impact we can have if we follow the correct strategy."

In early 1993, that strategy apparently changed and required abandoning Greenpeace for an organization with a confusingly similar name, Greenpeace London. When Alistair checked into the group, he discovered that it was a more radical environmental organization apparently not averse to using illegal practices to achieve its ends.

After Cartwright's escalated second threat, Alistair had no intention of returning to Hazelnut, but in light of Samuels' apparent increasing influence on Cynthia's thinking, he decided to try to persuade her to go on her own for a heart-to-heart talk with her parents about the ethical appropriateness of her new position and more especially about how they might overcome Anthony's objections to Cynthia marrying him. But, before Alistair got around to urging this course on Cynthia, there was another development. In April, thinking he was coming down with the flu, he left his office earlier in the evening than usual. As he turned the key and opened the door to their flat, he heard the door to the bedroom shut and the patter of feet on the floor. "Cynthia? Is that you?"

"Ye…yes, sweetie," she answered after a short delay. "What a pleasant sur—"

"Oh, good. I thought it might be a burglar." But, as Alistair walked past the living-room coffee table to the bedroom, he noticed a Bob Marley CD lying open—his *Legend* album of 1984. He rushed to the bedroom door and tried to turn the handle. "It's locked. Open it, will you?"

"Sorry. I don't know how that happened. I'll be right out, sweet 'ems."

"Just open the door for Christ's sake." Alistair detected a rustling sound at one end of the bedroom. "What the hell is going on?"

At last, Cynthia swung the door open. "Nothing, darling." But Alistair detected the sweet aroma of marijuana wafting towards him from the unmade bed. He marched immediately to Cynthia's walk-in closet, opened the door and pulled to one side the zippered plastic bags containing her dresses. "Please do be careful, sweetie, or you'll damage them."

He peered into the back of the cupboard until finally he saw the head of someone hunched on the floor. "Who the fuck are you?"

"I'm Vincent," a young man, undressed above the waist, answered politely as he stood up. "I'm pleased to meet you. Cynthia has told me a lot about you."

Alistair was totally taken aback by the response, and it was several seconds before he spoke again. "Well, I'm afraid I can't say the same about you…So…So, how long has this been going on?"

"Oh, sweetie, must you hold an interrogation right now?" Cynthia was hugging her dressing gown to her nude body.

"I just want an answer to that one simple question. How long?"

"About nine months, sir."

"Don't call me sir for Christ's sake. Let's not make this worse than it already is. Jesus! Nine months!" Alistair surprised himself by the calmness of his voice—the way he sounded almost as polite as Cynthia's lover. "Vincent, I would like you to finish getting dressed and leave the flat. I'm going for a walk now, but I'd like you out of here by the time I get back. I want to talk to Cynthia—alone."

"Certainly, I fully understand."

Alistair's thoughts were a jumble, and he wasn't aware of exactly where he was as he paced around several neighbourhood squares and up and down the mews next to Cynthia's. *How did this happen? Is it my fault for not following her to Greenpeace? Did she ever really love me? Do I really love her, or have I been kidding myself all along?* He didn't know the answers and wasn't sure he ever would, yet, to his surprise, he remained calm despite the shock of what had happened.

"I'll keep it short and simple," he said to Cynthia when he got back to the flat. "Do you still love me?"

"Yes."

"Then how could you do this? How could you jeopardize all that we have built together coming this far?" Cynthia began to cry. "Do you love Vincent as well?"

"Yes."

Jesus! Is this Cynthia I'm talking to, or Marianne? "More than you love me?"

"I don't know… Maybe… We see things the same way."

"Then I guess I should pack my bags and move out. Now, in fact. Is that what you want?"

Cynthia didn't respond, but that was all the answer he needed. He gathered his things together and moved right away into a cheap, short-term flat in an old apartment building near Victoria Station. From there, the next day, he called the person who was renting his Fulham flat and managed to negotiate a cancellation of the let in one month's time on the promise of a refund of the last three month's rent.

Shortly before he moved back to Fulham, he had an unexpected call at his temporary digs from Anthony Cartwright. "I'm glad I've reached you. Cindy has told me about this chap Samuels and that you two have broken off your engagement. I was very sorry to hear this." Alistair was astounded in light of his threats to Cynthia if they married. "I…I don't know what to do. She is so head strong, so radical, so different from me."

"I'm surprised that you haven't already done what you did to us," Alistair said sharply. "That ought to solve your problem right away."

"That's awfully blunt put like that, but I suppose what you say is fair. That is exactly what I am about to do."

"Well, don't take it out on Vincent personally. Actually, he's a nice young man, just a misguided idealist. Remember he is only in his twenties, maybe twenty-five. To him and Cynthia, you—and I for that matter—probably seem like old men out of touch with the times."

"I turned her into a rebel by being too controlling, didn't I?"

"Yes, I think you did. You needed to listen to Mary and take her advice. The world is changing and England, too. There are still wisteria-covered cottages along country lanes, and some, like your farmhouse, are even beside fields of grain, but that is not any longer most people's predominant image of the country."

There was a long, reflective pause before Anthony responded, "No… No…I suspect you're right."

Alistair quickly regretted speaking so bluntly again. "Well…no hard feelings. You probably saved me from a disastrous marriage."

There was another pause. "I'm going to miss seeing you here and having a glass of port together."

"Really? Maybe not when I tell you this. Before our first visit, Cynthia coached me on port etiquette."

"No! You sneaky devils." Anthony laughed loudly. "You had Mary and me completely fooled…Well, as you said, no hard feelings…none at all." After a long silence he added, "I don't suppose there is a chance of your forgiving Cynthia…if I can…if I can… induce her—so to speak—to give up Samuels."

Again, Alistair was amazed by Anthony's reversal. *Is this genuine or merely tactical? Has he simply decided that I'm less of a threat than Samuels?* "I most certainly won't. This whole thing opened my eyes. I see her very differently now."

"I was afraid you would say that. Anyway, whatever you may think of me, I am, indeed, sorry about the way things have turned out. And I'm glad I was able to reach you. It was good to talk to you again. All the best, Alistair. I mean that sincerely."

Alistair returned to his Fulham flat and his work at the *Sunday World*, finding it an escape from brooding over another failed relationship. Several times, he visited Cynthia's sons and explained how disappointed he was about the way things had turned out with their mother. "I was really looking forward to being your stepfather and doing all sorts of things with you." They in turn assured him that they felt the same way and wanted to see him whenever he had time for a visit.

Two years later, Peggy's elder sister, Gertrude, called to tell him that Mame had died. "I'm sorry to be so slow telling you. It was three weeks ago, but I have been very busy dealing with everything. Anyway, you couldn't have gotten here for the funeral. It was the next day. We did everything by the book this time. The reason I'm calling is that I need some information from you for all of the documentation."

"Documentation? I don't understand."

"For the execution of the will. As Peggy's husband, a third of the estate goes to you."

"No, no. That isn't right. I don't need it."

"Of course, it is, and Mame wouldn't have it any other way. She'd sit up in her coffin to object if you didn't get your share. I'm afraid, it's not much, though, apart from the house which obviously has gone up a lot in value."

Poor Mame. What sad final years, Alistair thought after they hung up. *She was quite a woman. I'm going to miss her…It's the end of another chapter.*

When the estate was settled, Alistair arranged to have his share deposited directly to his London account and was surprised to discover that the amount was substantially higher than he had expected. Then, in 1997, Jonathan called to tell him that several times recently their mother had fallen. He felt it was time to look into moving her to a nursing home and wanted to know what Alistair thought. He had always been troubled by having left it to Jonathan to carry virtually all the burden of checking regularly on their mother ever since their father had died, but now attending to her needs had become much more time-consuming for him. So, he commiserated with Jonathan over the situation, but asked that he not to do anything immediately while he looked into taking a leave of absence for a few weeks to come home and help.

Instead, he spent time calculating his financial situation, adding up his savings, the small pension he would be entitled to from the *Toronto Herald*, what he could expect from the Canadian government, his share of the Morganstein estate, and the probable value of what he would receive from the *Sunday World*.

What the hell. Mom and Jonathan need me there, and I wouldn't mind a change from working as an editor. I should be able to manage reasonably well, especially if I find part time employment somewhere in the media. Rather than a monthly pension, he negotiated a satisfactory lump sum payment from the *Sunday World* and submitted his resignation. Then, he arranged to end his lease on the Fulham flat and called Jonathan a week later than he had intended to tell him that he was coming home and that it would be for good.

Two days before he was to leave, he had a call at his flat from Charlie, sounding agitated. "Mummy called the *Sunday World* and learned that you have resigned. She says you're going home. Must you really? You know she's broken up with Vincent. It's you she really loves. She told me she'll fly out to Canada whenever you're ready to have her back. Is there a chance you might?"

"Not really, Charlie, I am afraid." Sensing the young man's concern, Alistair spoke as softly and soothingly as he could. "Not after what happened. But I'm really going to miss you and Jeffery. We got on so well together. Maybe you'll come to Toronto for a visit some time. I'd love to see you there."

"Oh, we're coming to Canada whatever happens. But please do consider the possibility of you and Mummy getting together again. We'd all like it to turn out that way."

Not to disappoint him, he said simply, "I'll think about it. That's all I can say."

The next day, he flew home. Ironically, it was in the same week that Princess Diana died in a car crash in Paris, shocking everyone in England and leaving them sad and dispirited. He felt the same way himself with the added burden of having little notion of what lay ahead of him for the rest of his life.

Chapter 35

WHEN HE ARRIVED in Toronto, Alistair's initial priorities were finding a place to live and deciding, along with Jonathan, what to do about their mother. He quickly located an apartment building near Yonge and Summerhill where he was able to obtain a six-month lease on a one-bedroom unit. Then he contacted the tenants at the house he and Peggy had shared in Cabbagetown, managing to arrange a termination of their lease at the same time that his on Yonge Street would expire. He and Jonathan quickly agreed that the only viable option with their mother was to move her to a seniors' residence, hopefully associated with a nursing home to which she could be readily transferred when it became necessary. As it turned out, that was only three months after she left the family home. In this new, unfamiliar environment where the routine was different from what she was used to and there was no space for most of her personal possessions, she declined quickly. A year after his return, she was dead. Sadly, it was just before he finished redecorating the Cabbagetown house where he had planned to have her for a meal to see it for the first time since he and Peggy had lived there. *Poor, Mom, I feel so sad not having been here to comfort her after she lost Dad…It must have been tough having two boys, consumed with their own lives. No empathetic daughter to hug and kiss when she wanted to cry.*

Before his mother's death, Alistair had launched on another task—finding part-time employment as a journalist to supplement his other income and keep him busy and mentally sharp. The search did not , however, go well. He received a courteous reception at the *Toronto Herald* when he dropped in, but there was only one person who seemed to remember vaguely the type of reporting he had done. All the city editor was prepared to do was to keep his name on file in case something arose, and to suggest that in the interim he try submitting a few freelance articles. At the *Toronto Star*, there was no interest in him at all. Times were tough in print journalism, he was reminded; they were downsizing more than they were adding new, "young" talent.

Before long, Alistair gave up the search and decided his only option was to retire fully, aged fifty-eight. After his mother's estate was settled, he re-evaluated his financial assets and calculated he would be just fine, especially if he sold the Cabbagetown house which had risen considerably in value. So, only two years after his return, he was back in an apartment, this time on Avenue Road south of St. Clair. It wasn't grand, but he was quite happy with it as his unit was freshly painted with a good view. *Bugger it, I forgot! If Cynthia's lads do come, I've got a problem with so little space… Well, I'll figure something out. Geez, what if Cynthia comes with them? Then what?*

His apartment looked south to Lake Ontario and the rapidly growing forest of high-rise buildings downtown. They were indicative of the extraordinary growth of Toronto since he and Peggy had lived there, an expansion that had made it a much more cosmopolitan, multi-ethnic, and dynamic city than he had known in his youth. As an old-timer, he did, however, find it disconcerting (rather than "concerning") that the Royal York Hotel, once visible at almost any angle looking downtown or up from the lake, was now so hemmed in by skyscrapers as to be virtually out of sight—a scrawny scrub oak amidst the towering pines. He was also put off by how so many people, especially those under forty, had taken to calling Avenue Road simply "Avenue." To his ears already ringing unpleasantly with tinnitus, that simply wasn't right!

The major question for Alistair now was how he was going to spend the bulk of his time productively. As he contemplated this matter on lengthy walks in his new neighbourhood and in near-by fashionable districts like Yorkville, Rosedale, Forest Hill and the Annex, he heard once again the familiar voices of the departed women in his life, pressing him to devote his time to the critical, worthy causes that they had adopted. Yet, he still couldn't rouse himself to contact a non-governmental organization and offer gratis his services based on his years of media experience. The issues just seemed too overwhelming and the possibility of having an impact so limited that he wasn't ready to make the necessary sacrifice. So, he restricted himself to occasional letters-to-the-editor, submissions to the offices of parliamentarians, and donations to a range of charitable organizations. Most of his time, he spent walking, reading, going to the theatre and movies, and eating out at the myriad of restaurants in his neighbourhood. When, before long, this self-indulgent lifestyle left him feeling unsatisfied, he decided to write a memoir chronicling his life working for newspapers and in the process discussing the major international issues of those decades that still bedevilled the world. He did not expect thereby to have any impact, but he hoped he might at least silence the voices of conscience within his head.

He had only just launched on his manuscript when Jonathan phoned him one evening. "I just had a call from an old buddy at the firm. Apparently, Colin Jameson died of a heart attack yesterday."

"Geez, no!"

"Yeah, apparently it was very sudden. He just worked himself to death, I guess. He would have been what? Sixty-two, I think."

"Poor Ginny, she must be devastated losing him at such a young age."

"For sure. I think I'll fly to Vancouver for the funeral. I haven't seen her for a long time."

When Jonathan got back to Toronto, he phoned his brother to suggest they go out for lunch, a custom they had adopted shortly after Alistair's return. "So how is she?"

"Pretty shaken up. But she's always seemed pretty resilient to me. I'm sure she'll pull through okay."

Alistair was certain his brother was alluding to his own break-up with her and the way she connected with Colin soon after. "When you talked to her, did my name ever come up?" Jonathan shook his head. "Maybe she doesn't remember me at all."

"Oh, I'm sure she remembers you alright. People never forget being jilted."

For several weeks, Alistair continued to work on his memoir, but he kept finding he was distracted, his memory roaming back to the wonderful times he had once shared with Ginny. *I guess it would be thoughtful to write her a note of sympathy… But what if she responds and we start corresponding? What might happen then? Jonathan said her mother is still alive and living in Etobicoke and one of her kids is here as well. She might periodically come east to visit them, and suggest getting together when she is here. Do I actually want to see her? Is it a good idea after so many years and at this stage in our lives? But what if she never answers or does so in an impersonal way? I would feel dejected, knowing that the wound I inflicted has never really healed. That would be worse than not writing and never knowing what might have happened if I did.*

Yet, the more he thought about all of this, the more he recognized that he did want to see her again—that he was, in fact, excited at the possibility, however slim the likelihood of its happening, and that he was prepared to take the risk of rejection. So, he phoned his brother. "I'm thinking of sending my condolences to Ginny."

"That would be nice."

"You don't think it is too late?"

"It's never too late to do the right thing."

"Of course, there's a chance she might take it the wrong way…You know, think I'm stirring up old embers."

"Nothing wrong about setting a fire burning if that's what happens. She's a widow and you've been a widower for a long time."

So, Alistair wrote her at the address Jonathan gave him. The first part of the letter he found easy to compose, extending his heartfelt sorrow at her terrible loss, especially when Colin was still so young. He noted as well how difficult it must be for their children as well as for their grandchildren whom he assumed she might well have and he apologized for his ignorance in that regard, reminding her that, while he knew they had at least two children of their own, he wasn't sure of their genders as his brother had told him only that he thought they were boys.

After that, it was much more difficult to know what to say. Should he just end it quickly, leaving it for her to decide whether or not to respond, or should he tell her that he would like to see her again? *I have to go for it. If I don't, the note will sound formal and detached.* The last line he had written gave him the lead he needed:

"It's obvious that a lot has happened in both our lives that we know nothing about. It would be nice to see you again and get caught up. As you'll note from my address, I am at last home in Toronto and here permanently on my own. Jonathan told me that your mother is still alive and living in the same house in Etobicoke and that one of your children is here as well. Perhaps we could get together sometime when you are in Toronto visiting them."

He added his phone number and repeated again his deepest sympathies at her terrible loss before signing the letter, "As always—well not really and maybe that is a good thing!"

It was only five days before he received an answer, but it seemed to him much longer. As he was finishing a simple supper alone in his apartment, the telephone rang. "Hello. Alistair?"

"Ginny! How wonderful to hear your voice!" They were words he had rehearsed several times before she called.

"You knew it was me?"

"Right away. You sound just the same."

"Well, I don't look it."

"Nor do I."

"Ah, now I recognize your voice. It—"

"Aw, oh! I hope it's not because I still sound cynical."

"No, no! It's good to hear it again."

They chatted amicably for several minutes mainly about Colin's death and how she was bearing up and, beyond that, simply acknowledging that there was much to talk about. At last, Ginny said, "I'm in Toronto from time to time to see my mother and my daughter, Rachel, and her family. They live just off the Danforth."

"Ah, one of your children at least is female! Jonathan got that wrong unless you had a third one later that he didn't know about."

"No just two. We had a boy first, Hugh, and then a girl. How conventional, I'll bet you are thinking."

"No, no. I'm just pleased to know their genders at last."

"I can't believe I failed to mention it when I wrote after Rachel's birth. Anyway, why don't I call you when I'm next in Toronto, probably in a month or two when things are more settled here? It would be nice to get together for a chat."

Alistair felt she sounded friendly but also rather reserved as if all she was considering was simply one meeting to discuss what had transpired over the years since their breakup. That impression was reinforced when she phoned two months later to say that she was at her mother's and could Alistair come for tea the next day. "That's the only time I have free. I'm busy dealing with doctors' and dental appointments for her and seeing Rachel and her family. I'm baby-sitting my grandchildren two nights as well."

"That's okay. I understand." *Her mother's? That will be tough.*

Chapter 36

ALISTAIR DROVE TO Etobicoke following the Bloor Street route he preferred and was pleased at least that Ginny was watching for him to pull into the driveway so that she could come out to greet him. Standing outside the car, they kissed on the cheek and hugged briefly the way any old friends might after a long interlude. For a moment, neither looked familiar to the other, the images they had retained masked by wrinkles and alterations in hair colour and length. But when Alistair focussed on Ginny's inquisitive blue eyes and caught the subtle scent of lavender that he had always detected when holding her in his arms, his initial impression receded, and she looked more the way he had remembered her. Clearly, she wasn't young any longer, but she didn't appear particularly old either. More importantly, she was easily recognizable as the woman he had known and loved. It was the same for Ginny, especially as a bemused expression crossed Alistair's face and when he spoke next, it was with a wry wit that she instantly recalled. "Well, now that we have noted the ravages of time, maybe we can talk about what lies behind them."

But they couldn't—because they had to go in for tea. Ginny's mother was certainly polite as she inquired into where Alistair was living now and where he had been over the years before his return to Toronto, yet she seemed distant and only vaguely interested in what he was saying as if she were talking to an unexpected visitor whom she had never seen before and was hoping would not stay long. So, he was relieved when after a half hour of small talk, Ginny suggested that they go for a walk and Mrs. Sloan declined an invitation to join them.

"Your mother doesn't like me, does she?" Alistair started the conversation as they strolled along the quiet streets of a neighbourhood he had forgotten was as attractive as it looked now with spring waving a wand that was turning its trees and lawns a myriad of shades of green. "I could sense that."

"It's not that simple. She liked you at the beginning, but obviously she was upset when you broke off our...our relationship, and she was angry with you for hurting me so deeply."

"She had every right to be. I have always been upset with myself about what happened."

"I know. I still have everything you wrote me. But when Colin and I got together, what had happened to us no longer mattered to her because she liked him and was happy for me. I think she almost forgot all about you."

"Just as well...Did you?"

"You know I didn't. I answered your letter after Rachel's birth."

"Yes, but that was years ago. After that?"

"Not really. For a long time, Jonathan gave me bits of information about your life. Mom didn't forget about you completely either because gradually she saw that my marriage wasn't perfect. But that's too long a story to get into now." *Does she mean we'll have another chance to talk?* Alistair felt a glimmer of hope. "Anyway, that made her wonder how things would have been if you and I had stayed together and that made her angry at you all over again."

"And now?"

"She doesn't dislike you. She's just suspicious of your coming to see me for my sake."

"Are you?"

"No... Not suspicious anyway...just not certain it's a good idea to be seeing you."

They chatted briefly about their lives without getting into details and then they were back at the house, and it was time for Alistair to go.

"Geez, I wish I could see you again. There is so much to talk about."

"Yes, it would be nice if we could…Maybe, I'll call Rachel and see if I can get out of dinner at their place tomorrow night."

"I don't want to disrupt your plans, but it would be great to see you again somewhere before you leave—at the airport even."

"Not at the Old Mill, though," Ginny laughed.

"No, not there. I don't want to see it ever again."

"I'll phone Rachel and let you know tonight."

• • •

"THERE IS SOMETHING I need to tell you," Ginny started her conversation with her daughter.

"This sounds ominous. What?"

"There was this man I dated before I met Daddy and—"

"He's come knocking at your door, right?"

"Not exactly. He sent me a nice letter from Toronto about your father and then I called him back to thank him. We agreed that it would be nice to get together for a chat the next time I was in Toronto, so I called him to tell him I was here. I've just had tea with him at Grannies."

"Grannies? Ooh, that must have been difficult for both of you…Did you love him way back then?"

"Yes. Very much. I cried for days after we broke up."

"Do you still love him?"

"I've no idea at the moment. It's been decades since I last saw him and it's too soon after Daddy's death to contemplate even. He does still seem sweet though and we had some wonderful times together."

"You want to cancel dinner tomorrow so that you can see him again to talk privately, right?"

"Yes, dear. You're so perceptive. Will you and Lei be okay with that under the circumstances? It's the only time I can see him before flying home."

"Of course. I understand, Mom. And if you do decide you still love him, go for it. We don't want to see you alone the rest of your life."

"Thank you, sweetheart. You're so understanding."

Ginny took the Bloor Street subway to the Danforth the next day and visited her family in the afternoon before meeting Alistair for dinner at a bistro at Yonge and Woodlawn Avenue that he had frequented when he first moved home and lived close by. Its food was traditional but good and it was a relatively quiet restaurant with well-spaced tables, making it possible to talk and be heard. And talk they did, barely noticing what they were eating. When the waiter uncorked their bottle of wine, questions flowed from Alistair in such a steady stream that they lost track of how much wine they were consuming and how much time was passing. He asked her about her life with Colin, her children and grandchildren; Vancouver, how much she liked it, whether or not she intended staying there; and what in general her plans were for the future. Quickly she remembered how he had always done that in the inherent manner of journalists even before he had become one. It was a trait that she had always appreciated because it had put her at ease talking to him and had reflected his genuine interest in her nature. Just as she was about to stop him and insist that he tell her more about his own life, he summoned the courage to ask the intimate question that he had wanted to pose the day before when on their walk she had hinted that she might be prepared to answer it. But he came at it obliquely. "So, from all you've said, it would seem you had a happy marriage." Then, before she could frame her answer, he apologized. "I'm sorry. That was impertinent of me. Don't feel you should answer."

She smiled at him—warmly, he felt. "Don't worry. I'm not offended. I know you're actually interested, not just looking for gossip."

"Oh, but I like that, too."

Ginny laughed and then formulated her answer carefully. "I guess I would say our marriage was okay, but our life together was rather boring, certainly not nearly as exciting as yours, judging from the little I know about it. Colin was so totally caught up in his work that he had very little free time to spend with the kids and me. He made a lot of money, so we lived well and in a large, attractive house, but it didn't feel like we were partners, at least not the kind who do things together. His partners were at the law firm and that was disappointing."

"But he liked to go dancing, didn't he?"

"Yes, but he never seemed to have time for it after we were married."

"What did you do on your own then? Did you get back to skating?"

"No. I didn't have much free time either and that was another problem. Because he was so busy at work, I did virtually all the raising of the kids. Often, he didn't get home until after dinner when I was putting them to bed. So, whenever he was free, he wanted me home. That meant I couldn't do much myself. I certainly couldn't pursue a career nor do a lot of volunteer work even. I did do some. Along with neighbours, we sponsored a family of Vietnamese refugees."

"Oh, yes. Jonathan told me about that."

"Colin supported that idea, but he was too busy to help much. Rachel, however, was terrific, getting their children settled in at school. It sparked a lifelong interest in Asia. Did I tell you that her husband, Lei, was born in Hong Kong? His parents fled there from the mainland in the fifties. Anyway, it's not like Colin forbade me to get involved, but I knew he didn't want me to have a real job and I was disinclined to upset or disappoint him."

"No. That was never in your nature."

"Well, remember, unlike you, I've never had a grand view of the world and its problems—a vision of how it ought to be and what I should do to help us get there. My goals have always been limited."

"I suppose it's true that for some time my ambitions were grand and global in reach but not anymore. I want simpler things now… but they are not necessarily any easier to achieve." Alistair wasn't even sure himself if he intended his response as a hint. "Is that also why you never left Colin; you didn't want to let him down?"

"I never considered leaving."

"Other women were increasingly frustrated by the inequality in their relationships and getting divorced. Didn't the women's movement affect your thinking?"

"Of courses, it did. I believe very strongly in gender equality, but I had made a commitment to marriage and having a family. Despite the changing times, I felt I had an obligation to him, and the kids and I intended to fulfill it however constrained I felt."

"Commitment. My old bugaboo, right?"

Ginny just smiled. "It's time for you to tell me your story."

But just at that moment, Alistair became aware of the waiter standing patiently in a corner of the room and staring right at them. "I'm so sorry," he said getting up quickly. "We've stayed much too long. I really do apologize. You must be exhausted."

"That's quite alright, sir. It was clear you two had a lot to say to each other. I much prefer that to watching a couple silently eat without exchanging a word."

"It's a good way to avoid choking, but that's about all," Alistair quipped.

When they left the restaurant, Alistair drove down Yonge to Bloor Street and turned right. "Oh! We're going to use our old route. Still don't like highways?"

"No, I hate them more than ever. There's always some idiot, right on your tail."

"So, you still anticipate trouble ahead?"

"I suppose, but not as much as I used to. And I don't take so long to make up my mind about things either. You can't when you are older."

"Good for you."

When they reached Ginny's driveway, Alistair asked if he could see her again when she was next in Toronto. "Yes, I'd like to. I'll call you when I'm coming."

"Great." Alistair kissed her on the cheek as she jumped out before he could assist her, walked to the door, and waved—cheerily, he thought—and then blew him a kiss. *Nice! I could almost feel that.*

A few days after her return to Vancouver, Ginny called him. "I just want to thank you again for dinner. It was lovely. And I need to apologize for doing so much of the talking. I want to know more about your own life."

"That would be better to cover in person when you are next in Toronto."

Ginny's call emboldened Alistair to telephone back a week later. "When you come, where would you like to go for dinner?"

"Why not the same place? I really liked it. Very private."

"Okay, when I know the date, I'll make a reservation."

Once again, Ginny telephoned him. "I meant to ask you before, do you still feel the way you used to about kids?"

"No, not at all, really. There were two boys I got to know well in London. They may suddenly show up in Toronto one day. Their mother… well, that's a long story. I'll save it until I see you."

A week later, Alistair's phone rang again. "I'm coming next week, sooner than I expected."

"What's up? Is everyone in your family okay?".

"Yes. I…I guess I just wanted to see you sooner. I…there is so much to talk about."

"That's great! I feel the same way."

When Alistair arrived to pick up Ginny, she rushed out to greet him and they kissed again, but just on the cheek. "I think I should go in and say hello to your mother before we go."

"Yes, that's a good idea. I'm sure she would appreciate it." They chatted with her for several minutes and afterwards, Ginny said, "I think that went well. She sounded friendlier than the last time. Gosh!" Ginny started to laugh. "Remember that first time you met her, and you had to skate around the question of religion?"

"I'll never forget it."

As they drove away, Alistair apologized for not meeting her at the airport. "You know me. That's one of those drives, I just can't manage."

"You're not the only one these days."

*   *   *

"You're back!" The same waiter as before greeted them at the bistro. "Still haven't finished that conversation?"

Alistair grinned broadly as he seated them at a secluded table. "What?" Ginny asked.

"Nothing. He just reminded me of another bistro…of how nice it is to be recognized, that's all."

This time, at Ginny's insistence, Alistair elaborated on all the places he had lived and the nature of the work he had done. He gave her thumbnail sketches of Peggy, Marianne and Cynthia, of his time with each of them, of Peggy's untimely death, and his eventual breakups with the others. "They were a result—well at least partly—of my inability to commit myself as fully as they did to their causes."

"Did you love them?"

"I certainly loved Peggy, but after I saw you again, I realized I never loved her the way I loved you, nor the others either." He could see tears forming in Ginny's eyes and at the sight of them he choked up and had to stop to compose himself. "Peggy was an amazing human being, extraordinarily courageous and totally committed to journalism—to seeking the truth and exposing people to the major issues of our times, convincing them of the need for action. But in a way she seemed like my big sister rather than my partner—smarter and the one in charge, pushing me to be a better journalist, disappointed in me when I changed direction.

"Marianne was movie-star beautiful, sexy, and fun. I lusted after her because I was alone and in Paris of all places. It wasn't until the end of our time together that her obsession with famine and poverty in Africa became evident. They concerned me as well, but not enough to give up my work and enjoyable life in Paris to work long-term in Africa. It wasn't until I was back in Paris on my own that I recognized how quixotic she was, that she was the type of person who fell easily in and out of love.

"Cynthia was there when I thought relationships were over for me. I guess I was flattered by the fact she seemed fond of me right from the moment we met and didn't care that I was way older. As I got to know them, I really liked her sons as well. Whatever, she buoyed me up. I knew she was spoiled and contradictory in nature, but that didn't bother me because my faults were similar. I didn't realize until it was too late how much her father's overbearing personality had affected her and made her a rebel, so I didn't see her commitment to the environment coming, nor her attachment to another, younger man because he was also a rebel."

Their conversation and their confessions continued until well after the restaurant emptied. It was only then that Alistair asked her, "Do you think if I had felt differently about marriage and having a family and I had proposed to you at the Old Mill that we could have made it work?"

Ginny's answer was simple and direct and, as she gave it, she began to cry. "Yes, I do."

"I do, too… Geez, you could have finished your graduate studies in Social Work and got a job with UNICEF that might have taken you almost anywhere abroad. I could have gone with you wherever you were posted and done travel writing from there. If only I had seen it that way!"

"No one did in those days. Even now, it's usually the man's career that comes first."

"So true." Alistair squeezed her hand. "Do you think we could still… still make it work, I mean?"

"I don't know," Ginny sighed. "So much time has gone by, so much has happened. I have my kids, my grandkids and my mother to think about…I would need to talk to them to see how they would feel about it. I know Rachel would be fine if we were to get together, but I don't know about Hugh. You would have to meet him and his family."

"But would you like to try?"

"Yes."

Alistair lifted her hand from the table and kissed it. When they left the restaurant and crossed the road to Alistair's car, he took Ginny's hand in his and held onto it tightly. They both felt the same tingle of excitement they had touching each other on their first date. As they drove away, Alistair felt Ginny lean gently against his shoulder; it gave him the nerve to take one hand off the wheel and squeeze her hand again. "So, are you still an agnostic?" she asked.

"An atheist now really. The more we comprehend about the universe, the more I find it hard not to be one. What about you?"

"Oh, I'm still an agnostic. You taught me to play it safe."

"Did I really?"

"Yes, just in case a thunderbolt strikes, and God suddenly appears to judge us all."

He laughed. "I'm amazed that I had that much influence over your thinking and that it stuck."

When they reached the driveway, Alistair got out to walk her to the door. "Hmm. No Christopher Robin leaping and digging his claws into me. I hope that's not a bad sign."

"I know he would if he were still around."

"Can I see you in Vancouver the next time?"

"Yes, I want you to come… and soon."

"Good. Then I'll call you there the moment I can." He bent over and they kissed—briefly, but this time on the lips.

"I think we can do better than that," Ginny said softly. They both smiled remembering that night and then a long embrace followed as tears flowed from both of them—tears of happiness and excitement at meeting again and still enjoying each other's company, yet also tears of sorrow at the loss of so many years that they could have spent together. "Promise you won't wait long before calling?"

"No longer than it takes to book flights."

"I won't need much time to decide…if…if, you, you know…if I think we can make it work."

"I know already."

"Oh, gosh! You are certainly more decisive thant you used to be. I can hardly believe this is happening." She hugged Alistair tightly and began weeping again. "I…We just need to see Hugh and his family first. I want to be sure they will be okay with this. It's so soon after Colin's death and Hugh was much closer to his father than Rachel was."

"I understand."

Two days later, Alistair called her and gave her the dates for his visit. "Two weeks! That's wonderful!"

"I've got a room at the Sylvia. It's—"

"The Sylvia? But I want you to stay here. Can you—"

"I booked it only for three nights."

"Oh…okay. I guess, in fact, that is a good idea actually. We can try and see Hugh and his family early on and if that goes okay, we're… we're—"

"…good to orbit the moon?"

"Yes," she laughed. "And the stars as well."

Chapter 37

Ginny met Alistair at the Sylvia Hotel in the West End of downtown Vancouver. They had a light lunch in the hotel restaurant overlooking English Bay and spent the afternoon walking the waterfront to Stanley Park and then the whole circumference of the seawall. They had dinner at the Rain City Grill Grill on Denman Street near the Sylvia from which they could see several freighters that had dropped anchor outside the bay—like snoopers who had deliberately moved close enough to overhear their conversation. "How did you get to know Cynthia's boys so well?" Ginny asked.

"Mainly from canoe tripping with them in Algonquin Park. It was much better than at Camp Comak. Of course, I didn't order them to massage my back and shoulders."

"Oh, I'm sure Cynthia handled that chore."

"I can't remember, but I don't think so."

"Well, I would have gladly."

"Ahh! I can just feel your delicate fingers pressing into my ribs. How wonderful that—"

"You're still awfully good at flattery."

Alistair laughed. "Anyway, at the *Sunday World* I was surprised how much I got out of mentoring young reporters. I hadn't expected that. I do look forward to meeting your children and grandchildren and, if things work out, playing some kind of supportive role."

"Good. I just hope that Hugh will be okay with our getting together. I phoned him before your plane got in. We're having dinner with them the day after tomorrow, but he said he thinks it's too soon after Colin's death for me to be with someone else."

"How do we deal with that then? I guess we just say we already know each other very well and we're too old to hang about looking for flaws that won't change how we feel."

"I think what's actually bothering him is his inheritance. He's rather acquisitive, just like Colin was."

"If that's the main issue, there's no problem. You can tell him I don't want a penny of your money."

"But that wouldn't be right. Counting the house, I have quite enough to satisfy everyone."

"No. Nothing for me. We'd spell it out. I'm fine as I am, and I have no dependents. Anyway, you'll outlive me, I'm sure."

The next day they went to the VanDusen Botanical Gardens, one of Ginny's favourite places where fuchsia, Hibiscus and hydrangeas of various shades were still in bloom. They lunched in its restaurant, not far from the formal garden where full-blown roses glowed like street lights flashing amber in the mid-afternoon sun. Afterwards, she took him to the market on Granville Island. "I'd rather have lived in this area than Shaughnessy—somewhere in Kitsilano at least. I like being near water and then I could have shopped here every day. I'm embarrassed for you to see our house."

They had dinner at the Wild Garlic on Broadway West. "Where do you want to live now?" Alistair asked.

"I think I'd like to move back to Toronto. I really miss Rachel and Lei and their children, and I would be of more help to my mother if I were nearer to her. Besides, we still have the cottage on Long Lake, and it would be nice to be able to use it again."

"I had almost forgotten about it. Do the bedroom walls still not reach the ceiling?"

"I doubt they've changed."

"What would you want to do beyond spending time together and having fun? Remember this is a hedonist talking."

"Not that much. Help out with my grandchildren, of course, maybe do a little volunteer work."

"You could finish your degree in social work, or study psychology. Then you could provide professional counselling services."

"Not now. That would mean too much time away from you."

"I get your services all to myself?"

Ginny laughed. "Now, don't be cheeky! You're incurable anyway… What about this memoir you were working on? Will you go back to writing it?"

Alistair shook his head. "Same problem. Writing is a lonely, isolated pursuit. I don't want that. I want to be with you every moment I can."

They had breakfast the next day on Denman Street near Alistair's hotel and walked from there along the waterfront to the False Creek dinghy dock where they took a little ferry across to Vanier Park. From there, they set out through Kitsilano, grabbed a sandwich near Jericho Beach, and took the bus to the University of British Columbia to visit the cathedral-like Anthropology Museum. "I think Freud would have liked to have had a totem pole in his office because they connect you to forgotten pasts." Alistair gently poked Ginny. "This is kind of like visiting Père Lachaise cemetery."

"Goodness, you do have a good memory, and you never give in, do you?"

"Yes, I do now…sometimes."

Afterwards, they walked to Hugh's home in West Point Grey. "The houses here are almost as grand as in Shaughnessy," Ginny whispered on the doorstep.

Dinner was a somewhat subdued affair at first, rather like tea had been with Ginny's mother. Yet all of the family was polite, and the atmosphere lightened dramatically when Alistair drew Hugh into an enthusiastic account of his golf game and his wife into a detailed description of the flowers in her garden.

"I'd say they liked you, my old con artist," Ginny sounded both relieved and joyful. "You can move into my place tomorrow if…if you're ready to."

"You know I am if you're sure you want to have me."

"Oh, naughty you, again," she said, kissing him.

Ginny picked him up at the Sylvia the next morning and took him back across the Burrard Street Bridge and south to Shaughnessy. "Holy, geez, you weren't kidding about the houses here. Who did you guys buy this one from, the mayor?"

"No, silly, but it's way too big for…for you and me. We'll put your bag in my room, okay? The bed is a king and it's much more comfortable than those awful little ones were in Europe."

At the end of a candlelight dinner in a solarium overlooking Ginny's garden, Alistair said, "Oh, I brought you something from Toronto. I hope you'll like it."

"Where is it? I don't see anything."

"It's in my pocket but first I have to ask you something—something rather personal."

"What? Don't be so mysterious. Just ask me."

"Will you marry me?"

Ginny threw her arms around Alistair and hugged him to her. "Oh, gosh, yes, my darling. I love you so. I don't think I ever stopped and now I love you even more because I understand better what it means."

They kissed until Alistair said, "Oh, I got carried away and forgot to give you this." He pulled a little box from his pocket containing a ring. It had a diamond in the centre—it wasn't huge but tasteful in size, he believed, and it was circled by smaller sapphires.

"I love it!"

"Good. Then I don't have to take it back."

Ginny pretended to shield her left hand from Alistair's grasp as she moved the rings from Colin to her right and placed the one from Alistair on her wedding finger. "You can't because it will never leave this hand."

An hour later, they were in Ginny's bed making love unrestrained for the first time. The climax was slower coming and not as high as it would have been when they were in their early twenties but that didn't bother either of them; they were together again in each other's loving arms and that was all that mattered. When it was all over, Ginny sat up in bed giggling. "Now I can tell my mother that at least we waited until we were engaged. She'll laugh at that today, I think."

Chapter 38

ITHIN SIX WEEKS, Ginny had sold her house and moved to Toronto where, at first, she moved into Alistair's Avenue Road apartment. Shortly afterwards, the Twin Towers in New York were destroyed in the nine-eleven terrorist attack. It reminded them both of the Cuban missile crisis and the Kennedy assassination when alarmed students had fled the dorms and they had been able briefly to sleep together. "I feel a little frightened again," Ginny confessed, "but not as much with you here and for more than a few days."

"Better sex now, too," Alistair joked.

Later that autumn, she and Alistair bought an attached red brick house on Alcorn Avenue, not far from his Avenue Road apartment. It was in a space that had once been part of a bakery and they decorated it to their eclectic tastes, including an apolitical original oil painting of a tugboat on the B. C. coast by E. J. Hughes that had been in Ginny's Shaughnessy home. In marked contrast, was a poster they hung on the staircase to the second floor, a large one of an old growth forest in the Carmanah Valley, with the caption "Trees Not Stumps." They were married in a civil ceremony at City Hall less than two years after Colin's death with all of their surviving family members present and a few old friends. The reception was at their home, and Alistair's old schoolmate, Melvin Steinberg, was one of those who attended. He had gone on from a business degree to establish a small chain of sporting goods stores, leading Alistair to ask him jokingly if he carried bows and arrows.

"Yes," he answered, "but only ones with rubber tips."

Hugh proposed the toast to the bride and Jonathan to the groom. "I never expected to be a match maker, but now I've done it twice for Ginny. So, I'm thinking I should start writing one of those advice columns. I'll call it 'Jonathan's Judicious Judgments.'"

After the speeches, hors d'oeuvres, and wedding cake, they rolled up the living-room carpet and the bride and groom began the dancing—alone and to ABBA. "Do you know why I suggested 'Dancing Girl' as the opener?" Alistair asked her.

"No. I like it, but, why?"

"Because in 1976, ABBA performed it at the wedding of the King of Sweden. You're my queen now, your majesty."

Ginny kissed him. "You never cease to amaze me with your knowledge of trivia!"

They went to bed that night tired but eager to make love. "Aw, oh! What's this?" Alistair shouted, surprised.

"What's what?"

"Our bed has been apple-pied. It's got to be Jonathan's handiwork."

Ginny laughed. "Will your competition with each other never end?"

"I doubt it. Oh. Look! He left us a bottle of champagne under the pillow. It's still cold. He must have slipped it in just before leaving."

"We only got them wine, didn't we?"

"I think so."

The next day, Alistair called his brother. "Thanks for the champagne but not the sheets. I enjoyed your speech, though. An advice column would be good for you. It would keep you too busy to pull more pranks."

● ● ●

ALISTAIR AND GINNY spent eighteen blissful years together doing the things they had talked about in Vancouver and, indeed, would probably have done years before if their initial relationship hadn't ended. They went to the theatre and concerts and visited galleries and museums. When the Crystal was added to the northern façade of the Royal Ontario Museum in 2007, Alistair pronounced it a "grotesque blister on the skin of a once dignified edifice that ought to be lanced," and Ginny responded, "It was designed that way deliberately to give you something new to complain about."

Naturally, there were other things that irritated Alistair as well. "What's that stuff called that you are fiddling with?" Ginny asked him one evening.

"It's called shrink wrap."

"Yes, that's it."

"And the goddam stuff is sealed on this bottle so tightly that I can't get it off. I don't know why they had to come up with all these new-fangled wrappers and jar lids. You need a degree in engineering to be able to get them off."

"I think they invented shrink wrap so that I would have something handy to seal your mouth."

"But then I wouldn't be able to do this." Alistair's crankiness had passed and he bent and kissed Ginny.

"Mm. That felt good. Why don't you pass me the bottle and I'll get the wrapping off so we can have a pre-dinner drink?"

"Okay, but that plus one or two at dinner won't be good for my libido."

"Oh, stop it! You'll be fine. I'll make sure of that."

Frequently, they drove to Etobicoke to see Ginny's mother and eventually they arranged for daily home care so that she could stay in her house as long as possible. Sometimes, while Ginny was doing chores for her, Alistair would take her for a walk. One day, she stopped and leaning on her cane, she confessed to Alistair, "You know, despite what I told Colin years ago, I never did take to the Beatles. I much prefer ABBA."

They dined out often, sometimes with Jonathan and Jennifer. Ginny enjoyed rekindling the friendship that she and Colin had developed with them earlier and Jonathan's wit always enlivened their conversations. "It's my bill tonight," he would assert, "'Jonathan's Judgments' is doing very well." Occasionally, they even went dancing together. "Maybe it's good that you guys split up in 1964," Jonathan quipped one time. "Otherwise, by now, I'd be ready for a second hip replacement."

They passed many winter evenings at home by a fire sharing books they had enjoyed while apart and finding that their literary tastes were still similar. They rented videos frequently to see films that only one of them had viewed but about which they were eager to have the opinion of the other, and they watched a string of movies familiar to them both from their years apart but which they wanted now to appreciate together.

Sometimes, Ginny would put on a CD, and they would dance around the living-room cheek to cheek. Oh, I love that song!" she cried when Alistair played "When I Fall in Love." "We used to dance to it, remember?"

Alistair nodded. "The first time was after that model UN."

"Of course! That's why I remember it so well. But who sang it?"

"Doris Day was first, but also Johnny Mathis."

"Oh, I thought it was someone else."

"Nat King Cole? He recorded it as well."

"Yes! That's the guy!"

On crisp, clear days when there was little wind, they went skating outdoors at Nathan Phillips Square or Harbourfront. Sometimes, when the ice wasn't crowded, Ginny would let go of Alistair's hand and glide swiftly around the rink doing simple jumps and spins while he stood at the edge proudly watching her.

In the summer, they went often to the old cottage on Long Lake where they discovered on their first trip that the bedroom walls were, indeed, still open at the top, leading Ginny to remark, "Now it's our turn to eavesdrop on the grandkids making out by the fire," and Alistair to respond, "They won't be inhibited the way we were, that's for sure. We'll hear them moaning with satisfaction."

They devoted some of their time to worthy causes as well. At Ginny's suggestion, one day a week, they served meals at a shelter in downtown Toronto, and along with Rachel and Lei, they sponsored a family of Syrian refugees, with Ginny providing counselling and Alistair language instruction. And, with Trump's electoral victory in 2016, appalled by his xenophobic racism and sexism, they marched in a women's demonstration outside the U. S. Consulate in Toronto.

They also travelled frequently. Their early visits were in Canada, and rather surprisingly to places that Alistair had gone with Peggy, Marianne and Cynthia, since rather than blotting out those years, Ginny wanted to use them to bridge the time they had been apart. Along with Rachel and her family they did a short canoe trip in Algonquin Park starting on Canoe Lake. "This is definitely the last one for me," Alistair grimaced near the end as he dropped a canoe from his shoulders. "My back feels like I've been stabbed with a knife." Afterwards, they said farewell to the others and spent three nights recuperating in the comfort of the Arrowhon Pines lodge. "Someday, I suppose we'll have to confess about this," Ginny said, climbing into a hot tub, "but not now."

Their first trip abroad was again with Rachel, Lei and their children to Hong Kong to visit his parents for the first time since the births of the grandchildren. From there, they went on their own to Singapore where Alistair showed Ginny the apartment he and Peggy had shared. On a subsequent trip, they flew to Paris and one day walked past the apartments where Alistair had lived on his own as well as the ones he and Marianne had shared. Later, driving along the Côte d'Azur, they stopped in Nice and lunched at Le Safari with Alistair charging the tab to his credit card. That evening, they had drinks at the Negresco where, as a joke, he had Ginny use hers. "Naughty you," she exclaimed, looking at the bill. "She certainly spoiled you."

Their last flight abroad was to England where they visited their favourite haunts from the summer of 1961. Yet, they also took the time to walk by Alistair's flat in Fulham and the one he lived in with Cynthia in Chelsea. They even drove through the Surrey countryside and right up to the gate into Hazelnut Farm. "You old honeybee. You smell that nectar he served you near at hand, don't you?"

For Ginny, these glimpses into Alistair's life did seem to contract the length of time that they had been apart, but they did not erase the realization that, given their advancing ages, this new period with Alistair would inevitably be shorter than they both desired.

Throughout these happy years together, there were moments in the middle of turbulent events that Alistair in particular felt guilty about his life—so easy had it been for a number of years and happier now than ever. When the United States and its allies invaded Iraq to overthrow Saddam Hussein, he had an uncomfortable picture in his head of Peggy still earnestly at work embedded with troops somewhere in the desert. And when Haiti was struck by a devastating earthquake in 2010, he wondered if Marianne and her husband might be there with Médecin Sans Frontières. "Given our close ties with Haiti," he said to Ginny, "she might have thought that we would respond to the appeal for help and that she would run into us. Good reason not to go there."

"Haiti. Where is that? Ginny asked. "I've forgotten."

"It's in the Caribbean, love."

The Trump administration's assault on refugees, including the separation of children from their parents at the Mexican-U. S. border, also horrified them both and several times, watching what was happening on television, Ginny broke down in tears. By then, however, they were distracted by a personal crisis that prevented them from reacting in any substantive way to all the damage and suffering that Trump's initiatives were wreaking.

One evening, Alistair was cooking spaghetti for their dinner while Ginny was making the accompanying salad. "They used to say these things were bad for you." Ginny held up an avocado she had sliced in half to cut wedges into the salad. "I've forgotten what they're called."

"Avocados."

"Yes, avocados. Anyway, now I think they say they're okay to eat."

It wasn't the first sign that something was amiss. There had been other moments when Ginny was unable to come up in mid-sentence with a word that she needed to complete a thought. Up until then, however, he had shrugged it off, persuaded by her conviction that she didn't have a problem. "It's nothing, just the inevitable forgetfulness that comes with age. You do the same thing."

The memory lapses were, however, becoming more frequent now, so Alistair urged her to see their family doctor for a checkup to make sure it was nothing to be worried about. "I don't need to see a doctor," she answered in an angry voice Alistair had never heard before.

Out for a walk together a few days later, they stopped to chat with a neighbour two doors away. It wasn't someone they knew well, but whom they had talked to several times. "Who is she?" Ginny whispered afterwards as they walked away. Alistair also noticed that she was forgetting more frequently where she had left her car keys and glasses, and struggling preparing meals from recipes she had known by heart. She was even forgetting subjects they had just talked about. She became distracted while cooking, leaving it to Alistair to finish the preparation of meals and when she was reading or watching television, struggling to understand what was transpiring.

Eventually, with Rachel's help, they were able to persuade her to be taken to see their family physician and subsequently a neurologist. Probable Alzheimer's was diagnosed. Alistair was devastated. It was clear their years of marital bliss were slowly drawing to an end. Yet, Ginny remained convinced it wasn't that but just old age. She was, after all, now seventy-eight. A grief-stricken Alistair did all he could to try to slow her decline. With difficulty, he persuaded her to take the medication the neurologist had prescribed; he coaxed her to go on eating despite her declining appetite and the narrowing range of foods she liked. He encouraged her to go on walks and even to skate until she complained that she couldn't any longer because her legs ached and felt weak. He read to her, and they watched old movies that were so familiar to them that he hoped she would still be able to follow them. Yet, at the end of *Casablanca* which they had both seen more often than any other film, she asked, "Who is that standing with the…the—"

"Gendarme?"

"Yes."

"That is Rick, darling. The actor Humphrey Bogart. He didn't get on the plane with Ingrid Bergman—with Ilsa—even though he really loves her."

"Oh, they've changed the ending. That's not what happened."

Finally, when Ginny was having difficulty climbing stairs and becoming incontinent, Rachel managed to convince Alistair that it was time to move her to a home. Shockingly, they discovered that none of the provincially funded long-term residences would have space available for up to five years. As a result, their only option was to place Ginny in a private home at over three times the cost. "It's appalling that we care this little about our elderly," Alistair raged. "Think of all the children with elderly parents who are no longer able to live on their own, but who lack the resources for private care. They're forced to have their parents move in with them, often totally disrupting their own lives. Here's another issue that needs more media exposure."

●　●　●

"I WAS HOPING this moment would never come." Alistair was walking Rachel back to her car the day they moved Ginny into the facility. "I thought that I could look after her at home right to the end, or that I would be dead before we got to this point. I don't know if I can stand watching her waste away in this place. She has always been so loving and caring. She is the last person who deserves to face this kind of end."

Rachel hugged him before getting into her car. "It will be awful for all of us and especially you, but there is no other option now. Fortunately, you are strong and resilient. You'll manage and don't forget we'll have the help of the staff. They seem very competent and pleasant, particularly that physiotherapist we met."

Chapter 39
Toronto

* * * *

The Present in December

ALISTAIR IS SITTING with Ginny at a card table in the nursing home's living-room. He is trying to play Scrabble with her, but she simply fidgets with the letters in her tray, unable to discern any longer what she is supposed to do with them. Alistair arranges them to form the word "love" and asks her to sound it out for him, but she can't. Another day, he tries Chinese checkers. She likes the shiny marbles, but the game is unfathomable to her now. There are no shouts of joy as there used to be at home when she discovered how she could make three leaps in one turn.

He wheels her along the corridors, a replacement now for the walks they used to take outside but which grew shorter with every outing. "Why, there is Mary Roberts," Alistair says, leaning over the wheelchair to get Ginny's attention. "Doesn't she look attractive today? Let's stop and chat with her." But no conversation ensues. He watches television with her although he realizes she isn't following anything she sees. She is simply drawn to the screen by the bright light and faintly flickering images, absorbed as much in the advertisements as anything else. It is the same with the Christmas tree erected in the living-room. She stares in fascination at the glowing white lights and the bulbs of different shapes but without comprehending why the tree is there.

Every evening after she is in bed, he reads to her from what used to be her favourite novels, books like *Pride and Prejudice* and *Sense and*

Sensibility. He knows she isn't really listening, but he is pleased when at least sometimes when he laughs or frowns at a good line, she does the same. "That's clever, isn't it?" he observes but there is no affirming nod of the head.

When he stops reading, tucks her in, and turns off the light, he sits in a chair, holding her hand and gently talking to her in a reassuring voice. "I will stay here until you are sound asleep."

Later, when Angela slips into the room, they tip toe out for a chat in the living-room. "How did you find her this evening?"

"The same." Alistair sighs. "Maybe a little worse."

● ● ●

Angela calls him one afternoon shortly after Christmas. "I think the end is near. She is lying motionless, and her breathing is becoming laboured."

He calls Rachel to advise her. "Lei and I will be there as soon as we can. I…I don't think I'll tell the kids yet, though. They wouldn't want to see their grandmother the way she is now. I don't want to spoil their memories of her."

When Alistair reaches the nursing home, he finds Angela in Ginny's room, holding her hand and she immediately passes it to him. "Just keep talking to her. The sound of voices is usually the last thing to go."

Angela leaves and Alistair climbs onto Ginny's bed. He kisses her on the cheek and goes on squeezing her hand. Her face is skeletal, her jaw clamped and jutting unnaturally. Her skin is sallow and leathery like the drying hide of a butchered animal. Her eyes are vacant like small, cloudy globes of glass, red at the edges. Her mouth is half open and periodically there is a clicking sound as she gasps for air.

Alistair puts his mouth close to her ear. "I'm here, darling. I love you. I always have and I will be with you wherever you are."

There is another quick, short inhalation. This time Alistair detects no sound of breathing. He grasps her limp wrist and searches for a pulse but cannot find one, and he notices that her eyes are no longer blinking. He kisses Ginny's lips and goes on holding her hand as he weeps, tears running down his face and dampening the bedsheets.

* * *

It is four days before Alistair returns to the nursing home.

Ginny's room is empty now, ready for repainting. Alistair has carried the last of her personal effects down to the car and is having a final look around the room. It appears even smaller now, stripped of furniture and everything else, an empty box waiting to be filled again. On Ginny's dresser, he spies a slip of paper, torn he presumes from a spiral notebook by one of the staff intending to use it to write something down. There is, however, nothing on it and, with even the waste basket having been removed, he scrunches the paper and stuffs it in his pants pocket. Suddenly, Angela is at the door. "You're ready to leave, I see. I'm glad I didn't miss you."

"Oh, I would have hunted you down before going. But I'll be back anyway. There are people here I need to come and see."

"That's what everyone says. But they don't. Life gets in the way. So, what are you going to do now?"

"Get a little supper, I guess. In fact, if I were twenty years younger, I'd invite you to join me."

Angela laughs appreciatively. "Ten and I'd accept."

"That few? Wow! I didn't mean it, though. I never could ask you out, not after being back with my 'It Girl.' She was the one for me, the only woman I ever needed."

"And I didn't mean this minute. I meant what are you going to do long-term?"

"Oh. Well, you already know my answer. In the long-term we're ether. It's the medium I'm not sure about. Visit Rachel and Lei and help them anyway I can. The same with their kids and now there is a great grandchild on the way."

"But what about goals of your own?"

"Oh, a few more emails and letters-to-the-editor about the state of the environment and other issues."

"There's that memoir you started years ago. Will you get back to it?"

"Geez, I don't know if I have the energy and enthusiasm for it now."

"You should finish it, you know. It would be good for you to have a project and, who knows, maybe what you say would really affect some people, even reach government ears."

"I don't know. I never made much progress on it, but I do have a title, *Troubled Conscience: Travelling a Bumpy Road from A to A.*'"

"Hmm. I rather like that. But it sounds like you'd be hard on yourself again. I guess, however, it's one of the things I like about you. I'm going to miss you, you know."

"Not as much as I will miss you, Sainte Angela. You were wonderful to Ginny—to both of us, in fact."

Outside, he stands on the nursing home steps zipping up his jacket. It is a grey and cold evening with a strong wind blowing. *Angela is right. I should carry on with the memoir. If I ever manage to publish it, I don't really think it will have any effect, but who knows, there is always a chance. Whatever, I shouldn't stop trying.* He walks down to his car parked in front of the residence. *You've reached the end when you give up. That's not the road to take.*

As he reaches into his pants for his car keys, the slip of paper from Ginny's dresser falls out. It lands on the sidewalk where a gust of wind, blowing down the road, picks it up and sets it tumbling down the street. Alistair watches it skitter away and feels guilty for not chasing to retrieve it right away, but he is tired, and his legs feel sore.

At last, the paper flutters onto the road and comes to rest in the gutter, fastening on to other litter lying there. He notices that his bit of scrap, at the top of the pile, is quivering like the wings of a wounded songbird about to expire. Only then does he hurry down the road, pick up the paper along with the rest of the garbage, and carry it to a city disposal bin across the road.

It is nothing really—just the tiniest of gestures. But he knows it is something Ginny would have done right away without any hesitation.

www.ingramcontent.com/pod-product-compliance
Lightning Source LLC
Chambersburg PA
CBHW032148050726
47591CB00001B/125